Charles John Cornish

Wild England of Today and the Wild Life in It

Charles John Cornish

Wild England of Today and the Wild Life in It

ISBN/EAN: 9783337095376

Printed in Europe, USA, Canada, Australia, Japan

Cover: Foto ©Andreas Hilbeck / pixelio.de

More available books at **www.hansebooks.com**

WILD ENGLAND OF TO-DAY

AND THE WILD LIFE IN IT

BY

C. J. CORNISH

Author of "Life at the Zoo"

*With Illustrations
from Drawings by Lancelot Speed
and from Photographs*

NEW YORK
MACMILLAN & CO.
66 FIFTH AVENUE
1895

TO

LADY WANTAGE

THIS BOOK, DESCRIPTIVE IN PART OF THE BERKSHIRE DOWNS,

IS DEDICATED

BY

THE AUTHOR

PREFACE

THE wild places described in the following chapters are so different—ranging from the Southern Cliffs to the Yorkshire Fen,—as to suggest the question how their wild character and the wild life in them has been so generally preserved?

Some, such as the Culver Cliffs, are in a measure self-protected. Some, like Abbotsbury Swannery or Blenheim Lake, are choice spots, which only pass from the possession of one great proprietor to another, and are preserved without change; others, like Christchurch Harbour and the southern estuaries, have natural features so attractive that rare birds never forsake them, in spite of disturbance. The Down country round "The Great White Horse" was always thinly peopled, and the change from arable to pasture has further reduced its human inhabitants. The Yorkshire fen is kept quiet by want of roads and deep rivers uncrossed by bridges. Other places described, such as the ancient meadows and Hampshire streams, are not wild in the sense of being removed from the homes of men, but convenience, or a sense of propriety, has kept them as they were. Most of these conditions are likely to last. But the "pine and heather country," and that round the lovely "Surrey ponds," will before long be in the hands of the builder, from the Bay of Bournemouth to Ascot Heath. It is worth while remembering that in this district Wolmer Forest is still Crown property, and might, if the New Forest Acts were extended to it, be preserved for ever "open and wild." Swinley Forest, and other royal forests in the south, might be similarly retained as "reserves" or natural parks, and the finest sea-cliffs which have no commercial value might be purchased and included in the protected area.

The greater number of the papers included in this book appeared in their first form in *The Spectator*, to the editors of which paper the author owes his best thanks for their encouragement, and also for permission to print them in their present extended form. Other chapters have been added, and many of the original papers re-written in greater detail. They are now presented in their natural order, grouped together as they deal with larger or smaller areas of wild England of the same type. For much minute and original observation of the wild life of the White Horse country I have to thank my brother, the Rev. J. G. Cornish of Lockinge, whose notes on the wild life of the Berkshire downs, and of other parts of England, have been constantly at my service. The greater part of the paper on Abbotsbury Swannery is also written from his notes.

C. J. CORNISH.

Orford House, Chiswick Mall,
　May 29, 1895.

CONTENTS

	PAGE
THE SOUTHERN CLIFFS.	
SEA-FOWL AND SAMPHIRE	1
THE CLIFFS AT SUNRISE	9
SEA-FOWL AND THE STORM	17
THE FROZEN SHORE	25
LAND WON FROM THE SEA.	
BRADING HARBOUR	32
SOUTHERN ESTUARIES.	
SALMON-NETTING AT CHRISTCHURCH	41
THE LAST OF THE OSPREYS	51
POOLE HARBOUR	60
THE SWANNERY AT ABBOTSBURY	67
THE PINE AND HEATHER COUNTRY.	
IN PRAISE OF PINE-WOODS	76
SELBORNE AND WOLMER FOREST	83
SURREY SCENES.	
THE SURREY PONDS	90
TROUT-BREEDING	97

CONTENTS

SURREY SCENES (*continued*)—

	PAGE
THE NIGHTINGALE VALLEY ...	104
THE HERONRY IN RICHMOND PARK ...	111
THE DEER IN RICHMOND PARK ...	118
FAWNS IN THE "FENCE-MONTHS" ...	124

HAMPSHIRE STREAMS AND WOODLANDS.

WINTRY WATERS	130
MAY-FLIES IN MARCH	137
THE WOODLANDS IN MAY	144
THE BUDS AND BLOSSOM OF TREES	150

ROUND THE GREAT WHITE HORSE.

THE LOST FALCON ...	156
THE PEEWIT'S HOME ...	166
MARCH DAYS ON THE DOWNS ...	173
"KITING" ON THE DOWNS	179
WILD RABBIT FARMING ...	187
BIRDS IN THE FROST FOG	195
ENGLISH ANIMALS IN SNOW	202
RUSTIC NATURALISTS	209

IN THE ISIS VALLEY.

THE ISIS IN JUNE ...	217
WILD-FOWL IN SANCTUARY	224

IN HIGH SUFFOLK.

SUNDOWN IN SHOTLEY WOOD	231
ANCIENT MEADOWS	238
SHOOTING RED-LEGS IN THE SNOW	246

CONTENTS

	PAGE
SOMERSETSHIRE COOMBS.	
A WHIT-MONDAY FISHING	257
THE EAGLE IN ENGLAND	266
CLIMBING IN ENGLAND	275
THE YORKSHIRE FEN	282
DUCK-SHOOTING IN A GALE	293
IS COUNTRY LIFE STILL POSSIBLE?	300

LIST OF ILLUSTRATIONS

EAGLE'S NEST	...	*Frontispiece*
SEA-GULL'S NEST	*To face page*	6
DUCK-SHOOTING IN A GALE ...	,, ,,	18
SWAN'S NEST, BRADING HARBOUR ...	,, ,,	38
SALMON-FISHING AT CHRISTCHURCH	,, ,,	46
THE OSPREY'S HOME, LOCH-AU-EILAN	,, ,,	56
FLIGHT OF SEA-BIRDS	,, ,,	64
SWANS AT ABBOTSBURY	,, ,,	70
THE HERONRY IN RICHMOND PARK	,, ,,	114
DEER IN RICHMOND PARK ...	,, ,,	122
THE FROZEN THAMES ...	,, ,,	132
PEEWIT'S NEST	,, ,,	170
GRASS-BURNING ON THE DOWNS	,, ,,	176
KITING ON THE DOWNS	,, ,,	186
KINGFISHER	,, ,,	222
TAKING CORMORANT'S EGGS ...	,, ,,	282

WILD ENGLAND OF TO-DAY

THE SOUTHERN CLIFFS

SEA-FOWL AND SAMPHIRE

THERE are still a few patches of the earth's surface left in England to which no "Access to Mountains Bill" or funicular railway will give admission; where Nature calls to man to keep his distance, and peremptorily forbids him even to set foot. Such, at least, is the warning, as we read it, written on the Southern Cliffs by the sheep-track that shrinks back from the scalloped edging of the brow, and the treacherous tide that prowls for ever at their feet, and piles round them the rotten *débris* of ocean death and land's decay. Yet the attraction of these great cliffs to the imagination and curiosity is as strong as the repulsion which sense dictates. When the air is still, we may sit by the verge and look over, while the white gulls swing out and float beneath; gazing, as it were, on some inverted world, where blue sea takes the place of blue sky, and birds are flying in the air below us. Or we may clamber down the face to some midway ledge, with cliff and sea beneath, and cliff and sky above, and sit level with the sea-fowl as they fly and float, and fancy ourselves in the cloud-city of revolted birds, that starved ungrateful gods by intercepting the sacrifices on their way from earth to heaven. Or, greatly daring, we may watch the temper of the tide, when the cliff—

> "Sets his bones
> To bask i' the sun, and thrusts out knees and feet
> For the ripple to run over in its mirth ;
> Listening the while, where on the heap of stones
> The white breast of the sea-lark twitters sweet."

But neither from its summit nor its feet, nor even from some jutting midway crag, can all the secret places of the cliff be seen ; and if the stranger desires to become familiar with the whole surface of the precipice, and learn the ways of its inhabitants, he must be content to gaze only on the forbidden land, and approach it, like good Ulysses, in his boat, over the wine-dark sea. Then, if he choose the hour aright, he may be in time to watch the sea-fowl depart for their long day's fishing, or their return to their sleeping-places in the inaccessible faces of the crag. But it is not every one who cares to face the discomfort of rising before daybreak, and of a long and chilly row along the shore, while the morning wind blows in cold and clammy from the sea. It is better to lie off the rocks on a summer evening—

> "Between the sun and moon along the shore,"

and watch the darkening cliffs, and the gulls and

cormorants flying in to roost, and mark the ravens and the peregrine falcon that still haunt the crag, to their resting-places among the seams and wrinkles of its face.

The lofty precipices of Culver Cliffs, in the southeast corner of the Isle of Wight, are still the breeding-place of the last two birds, and the first visit made by the writer to the spot had for its object to ascertain whether either, or both, had recently nested there. As long ago as the days of Queen Elizabeth, the falcons from these cliffs were famous, and they are said to have nested in the same eyries till the present day. The fishermen off the Foreland had just loaded up their boats with the lobster- and prawn-pots, five dozen in a boat, to shoot at the turn of the tide, and it was not without difficulty that a black-eyed, brown-legged fisher-lad was obtained to aid in managing the boat among the currents and rocks which the falling tide would soon disclose. Like most "longshore" fishermen, who look on the sea-fowl and rabbits in the cliffs as part of their yearly harvest equally with the produce of the sea, he was well acquainted with the habits of the birds, and soon confirmed the existence of the ravens. A coastguardsman had caught a young one newly flown from the nest a few weeks before, which ate so much that he had resolved to sell it cheap when he returned from his cruise with the mobilized fleet. After we had rowed quickly across the bay which separates the low land from the long line of Culver Cliffs, the first face of the precipice opened out,—a square-topped buttress of chalk, incurved and overhanging, with waving lines of flints running from top to bottom. For fifty feet above the water the cliff was covered with pale, sulphur-coloured lichen, and the surface was so smooth and hard as to afford no foothold even to the birds, except to the sand-martins, which, abandoning the burrowing habits of their race, had made themselves nests of chalk-pellets, like those built by house-martins beneath the eaves. The beams of the setting sun streamed over the top of the precipice, and against the light the tiny martins were visible, like gnats against the evening sky. The next wall of the cliff was hardly more favourable to the birds. A few gulls were sitting on a knife-like edge of chalk, which juts into the sea at its extremity, and the first cormorant launched itself heavily into the air, and flew out to sea. But as we approached the third and least accessible angle of the precipice, the cries and calls of the birds could be heard, and cormorants and gulls came flying round to see who were the disturbers of their evening quiet. At the extreme angle of the rock, the sea has bored two deep black holes in the chalk, and in one of these the body of the last of the Culver cragsmen was found some years ago, where the sea had washed it. At this point the cliff is, perhaps, more impressive than at any other, rising sheer, white, and lofty, untenanted by birds, and unmarked even by the creeping samphire. Beyond the "nostrils," as the black holes are called, the surface of the chalk alters, and is marked with long, horizontal lines and ledges of grass and samphire, and crowded with the old and young sea-fowl, which have made it their home for centuries. The long, black, snaky heads and necks of the cormorants lined the highest shelves, and sea-gulls sat quietly in groups and lines, like white doves against the short, green turf. Lower down, the beds of samphire hung in gentle curves one below the other, like the "festooned blinds" now so common; and among the wreaths sat the white and shining sea-fowl. The cormorants soon took wing, and flew croaking in wedges and lines out to sea; but the gulls were tamer and less inclined to move, though the whole colony raised their voices in loud protest against our intrusion. Amid the clamour and barking of the gulls, another sound was heard, like hundreds of kittens mewing; and this, we found, came from the young gulls on the lower ledges. The greyish-brown of the young birds makes them almost invisible against the grey chalk, which is, in this part of the cliff, of a darker colour than elsewhere; and it was not until the anxiety of a pair of parent gulls on one of the lowest ledges attracted our attention, that we discerned the young birds daintily walking along the shelf to a point of greater safety. The ravens had this year made their eyrie not in the chalk crag, but in the red sandstone under "Red Cliff Battery," nearer Sandown. The cliff is there so precipitous, that it would be possible to drop a pebble from the hand on to the beach beneath, which may account for the safe up-bringing of the young ravens. The nest no longer held the young; but one of the brood, apparently the sole survivor now that the protection of the Red Cliff had been abandoned, was sitting, apparently half-asleep, on a ledge of chalk about 100 ft. above the sea. It is not often that the chance comes of watching a wild raven at close quarters. It sat quietly in a sort of niche in the chalk, its head and beak in a line with the body, until our movements caused it to look back over its shoulder. Still it did not move. A gull then walked round the corner of the cliff, and black and white met face to face. The great size of the raven was then shown, as each bird sat looking at the other. Like most of the crow-tribe, the raven seems very drowsy in the late evening, and disinclined to move. When at last the bird became uneasy, it walked along a kind of covered way cut in the chalk, out on to a grassy slope, then poised, and swung flapping out over the sea, with loud, hoarse croaks. There it was joined by the two old birds, and all three went through those curious aërial gymnastics which ravens delight in, tumbling and taking "headers" in the air, like tumbler-pigeons. Otherwise, the flight of the raven is more like that of a gigantic jackdaw than of a rook or carrion-crow. But its voice and great size easily distinguish it from all other birds.

Where the broken rocks lay piled highest at the foot of the crag, we landed on one to gather samphire, and then turned our eyes from the dazzle of the chalk to the dark, translucent water at its foot. We were floating high above a luxuriant sea-garden, full of a rich and tangled growth of sea-ferns and sea-mosses,

Sea-Gull's Nest. *From a photograph by* M. Auty.

7

yet not so tangled but that each plant could be distinguished from its fellow when the eye became accustomed to the sea change suffered by the light in "the waves' intenser day." Our samphire-gatherer, after ascending to a point from which his form was hardly discernible amongst the giant fragments of rock, cast a great armful of pale-green aromatic cliff-herbs into the boat—samphire, and sea-poppy, and wild mignonette. Of these, the samphire is the strangest, with its thick, fleshy leaves like ice-plant, its salt and pungent scent and taste, and pale, uncanny-looking flower. To gather it in any quantity, it would be necessary to scale the most dangerous parts of the cliff, and it was while seeking this and sea-fowls' eggs that the cragsman was usually engaged, whose death we have mentioned. It was his practice to go alone on his perilous expeditions, and the exact manner of his death will never be known. It is more usual for two or three rock-climbers to work together. A crowbar is planted in the turf above, and two ropes are used. One goes round the body, and the other is held in the hand; the first is warped round the crowbar, so as to be let out at pleasure; the second is fixed to it by a noose, and when the cragsman wishes to reascend, he shakes this second rope as a signal, and the men on the top of the cliff haul at the waist-rope, while he assists by climbing up the second, hand-over-hand. The greatest risk is run when the climber throws off his waist-rope, and clambers along the shelving ledges of slippery turf which seam the cliff, where the least slip is fatal.

As the glow of sunset faded behind the cliffs, and the moon rose over the sea, the last flocks of cormorants came in from the channel, like rooks returning to roost. Then, as we set the boat's head homewards, a peregrine falcon darted from the cliff, and with rapid beats of the wing made a half-circle over the sea, returning to the crag in less than two-thirds of the time taken by a flock of cormorants which took the same course. We did not see the falcon's mate, or the young, as in the case of the raven. But they are said to have haunted the crag during the spring, and there is little doubt that the peregrine, like the raven, has never deserted the eyrie, which it has held for at least three centuries, in the chalk precipices of Culver Cliffs.

THE CLIFFS AT SUNRISE

(WHITECLIFF BAY)

SEEN from the verge of the southern cliffs, the rise of the summer sun presents a picture in curious contrast to the low and angry dawns of winter days, with their lines of red and tumbled cloud over tossing breakers, or the gradual and mysterious effects of sunrise in the forest, where the forms and masses of trees and woods are minute by minute separated from the clinging mists and vapours, as mere white light gives place to golden beams. The beauty of the summer sunrise over the sea is of the calm and silvery sort. There is no mystery of form to be disclosed on the quiet surface; the floating vapours are uniform and without visible outline, the sky as a rule cloudless, and merely receptive of the light. Thus while in the deep harbour valley which runs inland behind the cliffs, level masses of white mist are rolling and eddying like steam in a pot, and the trees around it appear as if fringing the margin of a lake, over which the black cormorants are flying high as if to avoid the fumes of some hidden Avernus, the aspect of the sea is like a level bath of quicksilver, veiled with pale-grey exhalations, similar in tone, but without reflected light, which appears only in the broad and shining track which runs from the shore across to the horizon and the sun. Only on the sea-level the south-east wind and tide seem to revolve the mass of water in an immense dimpled and revolving eddy, which has for one margin the whole semi-circle of the bay. The horizon, even where the sea whitens under the sun, is indistinct, and the division of water and vapour undiscoverable by a landsman's eye. Backed by the cornfields and bounded by the sea, the narrow line of cliff-face and beach enjoy at this hour a quiet and repose which seems for the time to allay the mistrust and fear of man of the wildest of the sea-fowl and land-birds which haunt the cliffs and precipices of the shore. Just after sunrise, in Whitecliff Bay, which, with its adjacent precipices of the Culver Cliffs, corresponds at the eastern angle of the Isle of Wight to Alum Bay and Freshwater Cliffs on the west, the writer found the ravens sitting on the juts of a sand-cliff, and almost as tame as the jackdaws, whom they had driven from the warm ledge on which they take their morning sun-bath. Except for the ravens there seemed not to be a living creature in the bay, though from beyond the chalk crag to the right, where the high cliffs face the south, the croak of the cormorants, and the screams and laughter of the gulls, rose above the measured suck and surge of the flowing tide among the shingle. The sand and clay-cliffs were full of small land-birds; pert, blackheaded stonechats were flitting from spray to spray on the furze-banks; butcher-birds and wheatears hovered in the cliff; and, strange to say, a large flock of sparrows had flown down from the cornfields in which they had been stealing wheat since daybreak, and were drinking and washing, with an immense amount of loud and vulgar conversation, where a stream of sweet water broke out at the foot of the cliffs, and trickled down through the sand to the sea. To descend the steep path of yellow clay it was necessary to doff boots and walk in "stocking feet"; for the boot-soles, drenched with dew, slipped on the clay as if on a surface of oiled and polished metal. The quiet bay was scored and furrowed by the violence of a great thunderstorm which had flooded towns and fields in the last week of August. A mass of water had collected in the hollow of a narrow valley above, and poured like a bursting reservoir over the cliff, cutting a channel 10 ft. deep and 30 ft. wide through the shingle banks, and laying bare the rocks and boulders buried deep below. The shingle was cleared away as if by hand, and pure water was still running over the smooth grey beds of shale below. Beyond the channel the shingle was spread fan-wise for a space of 60 yards, abutting on the sand beyond. On this sand, for many yards above the salt margin of the breakers, the surface was covered with neat round pits, the size of a penny. They were filled with water, and in the centre of each was a small round channel sunk,—probably the shaft leading to the shell-mouth of a buried razor-fish.

Two or three isolated rocks, covered with green and brown sea-weeds—"sea-ferns" would be the more appropriate name for the beautiful submarine fronds—lay in succession between high- and low-water mark; and between these the sand was marked in regular lines with crab-tracks, following, in the main, beaten paths, like rabbit-tracks on the snow. It is difficult to distinguish how many lines of footprints a crab leaves. It has eight small legs and two large ones, which last it usually carries in the air, though when not frightened it also uses them in walking. Consequently a crab-track looks as if a small wheel, with a number of spikes and projections, had been rolled over the sand from rock to rock. Most of these shallow-water crabs are "King-crabs," marked on the back with the distinct outline in profile of a royal crown, with the jewels studding the edges of the arches, exactly as it appears in the water-mark on official paper. Though useless for food, they are caught in numbers by the fishermen as bait for their prawn-pots. The monster crabs which are seen in rows on the slabs of the London fish-shops never live near the shore, but lurk in the seaweed jungles among the submerged rocks out at sea. The puzzle is how they ever get into the crab-pots, for in the largest of these, which are made in certain fixed sizes by the fishermen themselves, according to ancient and established tradition, the aperture at the top is only nine inches wide. Probably the big crabs, when they see any bait which looks and smells particularly nice, creep into the pots sideways.

The sea-fowl colony round the corner of the chalk precipice had a sentinel gull watching the bay, to give notice of any stranger approaching the point beyond which the chalk precipices rise to face the sun. This solitary white gull, flying at a great height above the down, kept up an incessant clamour, which, without causing the groups which were basking on the rocks to leave their stations, made them uneasy and alert. The Culver Cliff, like that on the opposite side of the island, might well be named "Sun Corner." The heat and light reflected from the 400 ft. of perpendicular white wall fill the atmosphere with warmth and brightness. All the birds were taking a quiet sun-bath, either on the cliff or on the flat rocks below. Rock-pigeons were sitting crooning to each other on a jutting ledge, and a colony of cormorants were basking on a ridge of turf which sloped back like a green roof from the perpendicular cliff. Best of all, a pair of peregrine falcons were quietly sitting not 300 ft. from the foot of the crag, their black-and-white breasts, and dark-blue wings and tails, even the eye and head, distinctly visible with the glass as they faced the sun. They were in no hurry to leave; but after a few minutes the pair launched themselves from the cliff and flew with lightning speed round a projecting corner of the rocks to some more secluded part of the precipice. A whole family of ravens, six in number, were perched in a grave and contemplative line on another part of the precipice. The two old birds were watching a young cormorant, which was sitting on a flat rock below them, and receiving from time to time supplies of fish from the parent birds, which were diving near the shore. A larger fish than usual was brought by the birds, and laid upon the rock at the feet of the young one, which, having well breakfasted, was apparently unable to swallow any more, and sat looking at the fish as if contemplating how long it would take to get up enough appetite to eat it. The ravens also saw the fish, and at once flew down on to the rock. Their method of robbery was, no doubt, in accordance with some unwritten law of the cliff colony; but unlike that which most birds adopt when they are dealing with a weaker, and, as in this case, quite defenceless neighbour. It would have been easy to make a dash at the fish, and fly off with it at once. But for some reason they did not choose to do so. The ravens, after a short croaking conversation, sidled up on one side of the cormorant, until all three birds were in a line, their shoulders touching. The ravens then proceeded to edge down upon the cormorant, gradually shoving it away from the fish, and towards the edge of the rock, all in a very gentle, friendly manner, with no appearance of force. The cormorant then shuffled in front of its fish, and turning round, set its sloping back towards the ravens, who found that as they pushed the bird, they only upset it on to the coveted morsel, on which it lay sprawling. As this did not answer, the ravens separated, and sat one on each side of the cormorant; one then gave it a push, while the other neatly picked up the fish, and both flew off with it to their own full-grown brood on the cliff. The probable explanation of this complicated manœuvre is that the ravens were quite aware that if frightened the cormorant would pick up the fish and dive with it out of their reach. Hence they adopted the trick constantly practised by watch-snatchers in town, in which one hustles the victim, while the other seizes his property. On the opposite corner of the island, by the Freshwater precipices, the rock-fowl are more numerous and of more kinds than those which haunt the Culver Cliffs. Only, if the visitor would see them all he must keep early hours, and be in his boat under the cliffs before daybreak. Long before sunrise, the gulls are awake, and uttering a hundred quaint calls and cries, laughing like children, mewing like kittens, whistling and whispering, screaming and crying, though no human footstep has trodden on the sand since last night's tide smoothed and pressed it, and bordered the damp edge of the sea-garden with curving wreaths of weed.

There are few better places for watching the sea-fowl than the cliffs of Freshwater. Not where the chalk presents its strongest face to the sea; for there the sheer crag denies a foothold not only to the birds, but even to the creeping samphire. But when the sun rises from the sea and flushes the more broken parts of the cliff, they may be seen in hundreds; rows of puffins in neat white waistcoats and black coats, like well-drilled City waiters; black solemn cormorants; guillemots and razor-bills; and long-winged, graceful gulls. As the red disc leaves the water, the gulls stream out over the sea, barking and whining like packs of hounds, to see if the herring-shoals have come in during the night; and the cormorants—"Isle of Wight parsons," as the sailors call them—launch themselves heavily from the lower rocks, and fly low along the shore in > shaped wedges. Only the puffins stay to gossip and wag their heads, and talk about the young rabbits they stole yesterday, and the agreeable change which they make in a fish diet. Presently, if no herring-shoals are in sight, the gulls come sailing back; the young ones first in their dusky feathers, and their grey-and-white parents later, some to line the rocks, while others settle on the water, and float like a fleet of yachts at anchor, and watch their visitor. If he be still and quiet, they will even alight near him on the sand, and trip daintily along where the waves break, stopping every now and then to examine the rolls of seaweed for dead crabs and fish. But these serve only to "deceive the stomach," as Mr. Stanley's phrase is. A gull's appetite needs more liberal diet, and the whole flock rise joyfully as an old white herring-gull flies in from the sea and screams to the hungry crowd. "Herrings!" he shouts, as plainly as may be. "Herrings! Hurrah!" the pack answer; and the air is full of white wings hurrying off to the distant shoal.

SEA-FOWL AND THE STORM

(BEMBRIDGE LEDGE)

THE great frost with which the year 1895 opened was preceded, about the beginning of January, by cyclonic gales of quite unusual violence. One of these sprang up so suddenly on the night of January 10, that the seaports received only three hours' warning, and the sea-fowl, who are often reputed the best weather-prophets, were caught by the storm with no warning at all. The wind struck the southern coast at midnight, and blew for forty-eight hours with a steady roar like the sound of machinery in a mill. As the day broke over the sea, where the long reef of Bembridge Ledge juts out at the north-east corner of the Isle of Wight, the whole stretch of waters seemed in motion towards the shore; the gale had mastered current and tide, and subdued all the minor conflict and welter of the narrow sea. As far as the sight could carry, the whole surface of the Channel was piled up in parallel lines of white-topped waves, hurrying fast and close, line after line, and breaking with a front of miles upon the shingle line. The swiftness and uniformity of the onset of the sea on a dead lee-shore in such a gale detracts something from the grandeur of the sight. But the coasting brigs and schooners forced ashore, seem almost to melt before the waves, and even the true sea-fowl, whose home is on the great waters, are starved and drowned, or driven inland until the tempest lulls.

For some days before the gale, while the frost lasted, the number of home-bred wild-ducks, as well as the true sea-ducks which winter in the Channel, had been increased by arrivals from the North. During the day these were seen swimming in little bands and companies beneath the tall precipices which broke the force of the north wind, or resting and sleeping just beyond the breakers. The sea-ducks and cormorants, which feed by day, were diving and fishing while the others slept, sometimes rising to the surface in the middle of the resting flocks, or taking long low flights from one feeding-ground to another. At dusk the sea was deserted by the birds, the cormorants flying heavily into roost in the chalk precipices, while the ducks, awake and hungry, took their nightly flight inland, rushing high in dusky lines over the heads of the fishermen lurking along the cliff with their long duck-guns, whose flash and roar were the nightly signal of the moving of the fowl. Those that stayed after dawn in the preserved inland waters had for some days paid a heavy toll to the gun. But so far, though the land-birds were pinched, and crowding to the houses and farm-buildings, the greater number of the sea-fowl had

Duck Shooting in a Gale. By LANCELOT SPEED.

suffered in no way from the wintry weather, and the ravens, which, according to tradition, always choose the site for their nest on New Year's Day, were playing and croaking in solemn gambols in the air, and evidently enjoying the annual renewal of their courtship, which is the pleasant custom of birds which pair for life. A few hours of storm broke up this sociable company. Even before dawn, the screams and calls of gulls flying round the houses and buildings had given warning that something had happened to disturb the usual order of life upon the shore ; and as the darkness gave place to uncertain light, their white forms were visible dimly drifting and circling among the trees, or soaring almost motionless against the steady current of the gale. These gulls were all of the smaller and weaker kinds, —mostly black-headed gulls, in wniter plumage ; the larger sorts had not yet succumbed to the force of the gale, but were flying high and steadily in noisy packs along the line of shore. On the edge of the cliffs, the sustained strength and violence of the wind was hardly less evident to the human spectator standing on the verge, than to the fowl which were struggling to maintain their usual place in the air between the summit and the sea. The gale still maintained its steady mechanical pressure, without gust or flaw, and the larger gulls were giving an exhibition of their powers of flight. A pair of the great black-backed gulls were the only fowl which still seemed able to disregard in a measure the force of the wind. They still maintained a place well out at sea, flying low with powerful beats of the wing, half-hidden by smoking mist, where the gale cut the crests of the waves and drove them on in clouds of greyish spray. Their course was at right-angles to the direction of the gale, and when its steady impulse drifted them shorewards, the big birds set their faces to the blast, and worked their way out to sea by sheer force of wing and muscle. The herring-gulls had abandoned the effort to keep the sea, but had not yet been driven from the shore. Unlike the black-headed gulls, whose habit is to nest inland, and who readily leave the coast for the fields whenever the supply of food is likely to be more abundant on the ploughlands than on the coast, the herring-gulls are true sea-fowl, nesting on the cliffs, and getting their living by fishing or picking up the sea-refuse on the beach; if driven inland, they are more often than not lost and bewildered, and being well aware of the danger they run if once they lose sight of the sea, their fight against the gale is strengthened by something more than the common reluctance of birds to leave their own familiar haunt. Unable to cruise over the water like the great black-backed gulls, and unwilling to drift inland, they held their place and maintained it throughout the day by the use of the power of soaring, or floating like kites against the wind. With wings extended and motionless, they floated edgeways to the gale, which gradually lifted them higher, and drove them towards the land. When carried backwards to a point above the edge of the cliff, they allowed themselves to fall downwards, and then, once more spreading their wings, soared up forwards and seawards with the impulse gained by their descent. All day long this manœuvre was repeated; and when night fell, they still held their places midway between cliff and sea. The wild ducks and cormorants, which have no such powers of sustained poise in flight, though the former excel in what M. Marey has distinguished as the *vol ramé*, or use of the beating wing, were in far different case. The inconvenience of this limited knowledge of the possible uses of the wing in creatures so intelligent as wild-ducks, was very obvious, and suggested the question why it is that though they have apparently discovered for themselves the exact distance and order of arrangement in which birds make best progress when flying in company—for wild-ducks not only adopt the wedge-shaped formation when flying together, but also preserve the distances between the files with the regularity of drilled soldiers—they have never acquired the art of "sailing" against the wind like sea-gulls, or even herons and pelicans.

Exhausted with the constant tossing out at sea, the ducks crowded to the edge of a long reef or ledge of rocks, and for a time rode uneasily just outside the breakers. But the rush of the tide soon drowned the rocks, and turned the ledge into a white and tumbling lake of foam. Then the ducks shifted once more out to sea, rising uneasily, and flying from place to place, like flocks of starlings. A pair or two of brent geese, looking as black and heavy as cormorants against the toppling waves, seemed determined to ride out the gale. But the constant rushing seas, which wrenched from their moorings and flung on shore even the fishing-boats anchored within the reef of rocks, soon wore out the strength of the ducks. Company after company rose and skimmed swiftly up and down, seeking some smoother and more sheltered spot, and finding none, turned their backs to the wind, and rising high and fast, abandoned the effort to keep the sea, and flew with extraordinary speed high over the cliffs. In half-an-hour after the rising of the first flock, every duck had left the salt-water, and flown in to face the dangers of the sheltered waters inland. The storm had beaten them.

As night fell the snow came. Carried on the gale, it rushed on in level lines, as if blown from a gun. The shore was silent and deserted. The nightly flight of fowl from the sea inland was suspended, and the only bird by the cliffs was a solitary owl, flitting in the dusk along the shore. Next morning the gale fell, and as the tide ebbed, we saw upon the beach some natural records of the forces before which the sea-fowl had retired. All the ridges of shingle had been cut away, and the beach relaid in an even and regular slope from the cliffs to the edge of the surge, brown and smooth, like bolted bran. The waves were thick with sea-weed torn fresh from the deeply submerged rocks. It lay in long wavy lines, wet and glistening, like the patterns on watered silk; brown oar-weed, with roots all crusted with pink sea-wet; green feathery sea-moss, and bright orange star-weed, and thin ribbons of a delicate sea-plant, so pale that it seemed to have grown in dark sea-caves, beyond the reach of sunlight. Mixed with the weed were bunches of orange eggs of sea-creatures, while jointed roots of mares'-tail washed from the clay cliff, and one or two big spiny-backed "sea-mice," as a fisherman called the big sea-slugs which are now and again washed up by the storms.

Beyond the bay, round the point, and under the chalk precipices, the storm had cleared away the deep beds of rotting sea-weed which usually lie there, and scoured and cleaned every rock by the batter of the large chalk boulders which are here rattled in the surge.

The evening after the gale we lay till dark beneath the crag, and watched the demeanour of the birds after the lull of the storm. Apparently they spent the whole day in fishing, in order to make up for their fast during the storm. Not a single cormorant and very few gulls were visible until it was dusk, though the peregrine falcons were flitting from point to point on the cliff face, and clinging to projecting lumps of chalk. When the cormorants did come in they flew in very low and heavily, like enormous bats coming out of the gloom in which the sky was only distinguished by a line of dull red glow from the dark uneasy sea. One of our party, who had done great things among the ducks in the harbour the evening before, was anxious to shoot a cormorant and make "scart soup," which is declared by some who have tried it to be as good as hare soup. But though the birds seemed within shot they failed to be bagged, and it is probable that their great size is often not taken into account by those who think them well within range. The flash of the guns and the eddying flight of the cormorants as they came swinging round the cliffs in the semi-darkness, with the screams of the gulls, made a wild and picturesque "good-night" to the big precipice, as the tide crept on to its foot with fast lessening waves.

THE FROZEN SHORE

(Freshwater Cliffs)

In the winter storms the sea-fowl ascend the rivers inland, and the land-birds seek the coast. In this, each kind acts according to knowledge : the sea-fowl, because they are truly birds of the sea, seeking their home on the deep and their living on the great waters, which are then too troubled and tempestuous to yield either food or shelter ; and the land-birds because they know that along the tide-way the salt-water kills the frost. Twice daily the mellow tide advances to undo the work of the encroaching frost, which has followed the ebb over shingle, sand, and rocks. Rivers are not the sole avenues by which the sweet waters reach the sea. Thousands of little land-springs, invisible in the summer droughts, trickle from the cliffs, oozing and dripping on to the fringe of boulders and large shingle which lies furthest from the sea, and meander down in channels cut between the sands till lost in the pools left by the ebb. Icicles soon form on the bents and brambles which overhang the channels where the rills leave the base of the cliff, and a film of white and rotten ice covers the sweet waters hour by hour as they trickle through the drying sand. In all other respects the shore remains unchanged, except for the greater symmetry and order worked by winter storms. The waves are the rakes and sieves and rollers which the sea sets to work to arrange the gravel-walks and borders of the great public garden which surrounds the island. They work, as Frank Buckland showed, on a uniform plan, and the storm, far from leaving confusion and disorder on the fringe of ocean, is merely an effort of Nature to work "overtime" and get things straight in a hurry. Doubtless many of the more fragile ornaments are broken in the process; but the order of the strand is never so perfect as when seen in the bright, calm weather which follows a December gale. The onward rush of the breakers carries the shingle with it in what would seem the reverse of the natural process. The largest and heaviest boulders, and the light and floating sea-weed are carried furthest, to the very base of the cliff, and are there sorted and piled, the boulders below, and the sea-weed above them in large level banks which steam and swelter in the winter sun. Next to this, in long escalloped bays, lies the pebble-bank. This, again, is lined by the shingle-layers, which are fringed in turn by the finest *débris* of the storm, the siftings and dust of the sea-wash, a yard of which will give delight for hours to the eye, and days of discovery with the microscope. Beyond this lies the finest layer of all —the irreducible and innumerable sands. The sea-siftings are the strangest medley in little of the components of the ocean fringe. In them are scraps and fronds of sea-weed and oar-weed, some ground to powder like coffee, others minute but undefaced fragments of the plant; with these pounded morsels of what once were planks of ships, green scales from copper sheathing, tiny beads of broken glass, dust of quartz and cornelian, globules of chalk and coal-dust, green threads of sea-grass and fibres of matting, myriads of tiny and most exquisite shells no larger than a pin's head, fragments of nacre from the larger shells, and white bruised limbs and skeletons of infant crabs done to death in the surge. The destruction of life among these small crustacea must be enormous. Yet few land-birds come to feed upon their bodies, except the carrion-crows and the rock-pipets, which are almost as native to the shore as the sandpipers and dunlins themselves. Beyond the sea-line, winter makes no disturbance in vegetable or animal life. The long sea-grass floats as green and luxuriant as ever in the shallow pools inside the rock-ledges, and the only sign that winter reigns is the flocks of brent-geese, which are pulling the grass and rolling it into neat packets before swallowing it, on the edge furthest from the shore. This grass seems to be the sole winter food of the brent, as it was of the swans at Abbotsbury, until, in 1881, the lifting of the ice in which it was embedded in the fresh-water of the " Fleet " carried the whole crop out to sea, and left the birds either to die of starvation or to take unwillingly to a new diet of grain. The geese and the wild-ducks from the north crowd the estuaries and harbours during the winter months, but the cliffs are silent and deserted, except by the cormorants and roosting sea-gulls. The puffins, the most numerous and amusing of the cliff tribes, have flown away to the Mediterranean, and the dizzy ledges of the cliffs on which the "sea-parrots" screamed and jostled and brought up their families during the spring are silent and deserted. On the last day but one of the old year there was not a sea-bird on the line of chalk precipices which runs out from Freshwater Gate to Sun Corner, near the Needles. The gulls were all away at the sprat and herring fishery, and the guillemots and razor-bills were out at sea, and would not return before night. Yet the day was one to tempt the fowl to leave the water and bask on the warm face of these southern cliffs. The summit of the down rose 600 feet above the water, clear of all clouds and frost-fog, into the light of the winter sun, which was shining in a broad lane of silver across the grey sea, and covered the face of the long line of bastions of chalk with a steamy haze. Flocks of starlings were feeding on the fine turf which clothes the down, and a brace of partridges rose from the verge of the cliff beyond the beacon. A pair of ravens were the only tenants of the awful precipice, which falls sheer down to the sea at this point. They soared level with the summit, one bird just above the other, in flight so evenly matched and uniform, that their movements seemed guided by a single will. Sometimes the bird above would even touch its mate, and the pair fall toppling down a hundred feet croaking loudly. After playing and soaring for half-an-hour, they flew out over Alum Bay and round by the Needles, perhaps to seek a site for a nest, which the ravens are said always to choose on New Year's Day. Beyond the beacon lies the still more awful precipice of Sun Corner. The cliff there is not perpendicular, but overhanging, and the voice of the gently heaving sea climbs so slowly to the summit, that it seems as if the sound of the breaker that the eye can see would be wholly lost on its way to reach the ear. On the highest point is an upright pinnacle of chalk, connected with the main line of the cliff by a narrow ridge, on which a man might sit astride. On the summit of the pinnacle, a peregrine falcon was quietly basking, looking inland, with its back to the sea and the sun. The bird was so tame, that it was possible to approach it and notice the colour of its plumage with the aid of the glasses. It was a young bird; and it may be hoped that for once the nest has escaped the hands of the cliff-climbers, who rob it annually. Ten years before, according to a record of a visit to these cliffs which the writer possesses, a peregrine was sitting on the same pinnacle, and was next day trapped by a fisherman. Further to the east, where the coast is lower, and long stretches of sand and rocks are exposed at low-water, the shore was covered with birds, each kind strictly limiting its feeding-ground to a particular belt of shore. Nearest the cliffs was a bank of sea-weed, covered by a flock of chattering foraging starlings. Next this a strip of dry sand, cut up by black malodorous streams which oozed from the decaying sea-weed bed. On this a flock of crows and rooks were busily digging for food. Beyond lay a zone of wet sand, on which a flock of small black-headed gulls were daintily tripping up and down on the margin where the ripples rolled slowly in. Lastly, in a shallow lagoon, a few big herring-gulls were standing quietly up to their breasts in water, some even sleeping with their heads half-covered by their wing. An old fisherman was anxious to sell some lobsters which he had in a pot among the rocks, and we followed him across the slippery ledges to where the pot and the lobsters lay. The creatures —never described as "fish" in the Isle of Wight— were alive, and as smart as a Lancer, in full uniform of blue and gold. Their backs were deep blue-black, and their tails mottled with two brilliant shades of Prussian blue. Their smaller legs were mottled to match their tails, but the two big claws were faced with brown and pink. The antennæ were pink also; but all the under parts of the body and tail were pearl-coloured, and the joints of their armour-plates edged with golden fringe. How to carry live and irritable lobsters without a basket was a difficult problem, but the two corners of a pocket-handkerchief tied in slip-knots made a safe means of transport. The pot looked like a prawn-pot—which it was—and we inquired of the man whether he had any prawns. "Yes," he said—"*one*—a beauty;" and taking off his cap he exhibited an enormous live prawn sitting inside! There is almost nothing which a sailor will not carry in his cap; pipes, tobacco, string, fishing-hooks, and bait, are all accommodated there,—perhaps because he rarely indulges in trousers-pockets. A man-of-war's-man has no pockets at all, and disposes of what surplus property he cannot carry in his cap, inside the loose front of his sailor's shirt, a habit which sticks to him after he leaves the service. "And do you ever put a lobster in your cap?" we inquired. "No, sir," he replied; "if I haven't anywheres else, I puts 'em in my buzzum."

LAND WON FROM THE SEA

BRADING HARBOUR

AMONG the many problems left by the smash of the "Liberator" Companies, that of the present and future management of the reclaimed lands at Brading, in the Isle of Wight, is the most complicated, though perhaps not the least hopeful. The nature of the appeal made by this wild scheme in the first instance to the daring speculators who, seventeen years ago, embarked the resources of the company in an enterprise of which not only the practical difficulty, but the financial worthlessness, had already been proved by actual experiment, as early as the reign of James I., will probably remain among the unknown factors of commercial failure. The belief in the possibility of getting "Something for nothing," due to the notion that land won from the sea is a kind of treasure-trove, may have quieted the first misgivings of shareholders. But the fact that Sir Hugh Myddelton, the engineer of the New River, though "a crafty fox and subtle citizen," as Sir John Oglander noted, had ultimately failed, not only to maintain his reclamation of Brading Haven, but to make it pay while the dam lasted, was well known in the history of engineering; and though the mechanical difficulties might be overcome by modern machinery, the nature of the harbour bottom for the growth or non-growth of crops and grasses could hardly have changed. Briefly, the past history of the Brading reclamation was as follows. In 1620, Sir Hugh Myddelton dammed the mouth of the river Yar, at Bembridge, opposite Spithead, and on the seven hundred acres of land so reclaimed he "tried all experiments in it; he sowed wheat, barley, oats, cabbage-seed, and last of all rape-seed, which proved best; but all the others came to nothing. The nature of the ground, after it was inned, was not answerable to what was expected, for almost the moiety of it next to the sea was a light, running sand, and of little worth. The inconvenience was in it, that the sea brought so much sand and ooze and sea-weed that choked up the passage for the water to go out, insomuch that I am of opinion," writes Sir John Oglander in his manuscript, "that if the sea had not broke there would have been no current for the water to go out, so that in time it would have laid to the sea, or else the sea would have drowned the whole country. Therefore, in my opinion, it is not good meddling with a haven so near the main ocean."

This experiment had cost in all £7000, when the sea broke in ten years later, and Sir Hugh Myddelton's fields once more became harbour bottom, and cockles and winkles once more grew where his meagre crops of oats and rape had struggled for existence. Some

D

years later an offer was made to repair the dam for £4400, but this fell through. No one thought it worth while to spend the money, though small arms and creeks of the harbour were from time to time banked off and reclaimed by adjacent landowners. The attempt which had baffled Sir Hugh Myddelton was suddenly revived by the Liberator Directors seventeen years ago. The sea was banked out, almost on the lines of Sir Hugh Myddelton's dam; a straight channel, of double the size necessary for the mere drainage of the higher levels, cut for the passage of the river and the holding of its waters during high-tide, when the sluices are automatically closed; and a railway and quay were added, with a hotel at Bembridge. Solid and costly as their embankment was, the sea broke in, steam-engines and machinery were toppled from the dykes and buried in the mud, workmen were drowned, and the whole enterprise was within an ace of becoming a little Panama. But at last the sea was beaten, 643 acres of weltering mud were left above water, and the reclamation, such as it is, is probably won for ever. But at what a cost! Four hundred and twenty thousand pounds are debited to the Brading reclamation, of which last sum we may assume that £100,000 were expended on the railway, quay, and buildings, leaving £320,000 as the price of six hundred and forty-three acres of sea-bottom.

As reclamation of mud-flats and foreshores has lately been much advocated as a means of providing "work and wages," and of adding to the resources of the country, the present state and probable future of the land won from the sea at Brading is a matter of some interest, omitting all considerations of the original cost. We may concede at once that, from the picturesque point of view, the reclaimed harbour is a great improvement on the ancient mud-flats. It has added to the Isle of Wight what seems a piece of Holland, covered with green pasture and grazing cattle. This area is as much withdrawn from the intrusion of man as the old lagoon; for as on the mud-flats there were no roads, no rights-of-way, and no footpaths, so the reclamation is a roadless district, secured absolutely to the use of the occupiers, and incidentally to the wild-fowl which swarm by its shallow pools and drains. The broad embanked river runs straight through the centre, and divides into two the level which lies like a green sea between the ring of surrounding hills and the harbour-bank. In this river, the waters of the ancient reclamations higher up the valley collect during high-water, when the pressure from the sea automatically shuts the sluices, and pour out during low-tide, when the pressure of the sea is removed, through the iron gates, near which lie, with the grooves still sound and sharply cut, parts of the sluices made for Sir Hugh Myddelton of English oak in the year 1621. The general shape of the reclamation is an oval, with one of the smaller ends facing the sea, and the other abutting on ancient dams near Brading, two miles higher up the valley. The whole of this has been converted into firm, dry land;

neither is its quality so inferior as Sir Hugh Myddelton judged. Possibly the improvement in the seventeen years during which the old sea-bottom has been exposed to sun and rain, has been proportionately more rapid than in the ten in which it was exposed to the air after 1620. Then half the area was described as consisting of "light, running sand of little worth," though the upper portion promised to become valuable pasture. Those advocates of reclamation of land from the sea, who propose to "leave it to Nature" when the sea has once been barred out, can see at Brading and Bembridge what it is exactly that Nature does, and how far art can help to make old sea-bottom into pasture for cattle, and even into a playground for men and women, in seventeen years. It must be remembered that in this case Nature has been hurried, and made to do her work before her time. Left to itself, the harbour would have silted up in the course of centuries, and the pastures would have grown of themselves, on land already covered with the alluvial mould. As it is, the sea was swept from the land, which had to take its chance as it was,—mud, sand, shingle, or cockle-beds, just as they came. There was not even an earthworm on the whole six hundred acres to move the soil and help the rain to wash the salt out of it. The wonder is not that the change has taken place so slowly, but that the change from a soil supporting marine vegetable growth in one set of conditions, to a soil largely covered with grass, clover, and trefoil, has matured so quickly. What was once the head of the bay is now good pasture covered with cattle, and letting at 30*s.* an acre—there are one hundred and fifty acres of this good ground. Nature has already prepared it in part—for it was mud-flat, washed from the valley above—and still preserves in contour, though covered with grass, the creeks and "fleets" in which the tide rose and fell. All round the fringes of the flat, where it joins the old shore, the earthworms have descended and made a border of fair soil. On one side sewage has been run into the hungrier soil; and there, on a natural level, the true use and place of such experiments is seen. Three crops of grass a year are cut from ground which otherwise would not fetch more than 5*s.* an acre—a hint, perhaps, for the disposal of some of the London "effluent." There remains a portion of dead, sour greensand on which no herbage grows, though the advance of soil and grass may be noted, like the gradual spread of lichen on a tree. Each patch of rushes, each weed and plantain, gathers a little soil round its roots or leaves, and the oasis spreads until all is joined and made one with the better ground. A cattle farm and nursery garden occupy the centre of the sea-weed curve. The farm is already surrounded by rich grasses, clover, and sweet herbage, and the garden is a wonder of fertility. Not only vegetables, but roses, chrysanthemums, carnations, lavender, and other garden flowers are there reared in profusion; and in the present month masses of mauve veronica are in blossom. In walking over what is now good pasture, the evidences of the recent nature of all this agricultural fertility crop up on every side. Where the turf lies in knolls and hillocks, the sea-shells may still be seen lying bleached or purple among the roots of the grass, and what would be taken for snail-shells elsewhere are found to be little clusters of the periwinkles and mussels for which Brading Haven was once famous. But perhaps the greatest success in the conversion of the old harbour to daily use is the present condition of the "light, running sand" near the sea. This sand must have a stratum of clay beneath it, for groves of poplar trees planted on it are now in vigorous growth. But for some years the land lay barely covered with cup-moss, lichen, and thin, poor grass, a haunt of rabbits and shore-birds. It is now converted into a golf-ground, and studded at short intervals with level lawns of fine turf for "putting greens," which daily extend their area, and promise before long to convert the "running sands" into a beautiful and park-like recreation-ground. The beauty of the whole scene is much increased by the number of half-wild swans, which are constantly in movement, either swimming upon the pools and streams, or flying to and from the sea. These swans are among the natural agents busied in aiding the reclamation of the land. They feed almost entirely upon the weeds which would otherwise choke up the dykes, and it is believed that two swans do as much work in keeping the water-ways free and open as could be done by a paid labourer.

The following notes on the reclamation, and the

Swan's Nest, Brading Haven. *From a photograph.*

garden now cultivated upon it, are from the pen of Mr. C. Orchard, the lessee of the latter, whose practical experience I give exactly as he communicated it to me, together with an extract from an article on the wild plants of the sand-hills which he contributed to *The Journal of Horticulture*.

"Some portions of the reclamation contain a sulphurous matter injurious to vegetation, and require a top-dressing of manure or other soil for the seed to germinate in. There are many varieties of soil and substances to be found throughout the whole area. The best for vegetation is a kind of loamy deposit of mud, on the highest parts; that is, above the strata of sand: in this nearly every variety of cereal and vegetable luxuriates and grows beyond all proportions. There are four acres included by a fence, and now cultivated by me, as a market- and flower-garden. The soil is rich in phosphates, and all kinds of vegetables grow wonderfully clean and of good flavour; the asparagus especially being noted for its delicious flavour, being in its natural element as a seaside plant. Apples, plums, and peas have been tried with great success, and flowers of all kinds grow and flower in great profusion; the bright colours coming out to the highest degree in the open and sunny position.

"Quite indigenous, the wild bastard samphire or glass-wort grows most profusely around the brackish streams and lakes. The horn-poppy also luxuriates on the sides of the road that forms the embankment, and on two distinct places I have found the very rare *Silene quinquevulnera*, which I believe has been found only in two or three places in England. The wild evening primrose, *Œnothera vulgaris*, is found both here and at St. Helens 'Dover,' as well as the sea-holly.

"The St. Helens 'Dover' is interesting on account of the beautiful and somewhat rare plants found growing thereon. It is a strip of land that stretches out and forms one of the arms of Brading Harbour (now better known as Bembridge Harbour), and composed almost entirely of sea-sand that has been washed and drifted up since the days of Sir Hugh Myddelton. It is covered entirely with vegetation peculiar to this soil, and the undulating surface of neat and fine turf, formed chiefly of the sheep's fescue grass, forms the very beautiful links of the Royal Isle of Wight Golf Club. In summer I constantly find patches of the great sea-bindweed, *Calystegia soldenella*, growing there. It trails and spreads over the sands, and twines about amongst the reeds and grasses, bearing a profusion of large, mauvy-pink, convolvulus-like flowers, quite $2\frac{1}{2}$ or 3 inches in diameter. The sea-holly, *Eryngium maritimum*, is another beautiful object that grows profusely; its silver-grey branches being surmounted by blue heads of teazle-like flowers. The common thrift or sea-pink, *Armeria vulgaris*, grows everywhere, and forms part of the ordinary turf. In the autumn, thousands of tiny heads of the light-blue autumn squill, *Scilla autumnalis*, spring up amongst the turf, and the white and yellow varieties of the common stonecrop abound everywhere."

SOUTHERN ESTUARIES

SALMON-NETTING AT CHRISTCHURCH

WITH the exception of the coracle-fishing in the Welsh rivers, the salmon-netting at Christchurch is perhaps the most ancient and primitive method of taking the fish which still survives in England. Moreover, the site of the fishery is unique, with surroundings of sea, land, harbour, river, and town of a kind without parallel or analogy on all the long line of British coast. The waters of the Hampshire Avon and the Dorsetshire Stour which meet at Christchurch, and hurry in great swirling pools past the grey towers and arches of the ancient priory, and under the many bridges of the town, are cut off from their natural impetuous entry to the sea by the long ironstone ridge of Hengistbury Head. Between the town and the sea this great dyke thrusts itself across the sky-line, and at flood-tide ponds back the whole of the tidal and river water into a broad lake, the exit from which into the sea might, for all that can be seen from this inland harbour, be by some subterranean passage beneath the cliff itself. The actual gate by which the outflow from the hundreds of acres of swollen waters escapes at the ebb into the sea, is a short and narrow channel, called the "Run," which cuts its way between two overlapping claws of sand-spit, the inner planted, down almost to its point, with gradually dwindling pines, the outer rising from flat shingle to moulded heaps of "sand-bennets," until it joins the ironstone rock of Hengistbury. It is in the narrow waters of the "Run" that the salmon are caught, as they begin to ascend the river at the turn of the tide. The mystery which the near presence of the invisible sea adds to the approach to this strange spot makes a visit a series of surprises and discoveries. Not until the last few yards are reached of the long road, which skirts the eastern side of the bay, does the scene suggest that the harbour is anything but a land-locked lake, dominated by the great pile of the priory walls and towers. The path runs along the claw of the inner spit, at the end of which are three or four old brown brick houses, with that bare, battered, salted look which betrays the neighbourhood of the sea. The pines on the left grow thinner and more gaunt, and as the view suddenly opens, there, within a stone's-throw, lie two long strips of sand, a short length of shining river, and beyond its mouth the long, grey, tumbling sea. On the left stretches the richly-wooded Solent shore; beyond, and across the water, the chalk cliffs of the Isle of Wight, the Needles, and the open waters of the Channel.

In the short channel through which the harbour

waters pour into the sea the net-fishing goes on without ceasing from the beginning of the ebb till the turn of the tide. The order of fishing is settled by agreement, and each boat in turn is rowed out into the stream carrying the far-end of the net, while the other is held upon the shore by a partner, who walks opposite as boat and net are swung down by the stream. Before the mouth is reached the boat completes its circle, and comes to shore, where both ends of the net are made fast, and the long line of corks swing with the tide till they lie in a deep narrow loop, parallel with the wet sand of the bank. Then comes the hauling of the net. Both men pull the wet mass rapidly in hand-over-hand, pausing now and again to fling out masses of sea-weed, until the last twenty yards of the net are reached. If the bosom cork is ducking under, if the gently bellying folds of the long-meshed trough are in a tumult, there is one salmon or more in the net, enough to repay the fishers for a score of fruitless casts. But in nineteen cases out of twenty nothing disturbs the even *sinus* of the floating line, and the meshes float on like clouds in the translucent waters, carrying with them only light and feathery masses of pink and crimson kelp. The words "we have toiled all night and have taken nothing" come home with a ring of human effort unrewarded, as net after net is hauled only to be found empty. But the Christchurch fishermen are not a complaining race. No sooner has one net swung at the bottom of the river than another has started at the top and is waltzing down with the stream. The fun is kept up like the gallop in a cotillon, each pair of partners hoping as they start that the caprice of fortune will give them the prize. It comes at last. The ebb has been running for an hour, at which time the salmon smell the fresh-water out at sea, and, fired with the sudden recollection of love and adventure in the river, rush, throbbing with impetuous life, into the narrow waters of peril. Gently the net swings with the tide, contracting and lengthening as if invisible fingers were drawing its centre downwards to the sea, until it lies in the still water by the bank, a narrow channel of cloudy meshwork some fifty yards in length. Before half has been pulled on to the dripping pile of net and sea-weed which lies behind the haulers, a rush, a great gleam of white and silver, and a splash tell without need of the sudden shout "A fish! a fish!" that a salmon is in the toils. Furiously he dashes from end to end of the yielding trap, sending water, sand, and spray flying on every side. Desperately he drives his shining head into the dragging, sluggish, invisible meshes. Had he only the one further gift of reason than that which his experience gives, he would leap into the air and clear the encircling lines before it is too late. But the net curves quickly in and closes over the fish, and in a second it is lying a broad silver bar upon the yellow sand. The symmetry and lustrous sheen of such a salmon seen within a minute of its return from its unknown life in the ocean, perfect in form, strength, and vigorous life, makes good its claim to be considered almost the most beautiful of living creatures, and beyond comparison the finest fish that swims in British seas.

The first fish taken in the day gives an impulse to the work of every boat. Salmon seldom come up singly, but rush into the fresh-water in little parties of two, three, or four, and not unfrequently the whole company are taken in a single net. The fortunate captors "track" their boat back to the ferry at the head of the "Run" to await their next turn, and meantime row across to the little inn which stands upon the point. To carry a 20 lb. salmon by the gills, a man crooks his arms in to the hip, and even so only just swings its tail clear of the ground. The arrival of the fish is awaited by a critical company of veterans, knowing in the subject, who have already guessed its weight and recorded their opinions with a minuteness and emphasis which show that reputations may be made and lost even in guesses at the size of a salmon seen at a distance of two hundred yards upon the sands. For the fishing is alike the sport of youth and the solace of age. Custom allows one share of the proceeds to the boat, one to the net, and two to the crew, and veterans who own the two first can afford to spend their day watching the efforts of the last to earn a living at all. The accuracy with which the size is guessed is surprising. Of a dozen estimates made of the weight of a salmon which turned the scale at exactly 20 lbs., a mistake of $1\frac{1}{2}$ lbs. was the utmost limit of error. No difficulty is made of selling the fish upon the spot; and any one who is so fortunate as to be present when the capture is made may purchase it at from 2s. to 1s. 6d. per pound cheaper than would be paid in a Bond Street shop. Fifty-two pounds is, we believe, the weight of the largest taken in the Christchurch river; three fish of $38\frac{1}{2}$ lbs., 26 lbs., and 22 lbs. at one haul fell to the lot of one fortunate fisherman quite early last season towards the end of April. But the fish are few and captures rare; rarer, it is said, than in former days, when one of the oldest men boasts that he once took nine great salmon in a single haul.[1] But if these scarce southern fish can still be caught in sufficient number to pay, what might not be the value of a restored Thames salmon fishery in which the catch would be numbered by hundreds, delivered fresh and unspoilt by ice at London Bridge?

The few Christchurch salmon which find their way into the London shops, are sold at one-third above the price asked for those from more distant waters. These fish are caught so fresh from the sea that the salt is hardly washed from their scales; in the very mouth of the swift fresh river, yet within a stone's-throw of the breakers, and so near to London by rail that the epicure may see the fish upon his dinner-table within a few hours of the time that it was thrown glittering upon the white sea-sand. Their

---

[1] Mr. M. D. Barton informs me that inside the harbour great hauls of flounders are made. "I once saw," he adds, "one haul of nearly 200 flat-fish, the greater part flounders. They took the appearance of one immense heaving flat-fish, in which live flounders took the place of scales."

Salmon Fishing at Christchurch. By LANCELOT SPEED.

freshness alone would justify their reputation in the London markets. But there is a quality and refinement alike of flavour and appearance in the salmon of Christchurch which lifts them into a rank just one degree higher than that enjoyed by any others, even of their justly honoured race. The delicacy of their flavour is beyond verbal description; and while some vainly point to analogies in this or that taste of other and baser fishes, or find a reason for their excellence in the luxurious food of the fish on the Solent shore, pointing to the fact that a Christchurch salmon fresh from the sea will look at no less dainty bait than the pink-fleshed tail of a prawn, others more justly claim that their flavour is due to their being taken at the exact psychological moment in which their spirits reach the acme of salmonoid exuberance, at the instant of leaving the sea and entering the river; and, as extremes meet, the taste of the salmon which has met its death in an ecstasy of pleasure may well excel even that of the sucking-pig to which a gusto may be imparted, according to ancient writers, if its death be caused by flagellation, in an intenerating ecstasy of pain.

Contrary to experience, the largest fish taken from the Christchurch river seem to have been captured with the rod. In the casts of fish in the room at South Kensington, which contains the collections of the late Frank Buckland, is one of a 52 lb. salmon taken at Christchurch with the rod. It was a female fish, in the very brightest and best condition. A middle-aged farmer, with whom the writer had a chat on the way from Christchurch to the "Run," gave the following terse description of the chances of sport with the rod at Christchurch. He was a sincere admirer of the "Run" fishing, which is a kind of social institution for the Mudiford gossips who sit in the parlour of the little inn on the spit, and drink their ale, while they watch the hauling of the nets, and discuss the annals of the fishery with others "in the fancy." "They pays a deal of money, and they fishes very industrious ; and what they catches they aren't always allowed to keep. And often it so happens as them as fishes hardest toils in vain. Others come, and fishes with a light heart, and happen on the luck." By this time my friend had got well into the narrative style and continued like a book. "Once there came here a cricketer ; he was a cricketer, not a fisherman, any one could see. He never changed his cricket coat, but he took a boat just as he was. Yes ; just as he stood in his cricketing clothes. And the said cricketer hadn't fished ten minutes before he caught a thirty pound fish, and he landed him, that's what he did ; and he might never live to catch another."

The fishermen of the "Run" mostly belong to the little village of Mudiford, which lies close by, and are without exception the best mannered and most taking set of men I have ever seen in rural England, though I have heard of a fishing community near Land's End, who seem to have much resembled them, and been even more closely united. The life on the spit, between the inland lake and the sea, seems to have cut them off from the rather demoralizing influence which the proximity of shore life always has on fishermen, and at the same time made them great sportsmen and fowlers as well as fishermen. Hence they are often in request to manage fowling-yachts, punts, and apparatus for that kind of sport. There is a kind of double harvest going on all the year round, of fish and fowl, and as the men draw their nets their big guns are seldom far off. In summer, when the fowl are protected, they keep up a constant warfare on the cormorants. The proceedings seem quite well understood both by birds and men. The cormorant colony is on the Needles and the Freshwater cliffs, many miles across the Solent. The birds fly over, and rising high over the lurking guns, go up the harbour and there catch trout and eels till their crops are full. They then fly back, and over to the Needles, to feed their young. The burden of fish makes it more difficult for the cormorants to rise clear of gunshot, and each as it passes is saluted with a discharge of swan-shot. But very few seem to be killed, though the men declare that every cormorant robs the harbour of fourteen pounds weight of fish per diem. As they approach the sand-hills near the "Run," they rise gradually in the air, and then fly at full speed, with necks stretched, out to sea, saluted by the roar of the big guns discharged after them by the fisherlads.

The winter shooting, especially in severe weather like that of last year, must yield not only amusement, but a certain return in fowl to those men whose houses are within sight of the tidal harbour, and in some cases almost washed by its waters. They shoot against one another, and seem out at all hours, day, night, or dawn, so that a stranger has very little chance of a shot. But this is natural enough, seeing that the men live on the spot, and have a kind of prescriptive right to the fish and fowl of their own harbour.

THE LAST OF THE OSPREYS

It has recently been made matter of complaint against the Christchurch fishermen that they shoot the ospreys, which yearly visit their land-locked harbour. The complaint is perfectly justified, and the worst of it is that nothing will induce the men to take the modern view of the matter, and think that a live osprey is a "thing of beauty" which ought to be "a joy for ever." On the contrary, they think they look better stuffed, and if not, that they are worth more to sell than a wild goose or a couple of duck.

"Did you ever shoot an osprey?" I asked of a young fellow, the eldest of a family of brothers who were working their salmon-nets in turn. He was as fine a young Englishman as I ever saw, with light curling yellow hair, blue eyes, straight nose, and dressed in the most picturesque costume for that Norse type, a white jersey and flat sailor's cap.

"No, I *never had that pleasure!*" he replied, in the polite phrase which these men seem naturally to affect. But he had tried often enough, and it was interesting, though deplorable, to hear what trouble he had taken to do so. The motive was a purely sporting instinct, and the only form of protection would be for the Hampshire County Council to pass a resolution forbidding ospreys to be shot; the Dorsetshire Council might do the same for their protection in Poole Harbour further west. In the long lagoon of the "Fleet," inside Chesil Bank, they are probably safe enough, as most wild creatures are on the estates of great proprietors. Of all the rarer creatures of Great Britain, there is none that deserves protection more than the osprey. It is unique alike in structure and in habits; the sole representative of its class among birds, with strong affinities to the great fishing-owls of the tropics, though itself a true hawk, high-couraged and singularly friendly to man, and of a size and strength approaching that of the eagles. The safe channels in the Hampshire estuaries are marked out by a curious and probably very ancient method of sea-marks called "leather and twig." On one side are posts surmounted with old leather buckets, or sometimes pieces of trace, or a horse collar; but the old buckets, being part of the come-at-able refuse of ships' stores, are the commonest. To the stakes on the other side are fastened old birch brooms, or branches of trees. As the posts are far apart and the channels intricate, this rough contrivance indicates which post is to be considered on the right and which on the left of the channel. These posts, often surrounded by hundreds of acres of water, are the favourite perches of the osprey, and on them it sits unconcerned, every now and again leaving its post to catch a flounder or grey mullet, on which it pounces with a rush like that of the solan-goose, striking the water with its thickly feathered breast, and driving its strong talons deep into the fish. At Christchurch, where they are known as the "mullet-hawks," the young ospreys on their migration may be seen every autumn; and one at least of the residents by the estuary makes it his business, when prowling gunners are about, to be on the water in his punt, and scare away the too-confiding hawks from the posts on which they sit. Most of these young ospreys are probably bred in Norway and Sweden,—the older birds which are seen on their way northwards in the spring being bound for the same shores.

But some of the Christchurch ospreys are probably British birds, and it seems probable that the breeding places whence they come in autumn, or to which they are returning in spring, may be known with some approach to certainty. In a report recently read before the Zoological Society, it was stated that there are but three pairs which regularly breed in Scotland; and in recognition of the protection extended to these survivors by the owners on whose property the nests were built, the Society resolved to bestow their silver medal on Donald Cameron of Lochiel, and Sir John Peter Grant of Rothiemurchus. To Sir J. P. Grant, whose death occurred a few days before the day on which the presentation was to have been made, belonged the credit of protecting what is perhaps the most ancient continuous breeding-place of the osprey in the Highlands.

Loch-an-Eilan lies in the narrow gorge between the Cairngorm mountains and the hill of Ord Bain, bordered by deep woods of tall and ancient pines, the remnants of the original Caledonian forest. Near the western shore, but wholly surrounded by the waters of the lake, is an islet, covered by an ancient rectangular castle, said to have formed one of the strongholds of the " Wolf of Badenoch." Looking at the castle from the nearest point on the shore, the angle on the left is seen to be strengthened by a square tower, that on the right is formed by a smaller turret, and piled on this to a height of several feet, broad and substantial and enduring, is the ospreys' eyrie. Year after year the birds have travelled northwards to their ancient haunt, reaching the old castle in the same week, and thrice, it is said, upon the same day, April 1st ; and the record of their success or failure in rearing their brood is probably more complete than that of any similar period of birdhistory yet preserved. The nest was seen by MacCullough, the geologist, in 1824. It was robbed by Gordon-Cumming, afterwards known as the most ruthless and destructive of all African hunters, who is fabled to have carried an egg to the shore "in his mouth,"—probably in his bonnet, held between his teeth, as Lewis Dunbar carried the eggs which he robbed from a similar eyrie, in company with St. John, about the same time. Even after that date ospreys built not only on the island castle, but in the giant firs on the bank both of Loch-an-Eilan and the neighbouring Loch Morlaich ; but the continuous felling of timber so alarmed them that their numbers were reduced to the single pair upon Loch-an-Eilan. It was shortly after this period, in 1872, that a disaster occurred which for a time left the nest on the old castle tenantless. A sportsman, seeing a strange bird rise from a burn, shot what proved to be the male osprey; and though for two years the female bird returned in the first week of April, and remained by the nest waiting for her old mate to join her, she finally disappeared, and for six years no ospreys were seen on Loch-an-Eilan. But in the first week of April 1878, a pair revisited the castle, and at once set to work to repair the deserted nest upon the turret. In due time the eggs were laid; and as no boat was allowed upon the loch, the young were hatched, to the delight of the whole neighbourhood, who made common cause in the protection of the brood. For ten years the visits of the ospreys were not interrupted, and the care with which the fish-hawks brooded and fed their young has been the most interesting spring sight on Loch-an-Eilan. "All that was visible of the hen-bird," wrote a visitor [1] in 1880, "was her brown back on a level with the twigs, and her erect head and flashing eye, which she constantly turned with the restless watchfulness of all predatory birds. She was looking up the loch when we arrived, a position which she seemed to prefer, but successively faced in all directions. She formed an interesting sight, with her grey crest and head, and the

[1] Mr. W. Jolly, in the *Leisure Hour*.

darker line round the neck—which gave her the appearance of wearing a cowl—her pure white breast, and the long, hair-like feathers of the upper part of the body blown picturesquely about by the wind. She generally sat quiet on the nest, gazing round, now readjusting the bleached sticks of her nest, then changing her attitude to settle down in watchful repose. The extraordinary devotion of so wild a creature to the trying duties of motherhood was most impressive. She seldom left the nest day or night, being supplied with necessary nourishment by her loving and unwearied partner." Of the male bird the same observer writes:— "We saw the male bird approaching high in the air from the south. He swept round in narrowing circles, and finally settled on the nest beside his mate. While on the wing he showed nothing in his talons, which were hidden in the longer feathers beneath; but he came not empty-handed, for he laid on the broad edge of the nest a shining fish, and this the hen proceeded at once to consume. . . . His behaviour to his wife was at all times modest, dignified, and attentive, as befitted a bird of quiet tastes, good character, and aquiline rank." It is difficult, indeed, not to feel a grudge against the selfish egg-collectors, whose greedy agents ruin all the hopes of such patterns of animal happiness and duty. The ten years of unbroken peace in this highland home were broken by a tragedy which was due, not to human molestation, but to a curious and inexplicable family feud among the ospreys themselves, which has once more left the eyrie on the castle desolate. In the April

The Osprey's Home, Loch-au-Eilan. By Lancelot Speed.

of 1888 a pair reached the lake as usual, though with an interval of a few days between the arrival of the male bird and its mate. The last was evidently a stranger, though possibly one of the young hatched the year before, but it took possession of the nest, and busied itself in preparing it for the summer. A few days later a second female appeared, and from the moment of her arrival the eyrie was the scene of continuous warfare between the rival birds, each endeavouring to drive the other from the nest. The first-comer was the stronger, and maintained her place, in spite of the savage attacks of the older bird, who, soaring above the turret, pounced upon her back, and tore her plumage with beak and talons. For two days the struggle went on from dawn till dusk, with little intermission. On the third, the dispossessed osprey seemed exhausted, but her efforts to turn out the intruder did not cease until the latter, suddenly rising from the nest, flew towards her enemy, and struck her a blow which hurled her senseless into the lake. The victor then pounced upon her, and driving her talons on to her body, tore the wounded bird with beak and talons until she floated dead. The osprey then flew back to the nest which had been the object of this fatal warfare, but in a few days left the castle and built a nest in a fir-tree at some distance from the island. No eggs were laid, and the pair soon left Loch-an-Eilan, never to return together. Each year the male bird has visited the castle, on which it sits and calls for its dead mate, and after hovering anxiously round the old home for a few days, disappears, and is seen no more till in the early days of the following spring it renews its melancholy pilgrimage. Another pair have nested in the woods near Loch Morlaich, at a few miles' distance, but the solitary osprey of Rothiemurchus has not yet found a partner for his home on the ruined tower.

Doubtless the Zoological Society's informants are correct in saying that there exist only three eyries which have been *continuously* inhabited. But there is good reason to believe that the fishing-hawks have not left the country, but have only retired from their natural eyries on the lakes to the deep and inaccessible fir-woods which now cover so much of the once treeless north. Mr. Booth, who travelled from loch to loch, and visited all the eyries best known by tradition on the lakes, found them all deserted. He then explored the dense pine-forests which grow on the steep hillsides or marshy lower ground. "It was necessary," he writes, "to force a way through a tangled growth of gigantic heather, entwined in places with matted bushes of juniper or bog-myrtle, while here and there waving bogs of green and treacherous moss, intersected by stagnant pools or streams, blocked the way. The atmosphere was stifling, screened from every breath of wind; and clouds of poisonous flies and midges buzzed in myriads round one's head." There, in the largest pines, he found the new homes of the ospreys, which, like the golden-eagles, are protected by the quiet of the great preserves. On some of the larger estates, two or even three nests might be visited in a single day. In the more open districts the birds have wholly disappeared, or are only occasional visitors to the scenes which were once their chosen home throughout the spring and summer.

POOLE HARBOUR

THE estuaries on the coast have an even greater variety of wild life to amuse and interest a sea-side visitor than the cliffs; and floating on their wide expanse of shallow waters, or threading the delta of mud-flats and rivulets that shift with every tide, is to many an experience as novel and interesting as the cries and forms of the birds which haunt them.

Sheldrakes, curlews, dotterels, plovers, herons, and the like, look very different when swimming or flying, and when hanging in a poulterer's shop. What strikes a new-comer most is the great number of the waders and other birds which he sees on his visits to any favourite estuary, such as Poole Harbour, or the Aldboro' river, especially when the flood-tide is making, and the birds are crowded together, busily feeding on such parts of the mud as are not covered by the rising tide. But it must be remembered that as all these birds feed mainly on the mud-flats, and can only do so at low-water, they are forced to meet at one time, and are obliged to feed in company, like city men at luncheon.

The best way to learn the habits of the fowl is to row up on the flood-tide with a boatman, if possible a local fisherman who knows the habits of the birds and the set of the tide. Yet the exploration of such harbours without local knowledge has its charms. My first visit to Poole Harbour was paid in the form which all history prescribes as the right one for approaching unknown shores, that is by sea, and on a voyage of discovery. In other words we were in a yacht—a large and comfortable steam-yacht—which had to be very carefully navigated into the harbour and over the bar. An hour spent musing over the charts in the chart-house on deck as we crossed the chord of the Bournemouth Bay, after rounding Hurst Castle, showed more completely than most maps the extraordinary character of this intricate estuary, for a chart shows the formation not only of the land, but of the sea-bottom, and the fathom-markings show the respective areas of shoal, deep water, sand, and mud-bank.

The chart not only showed how at Poole, harbour lay within harbour, like the outline of a bunch of grapes, but the enormous expanse of "slob-lands" in proportion to navigable water in these inland lagoons. One inlet runs for many miles up towards the "Trough of Poole," another, Hollesley Bay, lies at the back, and to the east of Poole town, which itself lies several miles from the narrow entrance. To the left another lagoon stretches inland further than the eye can see, surrounding islands of sound ground with trees and cattle on them. But we were not prepared for the positive beauties which the entrance to the harbour disclosed, though expecting that substitute for beauty — picturesqueness — which seems inseparable from harbour scenery.

As we came slowly in over the blue water, and passed over the bar, our surprise and admiration increased. On the right was a spit of sand-hills, covered with masses of purple heather and a few wind-blown pines. To the left lay Brownsea Island, with its castle and trees; to the left a wide inland sea, lying between Brownsea Island and the long sweep of Purbeck, with the keep of Corfe Castle standing up far off, black against the evening sun. In front lay the way up to Poole town, with quaint ports and sea-marks, and one or two pretty wooden sailing vessels dipping down with the tide. On either side of Poole the sea seemed to run inland till lost in heather and pines.

It was the first of August, the opening day for wild-fowl shooting, and bare-legged fishermen were standing on one or two shingle-banks just left by the tide, firing at flocks of ring-dotterels which were shifting about the harbour. We also caught the infection, and getting the yacht's dingy, rowed off towards the setting sun up the branch of the estuary. There is a singular charm in such an excursion into unknown waters. Even the minor problems of navigation, when a choice has to be made between different channels among thousands of acres of slob and sea-weed-covered ooze, serve to remind one of the difficulties which real explorers have to encounter in the unknown river waters which are so often the first road of entrance to newly-discovered countries. Beyond Brownsea Island were two hilly and bare islets. On either side the slob was emerging minute by minute, curlews and gulls were flitting to and fro, and the level beams of sunset lit up the flats with a blaze of mellow gold. On the left, beyond the flats, was a great plain of heather, gradually rising mile by mile towards the cliffs of Purbeck Island. Among the commonest and most interesting of the harbour ducks are the sheldrakes. They are devoted parents, and as the boat drifted up between the grey banks of ooze, the big black and white birds were seen watching anxiously by the harbour's edge, while the young ones, full-grown, but unable to fly, were swimming out in mid-stream. Presently the old birds rose and flew in swift circles, and the young ones dived. The boat being rowed quickly towards the places where they disappeared, they scattered, and when next they rose, showed only their heads above water, diving again instantly at the slightest movement. Meantime the old bird settled at some distance, and soon the young were seen rising from below water all round her, after which they swam off up the nearest creek.

If chased into a narrow channel, the young will sometimes leave the water, poke their heads into a crevice, and allow themselves to be caught. The eggs are generally laid in a rabbit-burrow in the great heather-clad plain to the left of the harbour, often at a considerable distance from the water. Sir R. Payne Gallwey states that he saw one, "when the tide was low, and she was unable to lead her brood to the sea, carry them on her back, each duckling holding on by a feather, having, while she lay down, climbed up and ensconced themselves with the greatest care." We were anxious to get a young sheldrake as a specimen, and rowed up the stream which flows down from Corfe Castle, in pursuit of another brood of the young ducks. Their skill and quickness in swimming and diving for a long time defeated us. But as the river grew narrower the space left to the birds for submarine tactics was contracted, and we secured one to take back to the yacht. It was of a white and cinnamon colour, not in the least like the plumage of the old birds, but a handsome creature, both in the tint and texture of its skin. Meantime the sun had sunk, the flats grew dark, and the broad stretch of water had changed into a great level mud-flat, fringed by dark heather and pines, and intersected by a winding, baffling stream down which we crept towards the yacht's lights in the distance. As the night drew on the whole harbour seemed alive with birds. Ducks, curlews, and waders flitted to and fro, and the air was full of calls and sounds quite unfamiliar to inland naturalists. Every now and again we heard the croak of a heron, as one after another they flew in and took up their stations for the night's fishing. Long after bed-time, as we lay awake listening to the lap of the water against the yacht's side and the rush

Flight of Sea Birds. *From a photograph by* B. Wyles.

of the tide on the cables, the cries of the coast-birds could be heard—the familiar noises of Neptune's poultry-yard, feeding round the threshold of the deep.

At the end of the great frost of the beginning of the year 1895 I paid another visit to the harbour; this time approaching it from the east, along the Bournemouth and Branksome sands, and following the coast-line to the extreme point of the sand-hills at the harbour entrance. Race-horses, frozen out from Newmarket Heath, were training on the edge of the sand, under the yellow cliff; the sun was bright and hot under the shelter of the pines, and the sea was slipping in in waves so tiny that they barely rose to the height of the horses' fetlocks. They were the merest pretence and fiction of waves—sportive, illusive—yet where the long sand-dam joins the upper cliff, and shuts in the right-hand haven of Poole from the sea, where the entrance would be, and may have been, before the sand-hills grew, was the fresh wreck of a thousand ton ship, her paint new, her fittings perfect, except the bulwarks, and her name still legible upon the stern. She had tried to make the entrance of Poole harbour, when caught in the gale, the effects of which upon the sea-fowl have been described in a previous chapter.[1] The Swanage life-boat came out gallantly through the " Race " which runs round " Old Harry Rock " at St. Alban's Head, but the boat was swamped and the coxswain drowned. Then

---

[1] The Sea-Fowl and the Storm, p. 17.

the Poole lifeboat came down, and saved the men on the vessel, who were in danger of death, not only from the sea, but from the certainty that if left on the stranded ship they would be frozen to death. Opposite the wreck, but on the margin of the shore, lay the backbone of an older wreck, part of a smaller vessel lost many years before. It is a curious tribute to the constancy of the set of the current in the gales most dangerous on this coast, that had the new wreck been able to drift right on shore, she would in all probability have laid her timbers on the bones of her predecessor in disaster. The sand-hills were quite beautiful even in the frost. The heather and moss which contrives to exist even on the sand were of the richest dark plum-colour and green respectively. The frost had nipped all the dead heather blossom off, and this lay in little piles and patches, like dark seed-pearls, daintily scattered on the sand. In other places the wind-blown sand had been quite freshly piled, and was covered with the tracks of mice, and strange to say, of rats, which had been out foraging for food the night before. On the other side of the sand-hills the wind was blowing down the harbour, bitterly cold. Nearly all the harbour was ice-bound, and the swans, to avoid being nipped by the ice, had collected together in a flock in one of the bays, where by constantly swimming and keeping together, they kept a little circle of still unfrozen water. All other fowl seem to have forsaken the harbour for some less frozen sea.

THE SWANNERY AT ABBOTSBURY

WHETHER judged by the strangeness and beauty of its surroundings, or the number and variety of the wild birds that make it their home, there is no more attractive spot for the naturalist, even on the line of coast which includes Poole Haven, Christchurch, and Lymington, than the Fleet, the straight lagoon which runs for nine miles from the Isle of Portland to Abbotsbury, behind the barrier of Chesil Beach. There is not an acre of water on the narrow shining lagoon, or a rood of shingle on the Chesil Beach which banks it in, that is not the chosen home of the wild-fowl of the river or the shore. During the winter, wild ducks and coots in thousands crowd the sheltered waters of the Fleet; in summer, the hot and hazy surface of the shingle swarms with the young of the terns and dotterels; and at the head of the water, in an almost tropical growth of pampas grass and fuchsias, and the rankest luxuriance of the herbage of the marsh, is the swan paradise of Abbotsbury. The nine straight miles of water below is only the playground of the birds; but in spring this is forsaken, except by a few pairs that nest on the inner side of Chesil Beach; and the rich and sheltered mead which fringes Abbotsbury Brook is white with the graceful forms of a thousand nesting swans. In this their ancient haunt, so ancient that although the hills behind are crowned with the ruins of votive chapels and ancient monasteries, the swans may claim for their established home an equal if not greater antiquity, all the favourite sites were, at the time of a visit paid early in April, occupied by the jealous and watchful birds, each keenly resentful of intrusion on its territory, yet in such close proximity to its neighbours that a space of ten or twelve feet at most divided it from ground in " separate and hostile occupation." Near the mouth of a small stream which enters the Fleet below a close and extensive bed of reeds, now cut down and stored for the use of the birds when building, lies the ground most coveted by the swans. There, between two hundred and three hundred nests, or sites for nests, were occupied on a space of two acres at most. So anxious are the birds to secure a place on this favourite spot, that they remain sitting constantly on the place when occupied, in order to maintain their rights against intruders, and there collect with their long necks every morsel of reed and grass within reach to form a platform for the eggs. At this time the swanherd visits them constantly, and scatters bundles of dried reeds from the stacks, which are eagerly gathered in by the swans and piled round and beneath them as they sit. These additions to the nest go on continually; and as the cock-swan takes his share, or even more than his share, of the duties of sitting upon the eggs, one of the pair is always at liberty to collect fresh material. This is mainly piled in a kind of wall round the nest, the interior being already finished, and often partly felted with a lining of swansdown from the birds' breasts. To the visitor who, under the guidance of the swanherd, walks on the narrow grass-paths which wind amid the labyrinth of nests, the colony recalls visions of visits to the island-homes of the great petrels or giant albatrosses in distant oceans. Many of the swans have built their nests so that they even encroach upon the paths; and each of the great birds as he passes throws back its snake-like head, and with raised crest hisses fiercely and rattles the pinions of its wings, or even leaves the nest, and, with every feather quivering with excitement, makes as though it would drive the intruder from the sanctuary. But the presence of the swanherd generally reassures the birds, though the hissing rises and falls as if from the throats of a thousand angry snakes. In view of the natural jealousy and fierceness of swans in the breeding season, the comparative gentleness of the Abbotsbury birds is somewhat remarkable. On the rivers and broads of Norfolk, each pair claims and secures a large stretch of water for their sole use, and constant and sometimes fatal fights take place if the reserved territory is invaded by another pair. There, also, the swans will occasionally attack not only strangers, but the swanherds themselves, who, owing to the extent of the streams and dykes along which the swans nest, are, of course, less well-known to the birds than are the keepers at Abbotsbury. Mr. Stevenson was told by John Trett, a marshman of Surlingham, that he was " attacked by an old male swan as he was examining the eggs in a nest, to which, being a boggy place, he had crawled on his hands and knees. The swan, coming up behind him unperceived, struck him so violently on the back, that he had difficulty in regaining his boat, where he laid for some time in great pain, and though he managed at length to pull home, he was confined to his bed for more than a week." Another marshman was struck on the thigh in the same manner, and described the force of the blow and the pain occasioned by it as something incredible. The Abbotsbury swans, though not pinioned like the Norfolk birds, and leading a life of freedom on the verge of the sea, seem to know by instinct that the protection and safety which they obtain at Abbotsbury is more than enough to compensate them for the loss of the freedom and independence which an isolated nesting-place must give ; and with the exception of about twenty pairs, they congregate as has been described, abandoning not only their natural instincts for isolation, but also much of the combativeness with which this instinct is accompanied. Fights between the cock swans do occur. But the swanherd soon restores peace. One fine old bird which had quarrelled with both of its neighbours, was made happy by a

semicircle of tamarisk boughs stuck in the earth around its nest, and so clearly defining its territory.

Whether viewed from the land seawards, or from Chesil Beach across the Fleet, the scene was alike rich in life and colour. The strangeness of the view from Chesil Bank inwards makes it perhaps the more striking. To the right stretches an apparently endless line of dark-blue sea, separated from the lighter waters of the Fleet by the golden shingle of "the Bank," which vanishes into yellow haze towards Portland Island. On the Fleet opposite floated hundreds of white swans, among which the black coots and cormorants swam and dived like imps among the angels. The further shore was again fringed with the dead-gold of the reed-stumps, backed by the rich green of the hills beyond. As the evening drew on, the birds and animals of the shore and the lake seemed to enjoy an exclusive dominion over their respective haunts. No human being was in sight, and the nine miles of Chesil Beach were probably untrodden by any creature larger than the hares which came hopping down from the hills to feed upon a wild vetch which grows among the shingle on the shore. The mackerel-fishing had not begun, and the men of Abbotsbury and Chickerel village were busy with farm work, leaving the eels and grey mullets which swarm in the Fleet to the cormorants and divers, which were busily fishing in the shallow water. Gregory Gill, the swanherd, and his boy had just crossed the water-meadows on their way to the village; every labourer had gone home an hour before;

and the writer, with an old swan and a hare which were sitting side by side on the shingle, were the only spectators. The variety of sound was as great as that of colour. The whistle of the ringed plover, the harsh cry of the coots, and the angry deep note of the male swan as he rushed at a rival, churning up the water with his powerful wings, with a noise like a distant paddle-steamer, rang out through the still air. The gulls were calling, laughing, and crying, and across the Fleet came the song of the land-birds from the poplar-grove behind the swannery. Then we saw the flight of the swan, a sight which the practice of pinioning these birds makes so rare in England. Four swans rose slowly from the mere, after a short rush across the surface, in which their wings beat the water into foam, and rose slowly upwards in Indian file, ascending steadily against the breeze. When they had gained the height they desired, they circled round the head of the lagoon, and from among the great flight-feathers of the beating wings there came back a measured sound like the ring of a tubular bell. Straight out over the meadows they flew, until they seemed like snowflakes over the church-tower a mile away, the bell-like sound growing fainter, but still heard, as it was echoed back from St. Catherine's Hill, and increasing in tone and volume as the birds once more circled back towards the mere.

The annals of the swannery, so far as the writer could gather its more recent history on the spot, are not without chapters of disaster to the white-winged community in the Fleet. The total number is at present 1002 ; but last year the cold and wet of the summer were so fatal to the cygnets, that out of 800 hatched all died but one ; 150 only were reared by hand. The birds are still 500 less than the total number of the flock before the year 1881. The frost in that winter caused the greatest disasters from which the swannery has suffered during the present generation. A heavy north-west gale drove so much water out of the Fleet, that when the frost came, the ice caught and embedded the top of the grasses which grow on the submarine fields below. As the water returned to its normal level, the ice rose with it, and dragged all the grass up by the roots, thus destroying over the whole area the main food of the swans. For the next three years the swans had to be fed with grain ; but at first they refused to touch the new food, and one thousand adult swans perished of starvation. Though the grass has now grown again, the birds have never lost their liking for the corn which they at first refused ; even the severe winter of 1891 did not injure them.

The history of this, which is not the most ancient swannery in our country, but the only one surviving in England, has been briefly summarized by Mr. Mansell Pleydell, in his *History of the Birds of Dorsetshire*. "There are records of a swannery," he writes, "long previous to the Reformation ; the abbots of the neighbouring monastery being its owners. At its dissolution, Henry VIII. granted it to Giles Strangways, the ancestor of the present owner (Lord Ilchester), who raised the number of the swans in the course of fourteen years from 800 to 1500." The heirs of Giles Strangways were successful in defending their right to the birds, when it was contested on behalf of Queen Elizabeth that the swans, *if marked*, belonged to him, though those which were not marked, "having gained their natural liberty by swimming in an open river, might be seized to the sovereign's use by her prerogative, because they are royal birds."

In August the cygnets of the year are nearly fully fledged, but are shut in pens with the old birds in order to keep them warm. By this time the swans begin to scatter over the whole of the Fleet, and even go into Weymouth Harbour. By this time the young terns, bred on the Chesil Bank, are also fledged and on the wing. The country boys catch them by putting a noose propped open with a straw just above a fish. The birds stoop down, and are caught by the neck. Later in mid-winter, the coots assemble on the Fleet, and in autumn sometimes an osprey. In March the ducks stay for a short time before going north, and the swannery waters are crowded with them. The few that stay to nest go up into the hills, and bring their young later down the streams to the Fleet. They have been seen swimming down the brook through the village in the grey of the morning.

Abbotsbury is one of the choice spots of southern England. The place is as interesting as the birds. Sub-tropical trees and shrubs grow in the gardens; there are the remains of the monastery, and the old chapel on St. Catherine's Hill, and the terraces showing the ancient cultivation of the soil when each man had a strip in the common fields. Game swarms, especially hares and pheasants. But there is probably no more ancient institution native to the place than the swannery, which has existed for 800 years, and there seems no reason why it should not continue for an equal time to delight visitors from the cities of men to the city of swans by the sea.

THE PINE AND HEATHER COUNTRY

IN PRAISE OF PINE-WOODS

THE southern home counties are at present the scene of a sudden change of ideas on the subject of "eligible building property," which must before long alter not only the general appearance of large tracts of country which have, until now, remained almost uninhabited since the memory of man, but also the character and mode of life of what were until lately among the most rural and primitive districts of the South. The rush to the pine-woods, with its transference of capital from the suburbs not only of London, but of the great towns of the Midlands and the North, to the heaths of Berkshire, Surrey, and Western Hampshire, is assuming the dimensions of an urban exodus. Measured by the standard of the realized wealth and spending power which it represents, it must be allowed to count in some degree as a makeweight against the loss to the rural districts by immigration to the towns. That the movement is not a mere foible of the hour, but based upon a strong conviction that the pine countries present real and abiding advantages for modern country life, seems clear from the insistence with which the newcomers cling to the heaths, and refuse the most tempting offers to build outside them. The villas follow the line of the sand as closely as collieries follow the line of the coal. Even the outlying and detached wastes, which, until recently, lay barren and uninhabited among the Surrey hills, or Hampshire commons, are parcelled out and covered with substantial houses; and there are signs that, before many years, the main tract of the pine country will be converted into one immense residential suburb, composed of houses graded to suit all incomes from £500 a year upwards.

The extent of the pine country is not so great as to render this surmise improbable. Though it reaches into the three counties of Surrey, Hampshire, and Berkshire, it covers a very limited area in each. Hampshire and Berkshire are, in the main, chalk soils; and the area of the Surrey heaths is more than balanced by the Weald, the mixed soils, and the downs. A line drawn from Bracknell, through Ascot, and thence to Weybridge, marks the northern limits of the true pine-country, which forms an almost equilateral triangle, with its apex at Liss, on the southern boundary of Woolmer Forest. This portion includes Fleet, Farnham, Aldershot, Bisley, Weybridge, Woking, and the Hind Head Commons. South of Liss, the Mæon Valley and the Chalk Downs block the way. Further south, in the "purlieus" of the New Forest, the sand once more appears, and finds its final limit, and the perfection of its peculiar beauties, in the pine-woods and cliffs of the great Bournemouth Bay, and by the shores of Branksome and Poole Harbour. In the larger northern position, which may be roughly estimated at 120,000 acres, the greater part is already marked with the present or proposed sites for building. From the heights of St. George's Hill to the desolate flats of Fleet, the roofs of the red houses stand thick among the pines, or above the birch and heather. The great common at the back of Hind Head is becoming a mere "hinter-land" to villa-gardens, except where the ground still remains in the hands of one or two owners of vast possessions; and by the cliffs and chines of Bournemouth, where, in the memory of living men, yachts' crews landed to fetch water from the little "bourne" by a solitary coastguard-station, a population of forty thousand inhabitants is imbedded in the pines, and thinks itself fortunate to secure a place in the groves upon the cliffs, at a price of from £1000 to £2000 an acre.

Bournemouth is the capital city of the new country, though placed at its extreme limit; there all has been done that money and forethought can accomplish, to anticipate the wants of the new settlers in this sandy Arcadia. The creation of Bournemouth is one of the economic puzzles of the century, quite as remarkable, and hardly less rapid, than the rise of Middlesborough or Barrow-in-Furness; for its population has gathered not to make money, but to spend it. The greater number were, in all probability, free to choose any other part of England for a residence. The reason for their building a "city to dwell in" on this long line of Hampshire sand-cliff, must be sought in some amenity of the site, not so obvious as to be perceived at once, or Bournemouth would have been built long ago, yet capable of appealing to the senses of the greater number of those who visit it. The proximate reason of any sea-side colony usually lies in some very direct appeal to sentiment or convenience. Beachy Head "made" Eastbourne, Brighton is London-by-the-Sea, Hastings lies on a sunny shelf, Scarborough and Whitby are the natural marine towns of the West Riding, Ryde and Cowes are the yachting centres, Ilfracombe and Lynton share the double beauties of Exmoor, and of coast scenery unrivalled in the West. Bournemouth can claim none of these special advantages. The long line of yellow cliffs, with the distant bastions of chalk precipice, Freshwater, and the Needles on the east, and the pillared cliffs of St. Albans Head to the west, beyond the wide blue waters of the bay, give to the seaward view a breadth and simplicity which grows upon the imagination. But it is not by its coast, or even by the bright waters of its sand-paved sea, which the wildest storm cannot discolour, that the place prevails on those who visit it, to make there an abiding home. It is the whispering of the deep pine-wood that lines the land, and not the voices of the sea, which they hear and obey. The pine-wood of Bournemouth is to the plantations of the sand country what the groves of Mark-Ash are to the beech-woods of the New Forest, the climax of an ascending scale of sylvan beauty, produced by the gradual and natural advance to perfection of a single species of tree, in a setting which varies in degree of beauty, but not in general features. What the charm of this pine-forest must have been, before it was discovered and inhabited, can only be conjectured, though the first care of the settlers has been to preserve the trees, so far as the construction of roads and houses allows, and their further felling is forbidden by the strictest obligations of leases, and the enforcement of local regulations against wanton burning and injury. It is a fact that the cross-bill, the rarest and shyest of the birds of the Northern forest, still breeds in the Bournemouth woods; and the ground is covered by half-gnawed cones flung down by the squirrels, which build their nests on the very verge of the cliffs. The trees in the oldest and thickest woods are not the Scotch fir, or the ragged spruce, which cover so much of the so-called "pine districts," but true Western pines, flat-topped and straight-stemmed, with a crown of upcurved branches, studded with masses of heavy cones, full of seed, and as prolific as on the shores of the Mediterranean. Many of these trees are more than a century old, and cover cliff and glen alike with high vistas of tall grey stems, lightly roofed by the intersections and multiplied upward curves of the branches which lace the sky, but admit both air and light to the ground below. Thus, in the oldest woods, though the mass of falling pine-needles makes the surface as soft and noiseless to the tread as in the thick and crowded new plantations of the Woking heaths, the bracken-fern has space to grow, and the soil between the trunks is filled with all the minor ornament of heather, woodbine, and wild-rose. In the hollows, masses of rhododendron grow self-sown, and where the sea-wind strikes the summit of the cliffs, a tangle of young pines makes a natural and complete provision for the shelter and quiet of the deep woods beyond. In their peaceful precincts, in the sound of the sea-wind in the branches, the subtle scent of the pines and heather, which no rough wind can ever dissipate, in the breadth and quiet of the sandy forest, in the dryness and clearness of its air, purified by trees and sea, the attraction of the newly discovered country lies. Were its area ten times greater than it is, it would hardly satisfy the wants of those who have yielded to its charm. It is already crowded, not from choice, but because there is not building space for those who desire to live there. The last thing to be desired as the result of the new exodus is a reconstruction of town life and amusements ; yet that is exactly what is taking place in the choicest districts of the pine country. If it becomes a matter of faith that this is the best soil, and the best air and surroundings to make life happy and prolonged, there is no price that will not be paid, within the scope of individual means, to secure its enjoyment. But the limits of space must control the limits of population, beyond which the peculiar amenities of the district cannot survive. There are signs that this limit is

G

already nearly in sight; though in the parts of Dorsetshire adjacent to the Poole district there is still a great extent of similar country available, and the question arises, Where else will be found the same conditions? Perhaps on the Norfolk heaths; or, if the climate of the East Coast is a barrier, we may see the growth of another and more perfect city in the pines, in the wide sand-hills of the Landes, between the Garonne and the Adour in sunny Gascony.

SELBORNE AND WOLMER FOREST

THE power of locality to form tastes, and its impotence to subdue character, are shown with curious completeness in the cases of Gilbert White and William Cobbett. The same district and the same soil—for Farnham is only twelve miles from Selborne, and both are lands of beech-hangers and hop-gardens, and both abut on sandy heaths—was the birth-place of the authors of the *History of Selborne* and the *Rural Rides*. Each formed in youth such binding ties with the land and those that live by it, that he was impelled to revisit the old home and the old scenes, and each has left descriptions of them unmatched by art. But at this point the power of locality ended. White, the contemplative, returned from Oriel and Oxford to become of free will "a stationary man," to spend his days in secure enjoyment and observation of the district he loved. Cobbett, when, after the third attempt, he had broken free from the ties of his father's farm at Farnham, returned only to look down from the hill-tops on his native land, and then, after "blessing it altogether" in some of the finest descriptive English ever printed, rode back to London to bombard his enemies in the *Political Register*, and denounce Pitt and paper-money. Sometimes the temptation came to him to abandon his warfare, not for a life of contemplation, like White's, but for one of rural progress and business success, the secret of which none knew better than Cobbett; and some such thought was probably in his mind when he remarked, on his visit to Selborne, that "people ought to be happy there, for that God had done everything for them." But the memory of private wrongs and hope of public reforms thrust the thought aside. "The delight of seeing Prosperity Robinson hang his head for shame! the delight of beholding the tormenting embarrassments of those who have so long retained crowds of base miscreants to revile me! . . . Shall Sidmouth then never again hear of his *Power of Imprisonment Bill*, his *Circular*, his *Letter of Thanks to the Manchester Yeomanry?* I really jumped up when the thought came across my mind, and without thinking of breakfast, said, 'Go, George, saddle the horses,' for it seemed to me that I had been meditating some crime!"

Selborne to-day is little changed since Cobbett visited it after a reader of his paper had sent him White's book; and the village itself can scarcely have altered since White wrote, except that his house has been enlarged, and there is a new rectory. To a visitor the first impressions of the village are perhaps disappointing, though the lofty beech-covered hill above it, and the romantic glen called the Leith, below the church, bear out all that has been written of them. The one striking feature of the place is the position of the church, on a promontory jutting out into this Leith valley, looking from which the square tower stands like some small fortress closing the steep and narrow glen, backed by the great beech-wood of Selborne Hill. The ancient yew-tree in the churchyard still flourishes, and the interior of the church, with its double row of massive pillars, has all the dignity which Norman or very Early English architects knew how to give to buildings, however small, and the monuments and fabric show every sign of decent and reverent care. Still, the features of Selborne itself are hardly such as might be expected to inspire a classic.

Wolmer forest, on the other hand, three-fifths of which lie in the parish of Selborne, is a strangely fascinating region, containing some of the wildest scenery of the South, full of strange birds and rare plants and insects, and improved, rather than lessened, in natural beauty, since it afforded White "much entertainment both as a sportsman and a naturalist." In his day it "consisted entirely of sand covered with heath and fern, without having one standing tree in its whole extent," but was studded with large meres and marshes. Now the waters have shrunk; but much of the forest is covered with plantations of pine, and even of oak. The fir-plantations were made by Cobbett's enemy, "the smooth Mr. Huskisson," and formed the text for a ferocious attack on him as Commissioner of

Woods and Forests; but though the price now fetched by the wood bears out the economical side of Cobbett's criticism, the trees add much to the beauty and character of the forest. "This lonely domain," says Gilbert White, "is an agreeable haunt for many sorts of wild fowls, which not only frequent it in winter, but breed there in summer,—such as lapwings, snipes, wild ducks, and, as I have discovered within these last few years, teals." During a spring walk in the forest, it was the writer's fortune to find the nest of every bird which White mentions as breeding there, except that of the black grouse, which, though introduced for a time, has become nearly as rare as in his days. At the northern end of the forest, near Walldon Hill, is a marsh, not a mere swamp in the peats, but such a marsh as hunted outlaws may have sheltered in, over which the flame of the will-o'-the-wisp may still dance on summer nights; a wide sheet of black water, with dead white limbs of drowned trees standing out from it, and winding labyrinths of dwarf alders covered with wet mosses and hanging lichens, and mats of bright green grass so firmly tangled that a boy can walk on them, and outside these quaking platforms thick beds of reed. This is the home and nursery of the wild fowl of the forest, where duck and teal, dabchicks and water-hens, bring up their young broods till the helpless time of flapperhood is over. But the ducks and teal do not nest in the marsh; and we found White's observations exactly true, the teals nesting at a considerable distance from the water, and the wild ducks in some of the furthest and driest parts of the forest. About a hundred yards from the marsh was a teal's nest. She had hatched her young the day before, but two eggs remained, of a pale ivory colour, and the nest, which was placed in deep heather under a seedling fir, was beautifully made of moss and speckled down from the bird's breast, which exactly matched in colour the lichen-covered heather. Had we risen at daybreak, we might perhaps have met the bird taking her tiny brood down to the water. A wild duck's nest was found on a steep, heather-clad hill, quite a mile from the water. There are few more difficult nests to find than that of a wild duck on a heath. But in this case a single breast-feather gave the clue needed, and after careful search a track was found winding among the heather-stems to a thick patch under the overhanging boughs of a young pine, beneath which was the nest. The eggs had been hatched for some time, and all the broken shells were buried beneath a layer of down. In a wet hollow near the outskirts of the forest was a snipe's nest. These birds are far less common there than formerly, owing, it is said, to the turf being no longer cut for fuel, so that there is less fresh ground exposed for them to feed upon. The nest was simply a round hollow in a wet tussock; but when their brood is hatched, the snipes are said to be most affectionate parents. This particular pair are said to have nested in the same place last year. Some men employed to dig sand close by were surprised to see a snipe fly up, which, after showing great unwillingness to quit the spot, perched on a rail about four yards off—a most unusual thing for a snipe to do—and remained watching them. Soon after, they discovered at the bottom of the pit four very young snipes lying together, which they took up and laid upon the level ground, whence they were soon called away by the mother-bird into the rough grass near.

Plovers nest on the swamps and rough hill-sides; and there are a fair number of wild pheasants and partridges on the sides of the forest. Squirrels swarm in the pine-trees, and live on the seeds of the cones. But perhaps the most interesting colony in the forest is the heronry. Perhaps this is a recent settlement, for Gilbert White does not speak of it. The nests are in a plantation of tall pines in the very heart of the forest, where one or two small brooks, deeply tinged with iron deposits, flow through the wood. The trees are so tall as to be inaccessible to the climber; and as the great birds launch themselves from their nests, and sail round with harsh cries above the tree-tops, the visitor might well imagine himself back in some bygone forest era. The trees on which the nests are placed are covered by a thick green lichen, and are readily distinguished from the rest. One rare bird, the Dartford Warbler, which haunts the forest, has been almost destroyed by the recent severe winters; and great numbers of woodpeckers have also died. But in the ring of lofty firs which caps the hill above the pool of Holly-water, there are a number of their nests, or rather the holes drilled in successive years for their nests, by the pairs which annually breed in this favourite spot. One of them had been robbed by the squirrels, which had sucked the eggs and flung the shells upon the ground. Higher up in the firs were the nests of carrion crows and hawks, robber birds which haunt this lofty eyrie, and, soaring round the hill, or perched upon the dead branches of the trees, keep a watchful eye upon the forest for miles around.

Wolmer forest is a good instance of a Government property managed with good taste and good sense. The forest fires, of which Gilbert White speaks, are now kept in check so far as the limited number of warders available can do so, and the wild life of the district is just apparently preserved to give that additional interest to woodland scenery, from the absence of which the forests of France suffer so greatly. If the origin of the sentiment which preserves these creatures were sought, it would probably be found in the writings of Gilbert White of Selborne.

SURREY SCENES

THE SURREY PONDS

Pools and still waters are as characteristic of the country in which they lie as rivers and running brooks. The beauties of a Highland tarn and a Norfolk broad are as separate and appropriate to their own surroundings as the rushing moorland stream, and the level and tranquil windings of the Waveney or the Yare. Even the clay-embedded water-holes of the Suffolk farms, surrounded by their ragged clumps of thorns, and peopled by ancient carp which burrow in the mud in winter, and welter in the thick and tepid waters in the summer droughts, have a certain interest native to the soil; and the moats of the decayed manor-houses, where rich franklins once kept their "bream and luce in stew," are still haunted by traditions of monster pike, the pets and familiar friends of past tenants of the farms. Among the bright heaths and moorlands of Surrey, and the adjacent corners of Hampshire and Sussex which meet near the sources of the Rother, the Wey, and the Deadwater, the "ponds" are perhaps the most beautiful and interesting features of the loveliest country within an hour of London. A glance at the map will show a hundred of these pools, some among the dry heaths on an impervious ironstone bottom, and often reaching the dimensions of small lakes, like Frensham pond, the Fleet, or Broadwater, near Godalming; others, perhaps the richest of all in bird and fish life, in such valleys as Chilworth, or the marshy meadows of the lower Wey. But the most picturesque, and perhaps the least known, are the long chains of pools which lie back among the hills. In the rich profusion of soils at the roots of the Hind Head, where hops and heather jostle, and the full-fed oak kisses the starveling pine, the head-waters of rivers gather in these ponds. Like the Spider Mountains of Argos, the hills spread their web where the three counties meet, and between their strands lie the lines of upland pools. Follow any of the hollows in the dry moor downwards, and the signs of subterranean waters are apparent. Oaks mingle with the pines, and the rabbit-turf grows greener and more compact. Loam takes the place of peat and sand in the banks, and beech and alder spring up in the hollows. Yet even there you may stand within a few minutes' walk of a chain of small lakes stretching for miles into the hill, and not know in which direction to seek them. The sound of falling water, the scent of wood and peat smoke curling up from a cottage chimney into which it seemed easy to drop a pebble, and the gleam of a pool seen forty feet below, were the first evidence to the writer that he had chanced on one of the beautiful chains of ponds which form the sources of the river Wey. Narrow peninsulas of sound turf jut out from either side of the glen, washed by the streamlet whose ripple was heard above. On one of these stands the game-keeper's cottage, and below it lies the pool. Trout, and not game, are the main objects of the keeper's care, and a jay sat flirting its tail and screaming its double note on a pine just opposite the house. The pool itself was a type of hundreds among the Surrey coombs. The streamlet, which enters at the head, runs straight and deep for a few yards with a rapid current. Feathery swamp-grass, tall skeletons of thistles and of willow-herb, and clusters of bright-green rushes, half-smothered in a russet snow of oak-leaves, fringe the banks; and where the morning sun falls, blunt-toothed fronds of oak-fern and young hollies sprout. Then the stream forks, and a miniature delta forms, covered with a tall growth of bulrushes. Below the delta stretches the broad, dark pool; pure, clear, and shallow, with sandy bottom strewn with fallen leaves, and hungry trout cruising up and down in the water made clear as crystal by a touch of November frost. Grey-stemmed, yellow-leaved, twisted oak, and dark and shining hollies fringe the sunny side, and on the shaded bank a line of weeping-birches dips into the pool. All is bright, clear, and clean, void of clay or mud or rottenness; even the dam at the lower end is built of crumbling, sandy loam, laced and bound together by the roots of oaks. The low November sun looks over the steep bank and beats into the sheltered coomb with a warmth that can be felt, though the opposite bank lies cold in deep shadow, with streaks of hoar-frost lingering beneath the birches. In front, the slender sparkling stream, so shallow that it must needs divide to run round tiny islands of gravel and jungles of cresses, meets again, and slips smoothly under a foot-wide plank, through the loam-bank, and into the pool below.

The keeper, tempted to linger and chat by the warmth and beauty of the day, explained the new and sensible trout-culture which now stocks the pools with thousands of dainty fish, in place of the chance supply of coarse jack and odious wriggling eels which were once their main inhabitants. In the warm days of spring, thousands of troutlets, about one-and-a-half inches long, bright, silvery little fish, with scarlet spots upon their sides, are caught in the narrow runnels of the water-meadows between the ponds, and placed in a long wooden cistern, through which a constant stream flows. The water is then drawn off from the pool below the keeper's cottage, and all the larger trout are removed to the other ponds in the chain. The sluice is closed, the pool fills, and the young fish are let loose, secured against all attack except the nightly visits of marauding herons from Stag's Wood, in Wolmer Forest. In eighteen months the water is once more run off, and the troutlets, grown into half-pound trout, are transported to the deep waters of the larger pools. These are divided from the breeding-pond by a "bottom," or a moist, green, squashy river of short grass, haunted by blackbirds, in which the stream is hardly visible, and often disappears below the surface, or is distributed among narrow strips of water-meadow. In the river-valleys of the lower ground, these "bottoms" are deep and oozy swamps, where red mud and slime stand and stink among the alder-stumps, and "quakes," or reedy jungles, spread in the open ground. The contrast between the sunny and the sunless bank remains: the latter dark, smooth, and steep, with a regular growth of birch, the former rugged and broken, studded with contorted oaks and ancient hollies. Flat-roofed caves lie under the oak-roots, in which sand is for ever dropping from roof to floor, like the dribble of the hour-glass; even the wren hopping and singing from root to root beneath the cave dislodges tiny avalanches of sand. Under a hazel-bush lay a pool in miniature,—an everlasting spring, fresh from the hidden cisterns of the hill. True springs like this are the nearest approach in rural England to the little "fountains" gushing from the rock, so dear to the poets of old Greece and Italy. The smallest of the "Waggoners' Wells"[1]—for these, like all ponds and pools, however remote, have their distinguishing name —could scarcely claim Horace's sacrifice of a kid; but

---

[1] Part of this chain of pools lies within the Hampshire border.

its tiny basin, scarcely a yard across, shows in miniature all the beauties of the larger pools. Ferns dip into its surface from the bank behind, thick mosses clothe its stones, and the crystal waters swell outwards in gently widening rings from some slow-throbbing invisible centre, where an unseen force is gradually raising tiny grains of brown rock, which linger and hang poised as if caught in water-cobwebs, or wander downwards, hesitating and reluctant, to the leafy bottom of the spring. A culvert of oak-logs leads this youngest mother of rivers to the central stream. Beyond the spring the banks of the coomb once more contract, and become lofty and precipitous. There, overhung by oaks and drooping pines, which jut from the high banks, sleeps a larger, blacker pool, deep and narrow, dammed at the lower end by a thick dyke over which the water rushes in cascades at either end. The pond covers a space of three or four acres, deep, and full of large trout, which are fed not from the clear waters and clean-cut banks of the mere, but by the vast quantities of insects carried down from the water-meadows above. At the coomb's head lies the queen of the line of pools—a straight and beautiful mere, two hundred yards long and a hundred wide. At its head is a lofty heath-clad hill, topped with a mass of upright pines, whose grey stems stand like rows of columns supporting the peaked foliage of their crests. On either side, black alders and the grey stems and ruddy leaves of oaks break the straight line of the water, and dip their branches in the mere. On the right lie sound lawns, cropped by cattle hung with tinkling bells; and at the lake's head a narrow bed of sedges harbours the few water-fowl which haunt the pool. Above, in the heart of the pine-woods, are tiny rills and basins, into which the trout ascend to spawn. Few cottages and fewer farms lie by these upland pools. Wood is the only crop, which needs a seven-years' season to mature, and no man to till the soil. Bad times and wet harvests do not touch the Surrey woods, or make the forester's or keeper's roof-tree cold. "Lonely? No, never," is the keeper's answer to our inquiry. "It's a deal lonelier in the woods; and what do I want with people? I want things quiet, and home is good enough for me when I come back." He, his wife, and children are almost as dependent on the "ponds" as the wild-fowl and the trout. The stream waters their meadow, fills their cress-bed, gives them perch and trout, seasons their withy-baskets, brews their tea and beer, and, in winter, supplies stray wild-duck and teal, shot in the grey dawn, and woodcocks snared in the "bottoms." The keeper would not take the warmest lodge in a lowland park in exchange for his cottage by the upland pond.

TROUT-BREEDING

It is now fifteen years since Frank Buckland bequeathed his museum of pisciculture to the nation. In connection with the question of re-stocking trout ponds, by other methods than those described in the previous chapter, it is worth inquiring what results have accrued from Frank Buckland's legacy of his museum of pisciculture to the nation. Those who regard the younger Buckland as something more than an agreeable writer on the curiosities of animal life, will be curious to know whether, in the period that has elapsed since his death, the cause which he had most at heart has made any real and effective progress. Fish-culture, in the sense not only of breeding fish from the ova, but of their protection, encouragement, and profitable maintenance in the running streams and lakes of England, was the serious object of Buckland's later years. In its advocacy, he was at once enthusiastic and practical, and so much before his time in the views he held as to the desirability of rescuing from neglect the productive forces of the water at a time when no expense or trouble was spared on improving those of the land, that he had to create a body of opinion in his favour. In this he partially succeeded, mainly by his personal charm and the readiness of his pen. When he died he left a number of reports bearing out the old proverb that an acre of water yields more than three acres of land, and a museum of objects connected with the industry of fish-farming as he conceived it might be developed, which he bequeathed to the South Kensington Museum. Had this been the gift of any one else less in earnest on his subject than Buckland, it might have been liable to suspicion as an attempt to secure posthumous interest in a hobby. But the Buckland collection speaks for itself. It is the best rough-and-ready advertisement and propaganda of fish-farming existing in London. Great part of the collection consists of casts of fish made and painted from life by Buckland himself. His object in leaving them for public exhibition was to show the size and beauty of the creatures which could be grown in our neglected rivers and pools. Each cast is labelled in Buckland's bold handwriting not only with the weight of the fish, but the river, and sometimes the very pool or reach in which it was taken. The common brown trout alone ought to raise the envy of every owner or renter of a stream or spring, however small, for every tiny rill can be made into a pool capable of fattening trout. There is a brown trout of $13\frac{1}{2}$ lbs. from Britford, near Salisbury; another of 14 lbs. from Alresford, in Hampshire. What Buckland intended to convey by their exhibition was probably something of this kind. "These common trout, taken from the Avon and the Test, are far larger than any wild edible creature produced by the manors through which those rivers run. A 14-lb. trout weighs as much as seven pheasants, fourteen partridges, five rabbits, or two hares, it is not less beautiful than the pheasant, and weight for weight, contains more food than any game bird or animal, all of which it equals or surpasses in flavour. Any stream with feeders coming from sand or chalk-hills will grow trout; why do the greater number produce few or none?" Trout are not the only fish neglected. Here is a 7-lb. silver eel, one of the best of river fish, from the humble little river Mole. Carp, the common fish of German ponds, are almost unknown on the country dinner-table in England. Readers of Carlyle's *Frederick the Great* will remember that the carp-ponds, with the waters run off, and a crop of rye growing in the mud for the fish to feed on later in the year, almost stopped the advance of Frederick's left wing and artillery of the Prussian army at the battle of Prague. As specimens of pond carp, Buckland left casts of two—one from Berlin of 27 lbs. weight, with scales as large as half-crowns, and one of the same size from Haarlem Mere. These round, blunt-nosed fish look like water-pigs, and are of about the weight and shape of a three-months'-old porker, minus the legs. They are mainly vegetable-feeders, and would thrive in most still ponds where water-weeds abound. The cause of the migratory salmon and salmonoids, the true salmon and the bull-trout, may be said to have been practically won since Buckland first spoke in their defence; and the question of the hour is not whether salmon shall be protected or neglected, but whether the salmon-fishery is of sufficient value to cover the cost of rescuing rivers from pollution by factories. "Obstructions" such as mills and weirs were the obstacles to whose removal or remedy Buckland more immediately addressed his attention. His casts of salmon smashed by mill-wheels, of spawning salmon seized at Billingsgate, with wounds made by poachers' gaffs and hooks, his models of salmon-ladders, and protective grating and guards for mill-heads and water-wheels, at South Kensington, are reminders of the danger of neglect in this direction; and his cast of the 70-lb. Tay salmon is left as a perpetual record of the return which a protected fishery may make.

Beautiful as the salmon are, they hardly come within the scope of practical fish-culture, except for the export of the eggs to the Colonies. The number of salmon-rivers is limited, and cannot well be increased. Moreover, the supply of foreign salmon is so large that the increase of the English stock could hardly affect the price. But trout, which can be reared in every one of the home and southern counties, are far rarer than salmon. They are hardly obtainable at the greater number of London fishmongers. Grilled trout makes probably the best dish for breakfast obtainable in England, as good as the monster prawns caught in the harbour of Rio Janeiro. Yet, on how many tables does it appear? Even at City dinners, where *truite au bleu* is often a part of the menu, the trout is more often than not a sea-trout, which lacks the distinctive flavour of the good brown-trout of the inland waters. In showing how the supply of brown-trout for stocking newly-made pools or existing but neglected streams could be raised beyond the limits of any possible demand by the artificial cultivation of the eggs in properly made hatching-places, Buckland completed the practical work of his life. His small hatching-pools, down which the water trickles from shelf to shelf, are still in use at South Kensington, and the young American brook-trout, hatched last year and the year before, are swimming in the tanks provided for them.

The Buckland Museum marks the point at which the industry of fish-farming had arrived fifteen years ago,—one hardly beyond the stage of suggestion. The degree in which its teaching has fulfilled the purpose of its founder is perhaps best shown by the account of the great trout-breeding establishment of the late Mr. Andrews at Crichmere and Guildford, contributed to the *Field* of January 19 by the well-known writer who takes the pseudonym of "Red Spinner." Mr. Andrews, like Frank Buckland, owed his death in some measure to a chill caught while superintending the work of spawning fish in winter. By education and profession he was a musician, and retained to the last the post of organist at St. Mary's Church at Guildford. But he early caught the enthusiasm for the new industry of which Buckland laid the foundations, and for many years was able, during the spawning season, to furnish trout eggs at the rate of a quarter of a million a day, for private fisheries and exportation. When he first began, the site of the Crichmere ponds was a water-meadow, with a few cress-beds in it. "When I first went to Crichmere," writes a correspondent of the *Field*, "there were eighteen ponds, and the last time I found them increased to thirty-five in the Crichmere meadows, besides pools and falls. Since then ten acres of additional land has been included, and a number of narrow ponds created. Very proud, too, was Andrews of his pet stud fish, magnificent specimens of fontinalis, fario, and Levens. They were fed with chopped meat for the amusement of visitors, and special friends were allowed the pleasure of casting for and landing one or two with a huge hackled fly, from which the barb of the hook had been filed. Except in Tasmania or New Zealand, it is only here that I ever fly-fished for and caught trout in January. The fontinalis would at first come boldly at the fly, and as the fish fought in the clear water their lovely colourings flashed there,—deep orange, silver-white bars to the fins, ruby spots set in turquoise, and perfect mottling on the back. There were over three thousand breeding females in the ponds, ranging from 1 lb. to 5 lbs. in weight. The extraordinary size of the Crichmere yearlings has no doubt been due to the rich natural food in the ponds. The eggs sent away every year are numbered by millions; there were orders on the books for all the Colonies and various parts of the Continent, and to execute them all the spawning has to be cunningly regulated, so that some of the ova may hatch out as late as April. In one year, I know, eggs were taken from one hundred females as late as March 24th. It demands the best of management to keep the proper balance of yearlings and two-years-old in stock, and the secret of the high reputation of the Guildford Hatchery must be sought in the extraordinary character of the yearlings. These always vary considerably in size, and occur from $2\frac{1}{2}$ in. to 7 in. or even 8 in. Marked results were achieved in hybridizing at Crichmere, and for years the ponds containing the hybrids have been one of the most interesting features of the Hatchery." The demand for the young trout has risen from the growing recognition by the owners of country-houses that trout-pools are both useful and ornamental additions to their gardens and grounds, and not less interesting than the poultry-run or the pheasantry. The successful making and management of a trout farm is a branch of rural engineering and economy which, though forgotten for three centuries and a half, is now better understood than it was in pre-Reformation times, when it was the common annex of every manor-house; and the credit of its revival is due to Frank Buckland.

THE NIGHTINGALE VALLEY

By the first day of May, through all Western Europe and Asia Minor, from the groves of "old Colonus" and the temples of Baal-bec, to the valleys of Andalusia and the coombs of the Surrey hills, the nightingales are in song, awakening, as they have for a thousand summers, the fancies of dreaming poets and the delight of the least imaginative of mankind. The poets of old set their own interpretation on the song of the nightingale. To them it was ever the voice of lamentation and mourning; Philomel weeps for Itys, and never varies the refrain. Modern fancy is truer to the facts of Nature To us, as to Keats, the nightingale is the

> "Light-winged Dryad of the trees,
> In some melodious plot
> Of beechen green, and shadows numberless,
> Singing of summer in full-throated ease."

In a side-glen of the Surrey hills, running down to the deep stream of the River Wey, lies the Nightingale Valley. Two tiny streams cut their way down the steep and sandy hills, and unite in a pool which almost fills the bottom of the hollow. The granary and buildings of a solitary farm rise almost on the margin of the pool, and give back an echo which the nightingales in the copses and thickets on the hillsides, and in the May-trees which overhang the water, never weary of answering. There are few villages without some garden or coppice in which the nightingale may not be heard in those counties which it visits; but this particular spot has always seemed to the writer its most favoured and best-loved home. The copses are full of the birds, and in the still nights a score of voices may be heard, first completing the full chorus of their song, then silent and listening for a moment, until the echo repeats the last notes, when its challenge is answered by a rush of tumultuous melody. Probably the faintness of the echo's refrain leads them to suppose that it is the song of a bird in some distant grove, and engages the nightingales in common chorus against their unknown rival.

The cock-birds usually arrive in the valley at the end of the second week in April, and spend at least a week in practising and recalling their song. At such times they are extremely tame, and the writer has often watched from a few yards' distance the singers, who show far less nervousness in practising before a stranger than is often observed in human vocalists. The first long-drawn notes are commonly run through without difficulty, but the subsequent trills and changes can no more be acquired without practice and training by the nightingale than by a human singer. The bird stops, and repeats the song, sometimes carrying it on with a rush which seems to promise success, and then breaking down helplessly. Now and then the complete song is sung so low as to be almost inaudible, and then triumphantly repeated with the utmost powers which the bird can exert. Prowling bird-catchers, with their traps and mealworms, are wont to find their way to Nightingale Valley at this season ; and the owner of the farm finds it necessary to give orders for the protection of the nightingales equally with the pheasants nesting in the copses. By the end of May the birds are sitting ; and the cocks sing to them throughout the night. Hard as it is to find a nightingale's nest, the number in the valley is such that quick-eyed searchers have seen as many as six in a day. The eggs and nest of the nightingale are both so beautiful, and so unlike those of any other English bird, that it is impossible to mistake them when once seen. The site is nearly always chosen among the brown and dead oak or Spanish-chestnut leaves which lie on the ground among the brambles or wild-rose roots, or have drifted into some hollow of a bank. Sometimes, though rarely, the position is open to every passer-by, with nothing to conceal it but the resemblance of the nest and sitting bird, with her russet back, to the surrounding colour. The outer circle of the nest is built of dead oak-leaves, so arranged that the rim of the cup is broken by their projections, a mode of concealment practised, so far as the writer knows, by the nightingale alone of English birds, though a common device in the nests of tropical species. The lining is made with the skeleton-leaves that have fallen in the previous winter, and completed with a few strands of horse-hair, on which the shining olive-brown eggs are laid. There are few prettier sights than that of a nightingale on her nest. The elegance of the bird, the exquisite shades of the russet and grey of its plumage, set in the circle of oak-leaves among the briars, suggest a natural harmony and refinement in keeping with the beauty of its unrivalled song. A pair of cuckoos also haunts the Nightingale Valley every spring.

The popular feeling in England in favour of the cuckoo is as unaccountable as the affection for the nightingale is natural and unquestioned. It is certainly of recent growth, for the old writers formed a just estimate of its character, and condemned it alike in metaphor and the plainest prose. Even to hear its voice was an evil omen—

> "It were a common tayle,
> That it were better to hear the nightingale
> Much rather than the lewd cuckoo sing."

Such is Chaucer's comment on the note, which, probably from its association with the coming of spring, is now so eagerly listened for in rural England. The cuckoo's coming is the certain sign that winter is over. "One swallow does not make a summer, but one cuckoo does make a spring," should be the amended form of the old proverb. And this the burden of the ancient catch—

> "Summer is ycomen in;
> Loud sings cuckoo."

As for the date of his coming, that is as uncertain as the arrival of the season itself. "He did use to come on Wareham Fair," said a Dorsetshire labourer the other day; "but now he seems to come just when he likes."

But except as a weather-sign, the writer fails to find one redeeming point in the life of the English cuckoo; and if the cuckoo-lore of the Old World, over which it roams from Lapland to the Equator, and from Connaught to Kamschatka, could be compared, it should bear out this conclusion. He is a "vagrom man," as Dogberry would say: a vulgarian, a disreputable parasite. Yet he is in some ways an interesting creature, and the world has always a fondness for interesting scamps. He is an impostor so complete, that the mere catalogue of his deceptions rouses curiosity. From the egg, which imitates in size and colour that of the harmless skylark, to the full and fraudulent plumage of maturity, which clothes the indolent cuckoo in the garb of the fierce and active sparrow-hawk, he lives for ever under false colours. Though he looks like a hawk, he is an insect-eater; he has two toes pointing forward and two backward, like a woodpecker; but he cannot climb. He is ἄστοργος,—devoid of natural affection; and never works for his wife, any more than she does for her children. There was once a cuckoo in Germany who hatched her own eggs; and another has been known to feed its young one, when the foster-mother, a hedge-sparrow, had been killed. But these instances are rare exceptions to the rule of cuckoo-life. In Spain, a large cuckoo is the especial parasite of the magpie, and lays eggs which almost exactly resemble those of the latter bird. Yet, in America, there is an honest cuckoo, which builds a nest though a bad one, and hatches its own eggs. This is the " cow-bird," so called from its note, " Kowe—kowe—kowe," which is uttered with gradually increasing speed until it somewhat resembles the bubbling notes at times uttered by our cuckoo. The American cuckoo will even decoy visitors from its nest by the affectionate arts which so many birds make use of to divert danger from their young to themselves.

It would be interesting to know which place "pays best," from the cuckoo point of view, and to try the result of contact with European cuckoo morals on the honest American cousin. If birds have the power of comparison, the contrast must be hard to bear ; for the career of the disreputable young cuckoo is one of worldly success from his first chipping the shell to his late departure from our shores. He is born with a special contrivance in the structure of his back, to enable him to hoist his foster-brothers out, and never rests till he has done so, and made things quiet and comfortable. The foster-parents then pamper the young cuckoo with a silly infatuation, due apparently to its size and appetite. " See what a fine child we have got ! " is the obvious feeling of a pair of wagtails or hedge-sparrows fussing round a young cuckoo, which though fully fledged is too lazy to feed itself.

Even other young birds, if placed in the same cage with a young cuckoo, soon begin to feed it. Yet after all the spoiling which it receives, the cuckoo is a thoroughly ill-conditioned, surly, and spiteful bird. A young one, which was daily fed by a thrush no older than itself which was confined in the same cage, pecked the poor bird's eye out because it ventured to eat a worm itself. Buffon speaks of a tame cuckoo which would follow its owner, flying from tree to tree, sometimes leaving him for a time to visit the cherry orchards. We much doubt whether cuckoos eat cherries. All the tame cuckoos we have known have been uninteresting and unfriendly birds. At the Zoo, where English wild birds and migrants are tamed in the large aviaries, and nightingales, wagtails, warblers, and even a woodcock live together on the best of terms, the cuckoos are wild and as much disliked by the other birds in captivity as they are when free. But the sounds of summer would be the poorer for the loss of the cuckoo's note. It is beyond all others the sylvan bird, certain to be found among the lofty oak groves and the glades of noble parks ; and its cry, heard even before the dawn, brings crowding memories of the lakes and woods of Selborne and Wolmer Forest, of Windsor Park, of Brockenhurst, and the wide woodlands of the South.

THE HERONRY IN RICHMOND PARK

WHEN the Duke of Fife kindly took the envoys of Gungunhana to see Richmond Park, they asked " where were his assegais ? " Such at least was the story current at the time, and it may well have been true ; for the park, with its deer, its game, its ancient oaks, pools, lakes, and heronry, is a typical piece of wild England, such as might well appeal to the sporting impulse of wild men like these African chiefs, and remains, almost unspoilt, within an hour's walk of the greatest city in the world. The contrast enhances the interest of this famous domain. But apart from the accident of site, Richmond Park can claim on its merits a place among the best of these enclosed " paradises " in which Englishmen take such pride and pleasure. In size it equals that of any private park in England except Hawkstone. Towards the sunset it looks over a riverside landscape of incomparable richness, and the whole is just sufficiently preserved for Royal sport, to maintain the proper character of a park, as a precinct devoted to the sport and recreation of a single owner. It is to this careful surveillance that Londoners owe the establishment of the heronry; for, strange to say, this is not a survival, but a new colony, and a unique instance of the migration of what are almost the shyest birds in England, *towards* rather than away from a populous city.

The original home of these herons was in the home park at Hampton Court, where the heronry had been for two centuries one of the ornaments of Wolsey's palace by the Thames. There, some ten years back, they were disturbed by the felling of some trees near their nests, and forsaking Hampton Court, they established their new home in the wood at the head of the two lakes, which are known jointly as the "Penn Ponds." There, protected partly by the care of the keepers, partly by the wary silence and stillness maintained by these nocturnal birds, the colony has increased from ten to fifteen nests, unknown to most visitors to the park, who possibly mistake the harsh and barking cry, which sometimes issues from the grove towards sunset, for the voice of a dog, or the challenge of a solitary stag.

A closer acquaintance with the inner life of the heronry, and with the nature of the wood in which it is situated, goes far to explain the heron's choice. Protected on the lower side by the broad waters of the lake, and screened from view on the south and west by a thick fringe of birch trees, the wood is the chosen home, not only of the herons, but of all the wild creatures in which the park abounds. The running stream which descends from the high ground towards the Kingston Gate, and forms the main feeder of the lake, passes through its lower side, and is joined by other springs which ooze up in the plantation, to form a miniature marsh, in which the young broods of wild-ducks and moor-hens shelter. Even the red deer, which come at evening and in the early morning to browse on the floating tops of the water-lilies, and to drink the purer water at the lake head, are sometimes tempted to cross the narrow straits, and crop the rank herbage of the marsh beyond. Once hidden among the tall oaks and rhododendrons, the trespassing stag will remain alone for days, enjoying the comparative silence and solitude which the fenced and locked enclosure affords.

The very dry and hot spring and early summer of 1893 were exceptionally favourable to all the birds and beasts which rear their young in the park. The last day of April was more like a hot June day, with all the freshness of young spring in the leaves of the trees ; and the newly-arrived birds, as well as those which had spent the winter in the park, were revelling in the warmth. It was the most joyous spring day I ever remember. The trees seemed all to have rushed into leaf together. The birds were almost beside themselves with happiness, which they showed each after their fashion. All the spring warblers, resting after their journey over sea, were practising their song, wild-ducks were flying in pairs high over the lake—presumably mallards that were unoccupied with their broods—the lesser spotted woodpeckers, the cuckoos, redstarts, and wood-pigeons were all uttering their spring notes. The deer were lying asleep, some of the stags stretched out with feet straight before them, and their chins resting on their knees, like a dog on a doorstep. Everything was happy, careless, and contented. The fringe of the wood, in the centre of which the herons were silently brooding their young, was alive with the melody of birds and the movements of the smaller beasts with which, in addition to the red and fallow-deer, the park is now so abundantly stocked. Swarms of rabbits, old and young, were moving or sitting-up in the tussocks of dead grass among the birch-stems, wood-pigeons glided from tree to tree, so tame as to be almost indifferent to our intrusion, and the song of the wood-warbler, the chiff-chaff, the cuckoo, and the chaffinch, came from all parts of the grove. Within the outer circle of birch, the character of the wood changes. Tall young oaks and dark spruce-firs, with scattered clumps of rhododendron, take the place of the thick and feathery birch; and the song of the smaller birds was lost in the harsh and angry cries of the disturbed herons. A carrion-crow flapped from her nest on a dead oak, and flew with loud and warning croak through the centre of the wood; and a trespassing deer, springing from its form in which it was lying concealed like an Exmoor stag, crashed through the thick growth of rhododendrons, and added to the alarm of the colony. Four male herons came sweeping high above the oaks in rapid circles to seek the cause of the disturbance; and at the same moment the first of the

The Heronry at Richmond Park. By LANCELOT SPEED.

nests became plainly visible. It was placed on the top of a tall spruce-fir, which was so thickly loaded with the solid pile of brambles, sticks, and reeds, that a sudden gale must endanger the safety of tree and nest alike. The hen-bird was sitting close, and as she slipped silently, like a grey shadow, from the nest, the faint cry of the young was clearly heard. The second nest was built in an oak, and a third and fourth in two spruces growing side by side. In a small group of spruce-firs further to the north, almost every tree held a nest, the spruces being evidently the favourite site for the herons' nursery. One large nest was placed in a beech, near the lake-side, and others in the oaks further to the north. In all there appear to be at least twelve pairs, in addition to four more building in a separate wood which crowns the hill to the north.

As each heron left its nest and joined the company of its fellows which were soaring above the wood, the scene became more wild and striking than is common, even in surroundings more often associated with English heronries than the centre of a London park. As the eye travelled upwards beyond the green summits of the oaks, the sky was filled with the forms of these wide-winged birds, sweeping in hurried and anxious circles between the tree-tops and the sun, and casting swift and intermittent shadows that cut and crossed the broken lights beneath. All the birds were thoroughly alarmed; their flight was extremely rapid; and the grouping of such a number of dark forms, moving swiftly against a limited space of sky, their plumage flashing alternately black and white as they faced or crossed the blazing sunlight, was a sight not to be forgotten. At such times the head is thrown back in a noble poise, the feet extended like a train far beyond the tail, and the broad flight-feathers of the wing stand out clear and distinct against the sky. Moving towards the lake, in order to allow the herons to return to their nests, we flushed a pair of wild-drakes from a shallow ditch, and almost at the same moment a lame duck shuffled distressfully from the same spot, and moved off slowly, with apparent difficulty, in a direction parallel to the lake. The counterfeit was so remarkable, that had we not caught a glimpe of a small black object dashing into the marsh which lay a few feet from the drain on the opposite side to the course taken by the duck, no suspicion as to the reality of her disablement would have occurred. Meanwhile, the old bird invited pursuit, lying down, as if unable to move further ; and, resolved to see the end of so finished and courageous a piece of acting, we accepted the invitation and gave chase. For twenty yards or more the bird shuffled and stumbled through the rhododendron-bushes, until she made for the lake-side, where the ground was more open. There, running fast, with her head up and discarding all pretence of lameness, for another twenty yards, she took wing, and flew slowly just before us, at about three feet from the ground, until she reached the limit of the enclosure, when, uttering a derisive quack, she rose swiftly above the trees and flew out over the lake. Anxious to see the sequel to this beautiful instance of maternal affection, we hurried back to the little marsh where the ducklings were probably hidden, and, sheltered under a rhododendron-bush, awaited the return of the herons to their nests and of the wild-duck to her brood. In a few minutes she reappeared, flying swiftly in circles among the trees, and after satisfying herself that the danger was past, she alighted among some wild-currant bushes about thirty yards from the marsh. There she stood for a moment, still and listening, with head erect ; and, seeing nothing to alarm her, ran bustling down to the drain. After realizing that no harm had overtaken her brood on the spot where they had been surprised, she climbed the bank and tripped lightly into the marsh, where, in answer to her low quack, we soon heard the piping voices of the ducklings, which till then had remained motionless and invisible in the few yards of grass and rushes near. In a few seconds the whole family were united, and we had the pleasure of seeing the old bird swim past at the head of an active fleet of eleven black-and-yellow ducklings, making for the centre of the marsh. The herons also recovered from their alarm, the hen-birds returning one by one to the nests, and, after some slight endearments, settling down to brood their young, while the cocks resumed their motionless poise on the surrounding oaks, to "dream of supper and the distant pool."

THE DEER IN RICHMOND PARK

In the winter of 1886 the deer in Richmond Park were seen to be suffering from some strange disorder. Several of them died; but it was not until January 1887 that the disease was proved to be rabies. I find the following notes made at the time of the results of several visits of inquiry. "The keepers have been doing their best to stamp out the infection, but with little success. For a while there are no fresh cases; then several animals are found to be infected at the same time, and have to be destroyed. At least 150 fallow-deer have already been killed, though the red deer seem so far to have escaped the contagion.

"When the disease was pronounced to be rabies the keepers were somewhat incredulous; but to any one well acquainted with the symptoms, the condition of the poor animals which were netted and brought for inspection could not be matter for doubt. Even when the fact was proved by experiment it was difficult to understand how the infection was communicated. Deer, it was said, do not bite when fighting, but use their horns. It was observed, however, that the rabid deer did bite others, inflicting very severe wounds; for though the stag has only a pad of bone in the upper jaw, the lower is armed with from four to eight very sharp incisors. They are also fond of licking each other, and it was found that the saliva of an infected deer was fatal to a dog; a healthy doe after being bitten by it also died rabid. It was hoped that the further spread of disease might be checked by isolating the animals infected: a plan which was rendered less difficult than might be supposed by a habit which the deer have, after the breeding-season, of dividing into separate herds into which intruders are not admitted. As the disease was apparently confined to a single herd, it seemed probable that by separating this from the others the disease might be kept within bounds.

"On the north side of the park near the head-keeper's lodge is an old enclosure, which was enlarged, and the herd were then decoyed into it by food placed inside. This was not difficult, as during the winter months the deer are always fed with hay, maize, and swede turnips, and the heavy snow made them tamer than usual. The ground was well suited for keeping them in health, as it is on a hill, with a good supply of water, and dotted with large trees and patches of bracken for shelter. In July about thirty stags and fifty hinds were left in the enclosure; the stags keeping in a separate herd and lying quiet, as their horns were in the velvet, when they are very tender. But though apparently healthy, several stags had been shot the day before my visit, and had no doubt left the seeds of further mischief behind them. Since then nearly all those first confined have been destroyed, and now another herd is enclosed as suspect. But this is not the whole extent of the mischief. Isolated cases have appeared in the park; and if these increase it will be difficult to know what further precautions can be taken, for the season is at hand when the old herds are broken up, and the stags join the hinds for some time." The disease seems gradually to have been extirpated by shooting down all suspected animals.

Though so many have been lost there are still more than 1200 deer left in the park, both red and fallow, and few parks contain a larger stock in proportion to their size. It was once supposed that the two species could not be kept together, and in some places, as at Grimsthorpe and Badminton, they are still separated. But at Richmond they live together peacefully enough, and I have seen the red and fallow stags feeding in the same herd. The fallow are true woodland deer, and their colour exactly matches that of the dead bracken; the red deer prefer the more open ground. Though the red deer of Richmond do not reach the great size of those in Windsor Forest, many of them are above the average of those in a Scotch forest.

Every year the largest red deer stags are caught and removed to Windsor Park, in case they should prove a source of danger to the public in the rutting season. Their capture is an interesting and exciting scene. In January, 1894, some twenty stags, all with large antlers, were in the large paddock or "purlieu," which adjoins the park, near the Robin Hood Gate, on the Roehampton side. This is dotted with fine trees, and lies along the slope of a hill. A brook runs through the bottom, which is much like any flat alluvial meadow, and is separated from the park by the ordinary high split-oak railing. Several riders, among them two ladies, had the exciting duty of chasing the herd, and separating the stags one by one from the main body. Very hard riding and much cracking of whips were necessary to do this; and the moment one parted from the rest, a brace of Scotch deerhounds were slipped after the deer. The object of the chase was not that the hounds should catch the stag in the paddock, but to force it to leave it through the only exit, a gate in the high split-oak fence, outside which the "toils" are spread. This classic contrivance for taking deer is a set of high nets, slenderly supported on poles, which "give" when the stag rushes in, and entangle him directly. Keepers, crouched on either side beneath the cover of the paling, stand ready with leather straps and buckles to bind the animals' legs, and transfer them to a cart. The first stag was so alarmed by the quick pursuit of the deerhounds, so unlike that of the cockneys' collies and terriers, which sometimes amuse themselves by a deer-course in the park, that it rushed at full speed straight for the fence, and charging it, burst quite through the barrier, carrying a yard of oak-rails before it, and came out uninjured in the park. The deerhounds followed, and a furious chase began towards the Sheen Gate. The stag, in far better condition than the hounds, beat them fairly, and the pair returned, panting and crestfallen, to the paddock.

The remainder of the herd were less bold, and less fortunate; but the scene was a curious reminiscence of the days when the Stuart kings used to take their diversion by hunting deer in the royal parks, though the result was neither cruel nor unsportsmanlike, but only an exciting and well-managed episode in the management of a "deer ranch." First a charge and chase by the riders, ending in the "cutting out" of a stag from the herd; then a splendid course round the ring-fence, the deerhounds stretching belly to ground, and the stag, with antlers lying on his back and muzzle stretched horizontally, flying before them until he came to the opening in the palings. One desperate bound landed him in the web of nets set beyond, and a rush of the keepers soon transferred him, bound and panting, to the deer-cart. The paddock, being quiet and not open to the public, is a favourite lying ground for hares, which kept rising from the forms and making away past the deer and horsemen. On September 1, 1894, the Duke of Cambridge and three other guns shot sixteen brace of partridges and forty hares on this side of Richmond Park, and on Coombe Farm, most of the hares being got in this enclosure.

In the beginning of the present year (1895) the hard frost made it necessary to postpone the catching of the larger stags for transport to Windsor until the end of February. Even then the ground was so saturated with frost that the riders could not gallop

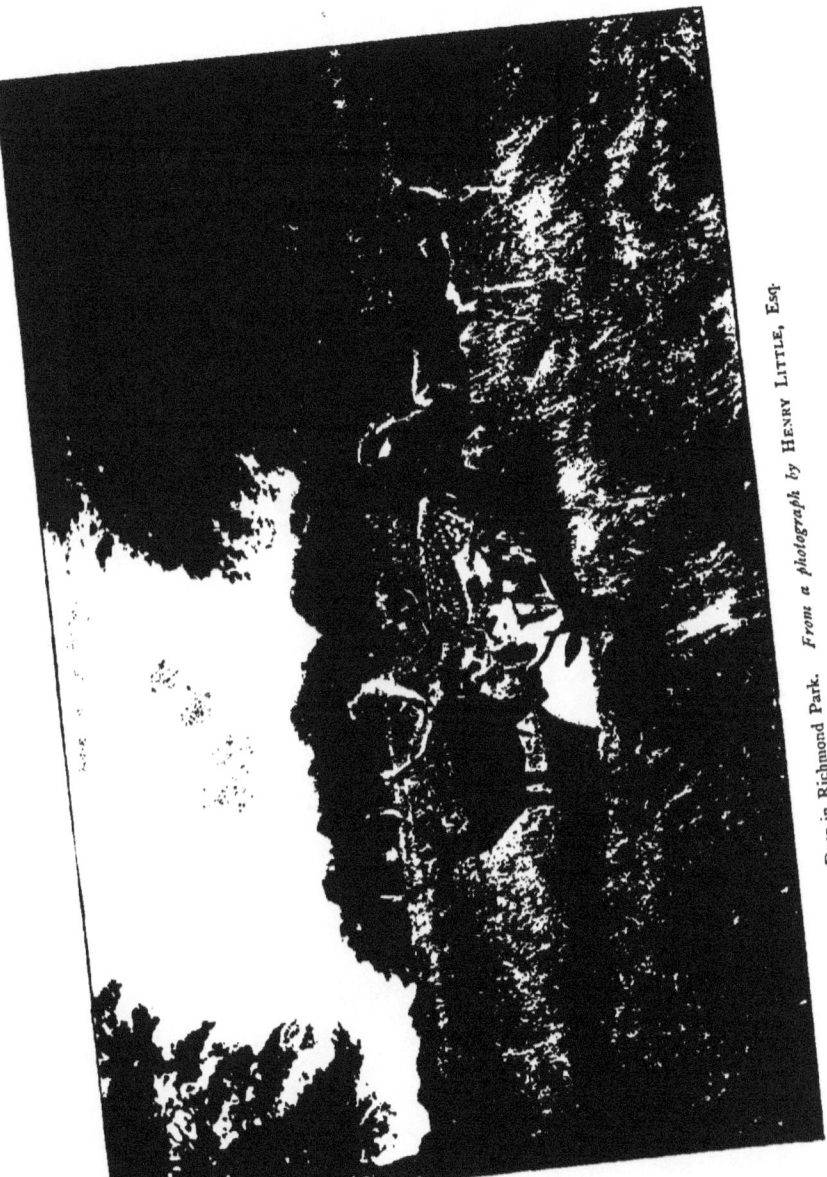

Deer in Richmond Park. *From a photograph by* HENRY LITTLE, Esq.

hard, and most of the work had to be done by the deerhounds. The stags were not driven into the paddock, as the escape of the animal mentioned above made it clear that the enclosure gave no special advantages for their capture. The nets were set between a thick plantation and one of the enclosures in which the deer had been fed during the frost. The hard weather had had no ill effects on their condition, as they had been liberally supplied with hay; and some of the finest courses ever seen in the park were witnessed. The "hunting" began at eleven, and did not end until three P.M., when four stags had been taken. The two largest beat the hounds cleverly, and have so far maintained their claim to stay in their native park as chiefs of all the herds during the coming summer.

FAWNS IN THE "FENCE-MONTHS"

"Défense de chasser" is probably the origin of the ancient term of venery which heads the notices, posted during May and June at the gates of the royal deer-parks, requesting that during the "fence-months" visitors will prevent their dogs from disturbing the deer. In the months of May and June the red deer calves and fallow fawns are born. When the young fern is up, and Richmond Park is in its fullest sylvan beauty, the three main herds into which the seventeen hundred head of deer in the park usually divide, are broken up. The stags have shed their horns, and steal away in small parties into the quiet parts of the park until their new antlers are grown, and the does and hinds are severally occupied in the most anxious care of their fawns. It is not until some weeks after their birth that these beautiful little creatures are seen in any number by the chance visitor to the park. Though both the red and fallow fawns can follow their hinds within a few minutes of their birth, the careful mothers hide them in the tall fern or patches of rushes and nettles, and it is only the older fawns that are seen lying in the open ground or trotting with the herds. When the fawn is born, the mother gently pushes it with her nose until it lies down in the fern, and then goes away and watches from a distance, only returning at intervals to feed it, or, if the wind changes, or rain threatens, to draw it away to more sheltered ground. They are not only most affectionate, but also most courageous mothers. Not long ago, a carriage was being driven along the road which skirts the wooded hill upon which the White Lodge stands. There is a considerable space of flat, open ground between the wood and the road; but a young red deer hind which was watching her first calf was so excited by the barking of a collie-dog which accompanied the carriage, that she ran down from the hill and attacked and wounded the dog with her fore-feet, until she drove it for refuge under the carriage. As she continued to bar the road, the carriage was turned round and driven back, but was all the way followed by the hind until it left the park by the Robin Hood Gate. Gilbert White mentions a similar attack made on a dog in defence of her fawn by one of the half-wild hinds in Wolmer Forest. "Some fellows," he writes, "suspecting that a calf new-fallen was deposited in a certain spot of thick fern, went with a lurcher to surprise it, when the parent-hind rushed out of the brake, and taking a vast spring, with all her feet close together, pitched upon the neck of the dog, and broke it!"

The oak-grove upon the sides, and the thick fern upon the flat top of the White Lodge hill, are the most likely spots in which to find the hidden fawns. The red deer seem to prefer the patches of tall rushes which grow among the oaks; and the fallow, the thicker shelter of the fern. There are also tall nettle-beds round the enclosure, in which the deer are fed in winter, and where in summer lumps of rock-salt are laid for them to lick. These uninviting nettle-beds are, strange to say, favourite *layettes* with the fallow hinds, and in them the writer has more than once found a sleeping fawn.

It would be difficult to see a prettier picture of young sylvan life than a red deer fawn lying in one of the patches of rushes among the oaks. Unlike the full-grown red deer, the fawns are beautifully spotted with white, and the colour of the coat is a bright tan, matching the dead oak-leaves which are piled among the rushes. If the spectator approaches from the leeward side, he may come within a few feet of the fawn, which lies curled up, with its head resting on its flank. Presently it raises its head, and looks at its visitor with grave, wide-open eyes, and if not disturbed, will go to sleep again. Otherwise it bounds up and is at once joined by the mother, who has been standing "afar off to wit what would be done to him." As the hind and fawn trot away side by side, the greater grace of the young animal is at once apparent. The head is smaller, the neck and back straighter, and the ears shorter in the fawn, and the eye is larger, and even more dark and gentle. The fawns of the fallow-deer are quite as distinct in appearance from those of the red deer as are the full-grown animals of either kind, both in colour and shape. There are three varieties of fallow-deer, and though these are often members of the same herd, the fawns of each seem generally to retain the colour of the mother, the dark mouse-coloured hinds having dark fawns, the white hinds cream-coloured fawns, while the young of the common spotted variety are white, mottled with light-fawn colour, which gradually takes later the dappled hue of the parent-hind. Occasionally a very light fawn may be seen, which is probably a cross between the white and dappled varieties. But none of the fallow-deer fawns have the grace of the red deer calf; they are less deer-like, and in some respects, especially by their long, thick legs, they suggest a week-old lamb; while the head is more rounded, and the muzzle less pointed than in the red deer. They seem to leave the fern and join their mothers earlier than their larger cousins, and are shyer and less easy of approach,—a wildness which seems difficult to account for in the young of a species which has been semi-domesticated for so many centuries. In order to approach them nearly, it is as well to take the precaution of walking up from the leeward side. Even park deer seldom become wholly indifferent to the scent of man; a score of hinds and fawns may be lying scattered under the oaks on the hill-side during a hot June day, enjoying the breeze and shade, and plainly unwilling to move. Yet if a stranger pass to windward of them, they will all rise, and when he comes in sight, move off to a distance. So when, in the winter, the keeper whom they know brings the hay to their feeding enclosure, they will scent him from a distance, and gather round the feeding-pen almost like cattle, some even venturing to pick up the hay as he throws it from the fork. But if a stranger be with him, not a deer will enter the enclosure, and few will appear in sight. Like wild deer, they seem to have greater mistrust of the danger which they can scent than of any object which they can see.

At the end of summer, when the fawns are weaned and the stags have grown their antlers, the herds re-unite, and in September the battles begin among the stags for the mastery of the greatest number of hinds. Then among the oaks of Richmond Park there are forerunners of the fights between the stags which are seen a month later on the Scotch mountains. The writer once witnessed a struggle of the kind, when belated in Richmond Park, about nine o'clock on a moonlight night in September. The moon was up over the Wimbledon hills, and the scene near the pool by the Sheen Gate was so beautiful, that he sat down by a tree to watch the night. In a few minutes a stag came up to the pool and challenged, and was answered by another from the valley, which soon trotted up to the other side of the pond. In a few minutes they charged, and the crash of horns was loud and startling in the still autumn night. After a long scuffle, the new-comer was defeated and chased down the slope towards the brook. It is on the flats by the brook between the Roehampton and Robin Hood Gates that the most formidable battles usually take place. A large stag generally takes possession of the ground on either side of the stream, and any invasion of their territory is so keenly resented, that the keeper of the Roehampton Lodge has occasionally preferred to make a very wide circuit by the southern path, to crossing the small bridge that leads directly over the brook to his usual beat in the park. When a stag is seen to put out his tongue and let it play rapidly round his lips, it is safe to infer that his temper is dangerous; and in that case it is always well to avoid disturbing the hinds. In Windsor Park, in September, the writer has seen as many as eighty hinds kept in sole possession by a single stag. At Richmond there are no such predominant masters of the herd, but no one can return from a day spent in observing them without feeling grateful to those who prevented the park being turned into a vast volunteer camp during the "fence-months."

HAMPSHIRE STREAMS AND WOODLANDS

WINTRY WATERS

(The Itchen and Tidal Thames)

Those who during the great frost of January 1895 cared to forego the attractions of the dead and frozen surface of the London lakes, found a strange contrast in the scene presented by the still living and moving surface of the London river. The tidal Thames for the moment changed its nature, and became a sub-arctic stream, deserted by man, whose place was taken by flights of wandering sea-fowl and a weltering drift of ice. Day and night the ice-floes coursed up and down with the tide, joining and parting, touching and receding, eddying and swirling, always moving and ever increasing, with a ceaseless sound of lapping water and whispering, shivering ice; while over the surface the sea-gulls skimmed in hundreds, sailing out of the fog and mist of London, flying over the crowded bridges, or floating midway between the parapet and the stream. These children of the frost became the pets of the river-side population, and bread cast from the bridges was the signal for a rush of white wings, and a dainty dipping of feet into the water as the birds gathered up the food, fearful, like Kingsley's petrels, that the ice should nip their toes. If a larger portion than common fell on an ice-floe, the birds would settle on the floating mass, with wings beating backwards like white butterflies, and guests, feast, and table alike travel up the river with the tide.

The scene beneath the bridges serves to remind us that it is not on the frozen pools, but upon the still open and running streams that the spell of the frost exerts its most pleasing powers. There it adds as much new life and novel form as on the still waters it destroys. It is hard to believe that the same powers have been at work on both. On the ponds and meres and slow streams the frost lays its hand and seals them like a tomb. As the ice-lips meet on the frozen bank, and nip the rushes fast, every creature that lived upon the surface is shut out and exiled. The moorhens and dabchicks are frozen into the ice, or leave for the running streams and ditches; the water-rats desert the banks, the wild-ducks have long gone, and only the tiny wren creeps among the sedges, or shuffles miserably among the bulrush stems. Even the fish are fast frozen into the ice, in which their bright sides shine like the golden carp on a tray of Chinese lac. Motion has ceased, and, with motion, sound, except that which

Sir Bedivere heard by the frozen lake, "among the mountains by the winter sea," the whispering of

> "The many-knotted water-flags,
> That whistled stiff and dry about the marge."

But there are hundreds of streams in the South of England which no power of frost can either freeze or stay ; and it may be doubted whether even the glories of spring buds, or the richest growth of summer by their banks, can match the beauty of these wintry waters in a strong and lasting frost. Take, for instance, the lower reaches of the Itchen, one of the most beautiful of Hampshire streams, with clear, swift, translucent waters springing warm and bright from the deep chalk that lies beneath the frozen downs. The river is so mild and full, that it runs like a vein of warm life through the cold body of the hills. Its water-meadows are still green, though ribbed across with multitudinous channels of white and crackling ice ; and to them crowd plovers and redwings, snipe and water-hens, sea-gulls, field-fares, and missel-thrushes, pipits and larks, and all the soft-billed birds in search of food. On and around the stream itself there is more life than at any time since the swallows left and the gnats died. That, at least, was the impression left on the writer's mind, when standing on one of the main bridges over the river below St. Cross, in the bright sunlight of New Year's Day. Though the banks were frozen like iron, not a particle of ice appeared on the broad surface of the river. A pair of dabchicks were fishing and

The Frozen Thames. By LANCELOT SPEED.

diving some fifty yards above the bridge, not altogether without fear of man, but apparently confident in their powers of concealment and escape. Coots and waterhens were feeding beneath the banks, or swimming, and returning from the sides to an osier-covered island in the centre. Exquisite grey wagtails with canary-coloured breasts, and ashen and black backs, flirted their tails in the shallows or on the coping-stones which had fallen into the stream. But the river itself was even more in contrast to its setting than the contentment of the river-birds to the pinched misery of the inhabitants of the garden or the fields. From bank to bank, and from its surface to its bed, the waters showed a wealth and richness of colour, rendered all the more striking by the cold and wintry monotony of the fringe of downs on either side. As it winds between the frozen hills, the bed of the Itchen is like a summer-garden set in an ice-house. However great the depth —and an 8-ft. rod would scarcely reach the bottom in mid-stream—every stone and every water-plant is to be seen as clearly as though it lay above the surface. For in midwinter this water-garden is in full growth. Exquisitely cut leaves like acanthus wave beneath the surface, tiny pea-like plants trail in the eddies, and masses of brilliant green feathery weed, like the train of a peacock's tail, stream out, in constant undulating motion, just beneath the surface. In other places the scour of the river has washed the bed bare, and the tiny globules of grey chalk may be seen gently rolling onward as the slow friction of the water detaches them from their bed. The low, bright sunbeams were still upon the water when, slowly and almost insensibly, from beneath the dark arches of the bridge there glided out two mighty fish,—not the bright, sparkling troutlets of West-country streams, arrow-like and vivacious, or the brown and lusty denizens of Highland rivers, but the solemn and sagacious monsters which only such chosen waters as those of the Hampshire chalk-streams breed, fishes which would have done credit to the table of such prelates as William of Wykeham, trout that are known and familiar to every inhabitant, honoured and envied while they live, and destined, when caught at last, to be enshrined in glass coffins, with inscriptions like embalmed bishops. Six pounds apiece was the least weight which we could assign to the pair as they slowly forged up stream and lay side by side, the tops of their broad tails curling, and their fat lips moving, looking from above like two gigantic spotted salamanders among the waving fronds of weed.

Clearly, in this water-world, the great change wrought on land by frost was still unfelt. The cold has no power beyond its surface; plants and fishes were unaffected. Yet on the bank, even at midday, the thermometer marked fifteen degrees below freezing-point, and at night a cold approaching that of Canada. The reason is not far to seek. The whole body of the river had maintained its temperature but little below that at which it issues from the chalk. Both at the surface and at the bottom, the quickly flowing water had a temperature of thirty-six degrees Fahrenheit; in the mill-race it was half a degree warmer; and only where very shallow and still did it fall as low as thirty-five and a half degrees. It is therefore possible for a chalk stream to maintain its heat, after a week of one of the severest frosts on record, at some fifteen degrees above the midday temperature of the land and four above freezing-point. No wonder that the birds seek its genial neighbourhood, and its own particular inhabitants feel neither discomfort nor dismay. We were curious to visit the famous salmon-pool at Swathling, some few miles lower down the river, and mark the effects of frost in a part where the river-waters are distributed in every form, from still frozen lakes and water-meadow channels to the mill-race, and the deep, swirling pool, in which a thirty-pound salmon may be caught, not two hours by rail from London. The Wood Mill pool is the crowning glory of the river. Two streams, one from the main mill-head, another from a tributary, rush into a wide horse-shoe basin faced with cam-shedding and concrete, where the waters whirl and spin in an everlasting eddy. Ice in powder, ice in blocks, and ice in sheets pouring in from the mill-head, followed the spin of the waters round, and showed the force of each minor whirlpool, clinking and shivering against the concrete walls, except where the long, thick strands of moss deadened its impact. At the back of the pool, a shallow beck was running below a covering of thin sheets, made up of ice-stars, with upturned edges fringed with crystal spikes, shifting and straining with uneasy motion. Higher up, the runnel was fringed with ice so formed as to lie just above the surface; and we fancied that we could detect a regular pulse or beat in the stream, which now brought the water level with the ice-fringe, and sent the flattened bubbles coursing below it, now left it dry and white and clear of the surface. But the strangest freak played by the frost around and above the salmon-pool, was the formation of *ground-ice*—or " anchor ice,' as it is sometimes called—deep below the unfrozen surface of the water.

The hanging mosses, at a depth of from three to four feet, were covered with thick and clinging ice; and in the deep but rapid waters at the inrush by the mill-head, rocks and stones far beneath were seen coated and crusted with a semi-opaque and rounded glaze of crystals. How it happens that ice, which should float on the surface, forms and remains below waters which are themselves apparently too warm to freeze, we are not prepared to explain. But in this case we forebore to test the stream, lest our operations with a thermometer at the end of a string should be mistaken for some new form of fish-poaching,—a view clearly taken by one observer of our experiments at Winchester.

MAY-FLIES IN MARCH

(ITCHEN ABBAS AND AVINGTON PARK)

"DAYS of promise" are a common feature of the English spring, when the rough winds sink and shift into the west, and the cold rain draws odours from the earth, and song from the birds, that remind us that winter is left behind. Even then the response of Nature is as hesitating and uncertain as the shifting moods of the March sky; and the influences which appeal to man seem too subtle or too transient to change the winter habits of birds or beasts.

Far different is the result of the first really hot days of early spring. When such weather comes in the middle of March, and lasts for more than a day, it affects all wild animals like some beneficent spell. The physical contrast of summer and winter, marching, as it seems, hand in hand, is alone almost sufficient to account for the change. The night frosts are forgotten in the heated air, which dances over the withered grass; yet the dust, scattered in the high-road, falls on ice-covered pools in the shadow of the fence; and the tortoise-shell butterflies, which flit from side to side of the lane, alight alternately on leaves and twigs powdered here with dust, there with crystals of hoar-frost.

The scene in the water-meadows at Itchen Abbas, above Winchester, on such a day in March at the beginning of the hot dry spring of 1893, was in strange contrast to that presented by the wintry waters in their setting of iron-bound earth and icicle-fringe during the great frosts at the opening of the year. Then the warm and life-giving river supported by its bounty thousands of strange and suffering birds, forced by hunger to leave their native haunts, and to seek food by the still unfrozen stream. Now the river and its valley was peopled, not by hungry strangers, but by all the wild creatures native to this chosen spot, not struggling for existence, but enjoying the most complete form of happiness known to animal life,—warmth, quiet, security, and plenty. There is, perhaps, no district in the South of England where Nature has done so much for man as in the upper valley of the Itchen. The downs on either side shelter it from rough winds, the parks and villages at their feet form a continuous line of garden and spreading timber, and at this season of the year the visitor may walk for miles without ceasing to hear the cawing of the nesting rooks. Rooks are still "free selectors" in our old-world country, and their presence is a guarantee that the land is good enough not only for man, but for the most civilized and critical of bird-kind. But the exuberant life of the valley is supported, not by the timbered parks or rich gardens under the hills, but by the great chalk-stream, which, like the river of Egypt, winds through the centre of the land, and distributes its waters in a thousand swift and shining streams over the thirsty meadows on its banks. There, while the grass upon the hill-sides is still grey and sere, the hay already shows half a crop, and the wide green blades seem to suck up the moisture visibly from the streams which trickle through their waving stems. Each furrow is a flooded watercourse, not stagnant and foul, like the muddy drains of Eastern fens, but bright and swiftly flowing, a miniature of the great chalk-stream itself. Where the valley narrows, as at the bridge of Itchen Abbas, opposite the tall limes and avenues of Avington Park, the teeming life of the river and its vale may be viewed at close quarters. There, as the strange and sudden heat of the March sun burnt and increased, and the yellow coltsfoot flowers spread their petals wide, like arms and bosoms, to the rays, we watched the whole wild-life of the valley abandon itself to the sense of exquisite happiness given by the first burst of light and heat in the year.

Those who would blame man for his interference with Nature should at least give him credit for building the water-mill, with its dam and mill-stream, its foaming " tumbling bay," its weir and double bridges. The result at Itchen Abbas is to divide the river into a wide and dancing shallow, studded with sedgy islands above the mill, while below the two streams unite in a swift and rushing current. The islands and reaches above the bridge are the chosen home of wild-fowl; the pool below a very paradise of monstrous Hampshire trout. Up till mid-day the wild-fowl were still feeding, or moving from one part of the marsh to another. Two or three pairs of dabchicks were busy diving just above the bridge, their plumage almost black, and looking, when they appeared as if by magic on the surface, as if clothed in velvet. Moorhens and coots swam out from the sedges, the former in their best summer suits, with beaks red as sealing-wax, and neat white borders to their tails, crossing the river with that peculiar ducking and jerking motion of the head which distinguishes them from all other fowl upon the water. But at midday the sun asserted his dominion even over the water-fowl. For some time the land-birds had been flying in from the hot and dusty hills, and settling in the water-meadows to drink, feed, and wash themselves. First, a pair of partridges came skimming over the road, and dropped among the dry flags on one of the islands in the stream. Then a flock of plover came floating down, one by one, just clearing the gables of the mill, and settled in the water-meadow beyond, where they first drank from a shallow rill, and then bathed elaborately. The flutter and splash of the black-and-white pinions was clearly visible, until their toilet was completed by running up and down on the bank with wings expanded to the sun and wind. Then the rooks came down to drink, one by one, and a pair of wood-pigeons followed; but the birds had come, not merely to bathe or satisfy their thirst, but to stay.

Plovers, pigeons, and rooks settled themselves down upon the grass, drooped their wings, stretched their feet, and lay basking in the sun. For rooks, the most industrious of birds, to abandon themselves to complete idleness and sleep at midday is, so far as the writer's experience goes, a most unusual indulgence. Not till the day's work is over, and the low sun is lighting up the elm-tops, do the rooks allow themselves to take a brief hour's gossip and idling, and then only before the young are hatched. As it was, one pair, who had been busy close by nest-building in the earlier hours, kept up appearances long after the rest had yielded to the drowsy influence of the sudden heat. The hen flew up to the nest and pretended to "sit," though the eggs were not yet laid; while the cock-bird, who was basking on the grass below, started up at intervals, as some comrade flew overhead, and pretended to be looking for food with a sham earnestness most comical to behold. Meantime, the water-fowl were fast leaving the river for the meadows, in order to enjoy to the full the genial warmth. An old mallard stole quietly from one of the water-channels, and, after standing with his green head erect to reconnoitre for some minutes, he lay down on the grass, turned on his side, and slept as tranquilly as a farmyard duck. One or two other mallards followed his example, each lying down on the highest point of the ridge between the water-cuts, like a hare in its form. An old gander, who with his mate was swimming in the mill-stream, took a walk in the road, and finding that the warmth was to his liking, flew back in a hurry, and after some conversation both climbed the bank, and went off in a vast hurry to the strawyard, where they also composed themselves to sleep. By this time every one of the larger birds in sight was dozing, and the writer so far followed their example as to move to the sunny side of an old brick bridge, and there, with the warm wall behind, and the shining river in front, to watch the trout, and lunch. The sun was at its hottest, when a whole flock of chaffinches came hawking down the river, in eager pursuit of something which had not, till then, appeared upon the scene. We looked, and there over the surface of the water were hundreds of "May-flies," hatched by the sudden heat. Of course they were not true "May-flies"; but for all that they were true *Ephemeridæ*, with long white tails and transparent wings, "March browns," we believe, in the language of the fly-fisher. Poor creatures! What with the chaffinches above, and the greedy trout in the water below, even their brief day was shortened. The trout were in ecstasies. Before the appearance of the swarm, they had been leaping from the water in sheer exuberance at the fine weather. Now they settled down to the serious business of eating. Not ducklings and early peas, strawberries in February, ortolans in vine-leaves, or the first plovers' eggs, could move the epicure so deeply as the first dish of early "May-flies" in March touched the imagination of the Hampshire trout. The fish lay in lines across the river, each in his favourite part of the stream, like sportsmen in a row of grouse-butts. Constant quick rises—just a ripple, as the broad nose, followed by the back fin, and a triton curve of the tail, broke the surface of the water —showed where each struggling fly met its fate. The flies then vanished as suddenly as they had appeared, and the dinner of the trout was over.

THE WOODLANDS IN MAY

THOSE whom choice or fortune has led to spend a fine May day in the deep woodlands of the south, will have learnt to prize the unrivalled splendour of the English spring, when lasting and unbroken sunshine has called every tree and bush, from the oak to the trailing sweetbriar, into leaf together, and the beauty of the woodlands appeals to the senses with a force and freshness which the maturer months of summer foliage can never weaken nor efface from the memory. There is an unwritten law in some of the villages of America that on a certain day every able-bodied inhabitant shall go forth, and not return, until on land, either set apart or otherwise suitable for the purpose, he has planted a tree. Now, if ever, such an example of the duty of man to Nature should appeal to every Englishman. Even though the craze for destroying the beautiful hedge-row timber, which, massed in the distance, makes the foreigner believe that he is for ever approaching a forest, which for ever recedes before him, no longer forms part of the enlightened farmer's creed, there are still many counties which the axe has left treeless and bare; where the countryman never sees a real wood, or knows the delight of walking for hours where the low sky never shows between the distant trunks, and the sound of the labour of the field does not penetrate. Yet there are still many counties rich in forest scenery, even in the south; and there is no need to visit the famous cluster of great estates in the Midlands, where the woods of Clumber, Welbeck, and Mansfield unite to cover the site of the old Sherwood Forest with an unbroken tract of woodland, in order to realize the full-dress beauty of the early spring. Hampshire, for example, may claim, apart from the New Forest area, a foremost place among the woodland counties of the south. Of its million acres, a hundred thousand are covered by permanent and ancient wood, not sprinkled in scattered patches, but deep and connected areas of trees and copse, in which timber, large and small, is regarded as the staple crop, with stated times for cutting and harvest, equally with the produce of the meadow or the field. Trees are native to the soil. On the uplands between the deep and fertile valleys of the Itchen and the Test, the transition from natural woodland to the spreading forests, which owe their present form to human care, may yet be traced. The down stands thick with ancient and self-sown hawthorns, fragrant with the heavy perfume of the May-blossom, and interspersed with tall patches of gorse and feathery birch, among which the partridges nest, and the young plovers, driven by the drought from the open downs, seek food and shelter. In the woodlands beyond, each and every tree and shrub to be found in the southern counties is in its full raiment of young and tender leaf. Even the ashes have burst their black buds, and the flower-clusters hang like bunches of keys thick upon the branches. The maples are in flower; the cotton buds of the broad-leafed willow are rolling on the paths before the wind; the young oak-leaves are crisp and curling; the ground-oaks show clusters of longer leaves of flesh-colour and green; the white-beam glistens with grey and silver, and flat white flowers; the beech-buds have dropped their brown night-caps, and the sun has smoothed out the creases; the elm branches are covered with almost summer drapery, and the senses are at once stirred and soothed by the ripple of the light air over the foliage, and the fresh smell of young green leaves. Beneath the timber-trees the copse-wood grows so strangely thick and strong, that a hundred stems seem to spring from every crown, and arching upwards and outwards, meet and overlap to form a continuous roof of clustering foliage, various in kind, but alike in strength and vigour. In the low lanes beneath, cloistered by this natural canopy, stretches in endless lines the flower-garden of the forest. Every foot of ground between the tree-stems and coppice-clusters is set thick with dark-blue hyacinths; and if we stoop and look up the long corridors between the thickets, with roofs so low that nothing larger than a fox could thread them, the distance merges into a level sheet of purple. Over hills and valleys, banks and glens, the hyacinths spread, with no difference in number or size, except that in the open spaces where the copse was felled last winter the spikes are taller and richer in scent and colour. Where the clay crops up, the hyacinths are mixed with primroses, small, but strongly perfumed, set as in a garden, in cushioned beds of moss. Standing on the hill-side at the margin of the wood, and facing the wind which blows over miles of similar forest-ground, the air sweeps by us fresh and clear, yet loaded with the perfume from hundreds of acres of this hyacinth-garden, like the scent of asphodels from the Elysian fields.

In spring, while the sap is still running upwards, these woods are as silent and deserted by man as the wheat-fields in June. The fallen timber lies ready for carting; but the grindstone stands dry with rusted handle, until wanted to sharpen the axes in autumn, and the young fern and flowers are twining among the stacked faggots and piles of wattle hurdles, which will not be moved till the fall of the leaf. There are few or no villages in the forest-country. The homes of the woodlanders are scattered and remote, and, when found, present a strange and pleasing contrast to those of the labourers in the cultivated country. For the former, the choice of site has not been limited by the artificial value which accrues to land in the neighbourhood even of the smallest village, and too often robs the labourer's cottage of the light and space which should be a countryman's birthright. The woodman has usually been a "free selector" in the choice of his dwelling-place, and it needs a wide acquaintance with these sylvan homes to weaken the first and natural impression that each and every one of these solitary cottages enjoy some peculiar and accidental advantage of setting and surrounding to which it owes its charm. The real reason for their beauty and their comfort is not far to seek. The cottage was built where it stands only because Nature had marked out the spot as a natural home for man. Shelter from the wind, water for the pony and cattle, a patch of good soil for a garden, and a glade of green grass for the cow to graze upon, may be all found together for the seeking in the wide woodlands; and the spot where a company of hurdle-makers choose to light their mid-day fire, and raise a faggot-shelter in the winter, soon sees the growth of the woodman's home. A little reflection soon shows the reason, and even the *necessity*, for the beauty of the whole. The water in the little stream was the first condition of the building of the house. The stream made the rustic bridge necessary, and its own moisture decorated the under-side of the planks with moss and tiny ferns. The ancient trees, with the close turf under them, are not accidental either. The woodman wanted a few rods of pasture, and found it where the spreading oaks and sycamores had killed the undergrowth below. His orchard flourishes, and fallen apple-blossom smothers the garden-plot, for where the oak grows there the apple grows also, and the autumns of centuries have enriched the ground with vegetable mould. The woodlands are the poor man's best home; and while Nature gives the stream, the tiny park and paddock, the good soil, and the fostering shelter of the forest, the owner himself is seldom backward to use the sylvan gifts. His work among the timber makes him master of the use of woodman's tools, and the split-oak fence of his garden, and the well-built sheds for cattle and stock, show a sense for order and good workmanship in strong contrast to the makeshift shanties around the field-labourer's cottage. In his daily fare he still tastes the forest dainties which have for ages been regarded as his right—

> "I'll show thee the best springs; I'll pluck thee berries;
> I'll fish for thee, and get thee wood enough;
> Show thee a jay's nest and instruct thee how
> To snare the nimble marmozet; I'll bring thee
> To clust'ring filberts, and sometimes I'll get thee
> Young scamels from the rock,"

says the woodland monster in *The Tempest*. The forest children are adepts in these, as in other forms of woodcraft, and bring in tribute of brook-trout, young wood-pigeons, mushrooms, and wild fruits to the cottage table,—sylvan gifts. The woodland children, and even the woodland dogs, seem to feel the influence of the quiet and loneliness of their lives. Both seem to long for human society and human sympathy, and the little sons and daughters of the cottage, with their dog companions, are happy and content to lie down and wait near the temporary resting-place of visitors to the woods, the children amusing themselves by weaving wreaths of moss and flowers, and asking no more proof of good-will than that implied in a kindly toleration of their presence.

THE BUDS AND BLOSSOM OF TREES

"A belt of straw and ivy buds
With coral clasps and amber studs."

THOSE who live among the woodlands maintain that to know the beauty of trees they should be watched from the first day of the New Year. To wait till the young leaves clothe the branches is to miss half the early graces of the woods; for the trees, like the sunburnt maidens of the Southern Sea, wear ornament before drapery, and lightly wreathe their limbs with beads and coral stars and studs, little coquettish jewels, like shells and flowers, and, like them, often thrown away before the day is done, or exchanged for ornament more lasting and complete.

Nothing in the full foliage of summer is more beautiful than the early buds and blossom of trees; yet no "flower of the field" is more often doomed to blush unseen. The gaze, which is at once bent down towards the crocus or the primrose, is seldom raised to the crimson blossoms which now cover the tops of the elms like drops of ruby rain, or to the pendent blossoms of the poplars, the little golden brushes on the

THE BUDS AND BLOSSOM OF TREES

ash, or the pink flowers which stud the larch boughs like sea-anemones. These are blossoms which appear on the naked limbs of trees. Later, among the young leaves of the oak and sycamore, the bunches of pale-yellow bloom are confused with the young leaf; and it is not till the ground below the last is piled with golden, dustlike petals that we wonder whence they came, and what the flower was like that bore them.

One only among the hundred buds of trees is well known, and used for ornament in England—the " palms "—which are gathered by every stream and pond the week before Palm Sunday. Even they have as many phases of beauty as the rose;—first, the tiny pearl-like studs of satin-white; then egg-shaped buds bound in grey plush like the lining of an opera-cloak; and lastly, rounded golden thimbles, set with tiny blossoms. Or to follow the fancy of the Cheshire children, the young buds are the goose's-eggs, and the golden flowers the goslings, hatched by the hot March sun, and bending to the river. But the beauty of the buds of trees is almost invisible against the sky. They are lifted too far from the eye, and their forms are too minute and their colours too pale to break across the line of sight and play a part in broad effects of sylvan beauty. To be appreciated in mass the buds of trees must be viewed from above, from the opposite side of a glen, or in a copse below the observer. In the deep woods which cluster at the foot of the Hind Head, in the broken hollows near Haslemere, the millions of buds and catkins so pervade the upper level of the copse that the distant trees seem to rise through vapour and smoke. Nearer, the smoke resolves itself into motionless flakes of white or grey, dotting each upright wand and branch like seed-pearls sewn on a velvet scabbard. But at a distance the whole wood seems blurred with motionless puffs of white vapour, merging in the distance into a greyish haze. Plunge into the copse, and the source and shape of the misty mirage is explained. Every clump of underwood is studded with bud or blossom, though hardly a leaf is out from fence to fence. The catkins of the hazel and the tiny pink star-fish flowers are almost over, but the cornel buds are formed and the masses of blackthorn are powdered over with tight little globes no larger than a mustard-seed, in which lies packed the embryo blossom. The black-poplars are still as leafless as in the bitterest December frosts; but their topmost twigs have lost their rigid look and are decked with little funeral plumes of sooty-black flower. At all the joints of the woodbine green buds are peeping out in pairs, and on the sunny edges of the copses the dog-rose is opening its leaves to the wind and frost. The elder is the only other native tree in leaf so early, though why this, the softest and weakest of the woodland shrubs, should share with the climbing woodbine and rose the honour of being the first to wear the colours of spring, is still among the secrets of the wood. On the wild-cherries the flower-clusters are shown in miniature globes, which stud the upper branches with whity-brown knobs and clusters, and the Lombardy poplars, as yet leafless and dry, have a false foliage of splendid crimson catkins, which lie tumbled, like crimson and yellow caterpillars, upon the ground below. But the buds of the willows are the main feature in the phase of beauty in the woodlands in March which precedes the bursting of the leaf. The tall osier rods are of all colours, grey and green, yellow and scarlet, maroon and black, and these, from root to top, are studded with white satin buds. The most beautiful of all have a deep purple bark which shines with a polish like Chinese lac, against which the velvet-white of the buds stands out in perfect contrast of texture as well as of colour.

It is these beautiful and exactly placed ornaments that make the silver haze in the woods before Palm Sunday ; and it is perhaps of their silver fleeces that Shelley thought when he wrote of the spring—

"Driving sweet buds like *flocks* to feed in air."

In the sunny March mornings, when the sun is up at seven, and a choice band of native songbirds, the thrush, the blackbird, the robin and the hedge-sparrow, are singing their pertest and loudest, un-challenged by a single note of song from the earliest of the warblers from beyond the seas, every tree shows some slight, half-hinted shadow of spring change. It is like the change of breathing as sleep is ending, or the swelling of wetted grain. At every joint, and at the end of every twig, there is ever so slight a swelling of the bud ; and though the change of shape and colour in each is hardly discernible till held in the hand, the multiplied myriads of tiny curves change the whole aspect of the tree. In the sycamore, the points of the lower buds are slipping from their sheaths, like long green olives of Italy. The downy sumach tips are rough with swelling knobs, the laburnums are flecked with silver-grey, and even on the planes, where last year's fruit still hangs, the buds are swelling. But perhaps the most beautiful of all are the sprays of the hawthorn. Where each thorn leaves the stem, a tiny, gemlike globe has appeared upon the bark, laced on the sides with green and gold, and tipped with rosy carmine. The sharp thorn mounts guard above it, and protects it from harm,—one thorn to a bud, all the tree over. But where the young shoots end—where there is no protecting spear—there the buds are clustered, that if one fail another may take its place.

It is true of most English woods and gardens that the larger the tree the smaller is its flower. Few people could describe the blossom of the oak, or trace its change from the tiny pale-green flower to the infant acorn, in its miniature cup no bigger than an ivy-berry; or paint from memory the flower-clusters which nestle among the beech-leaves in early June. Except the horse-chestnut, we have no native flowering timber-tree to take the place of the tulip-tree of North America, or the mimosa groves of the African plains. Yet the tulip-tree, with its broad, flat-headed leaves, and fine orange blossoms, like single inverted bells of the crown imperial, will flourish like the poplars in an English garden or hedgerow, and is far more useful as timber than the quick-growing and ornamental abele. We need another flowering tree. Even the blossoms of the lime would be less seen and admired were it not for their scent and the attraction which they offer to the bees. Were the flowers of oak and elm, of poplar and of fir dependent on the bees, rather than on the wind, for fertilization and the carriage of the pollen from flower to flower, they would be better known and appreciated than they are. But the pines at least attract the early bees. In the hot spring of 1893, the upright spikes of yellow, clustering flowers on the Austrian pines were crowded with the working bees, which laboured among the dusty piles till their bodies were covered with pollen, like flour-porters in the docks. The blossoms of the silver firs, the "balm of Gilead" of rural botanists, usually borne so high on the lofty summits that no bee would soar to reach them, studded even the lower branches, and revealed to ground-walking mortals a new feature of the flower-garden which lies in the upper storeys of the woods. Now that the pear and the cherry, the peach and plum, the apple and the quince, and, above all, the early and beautiful almond, are once more hastening into blossom, can we not take a lesson from Japan, and plant, not in isolated trees, but in orchards and groves, the double plum, and the pink-flowering cherry, which, for a few weeks, will fill our parks and gardens with the blossom and colour which even March winds cannot kill?

ROUND THE GREAT WHITE HORSE

THE LOST FALCON

It was three o'clock on a winter afternoon. The air was filled with frost-sounds—of twigs snapping, and ice tinkling as it formed and fell. On the lawn lay the limbs of an ancient cedar, snapped by the weight of snow. Hard by, on her block of pinewood, sat a trained falcon, her plumage compact and glossy. Though indifferent to the cold, she moved impatiently from time to time, jangling the tiny Indian bell upon her ankle. Feeding-time was near, and her appetite was sharpened by the frosty air. As we watched the bird a great white owl flapped, moth-like, across the open—perhaps disturbed before her time, or disappointed in her catch of mice the previous night. The hawk caught sight of her also, and instantly changed her attitude. In general, though keenly observant of every living thing that passed her station, she knew the limit of her range. But instinct is stronger than training. As the owl passed, uncertain, slow, bewildered, the temptation was irresistible. Tethered as she was, the hawk raised her wings, poised herself for an instant, and darted from the block. The leash, insecurely fastened, gave way, and she dashed off in chase.

Falconry has many anxieties and disappointments; but few mishaps occasion more concern than the flight of a hawk before the "jesses," or straps which secure her ankles, have been separated. In this case the thin leather strap or "leash" which is used as a tether was still attached to the jesses at one end. Consequently the danger of her being entangled in a tree or hung up by the heels to die miserably of exhaustion was increased. If, as was most probable, she killed her quarry, she would be likely to remain in the enclosed country. But beyond and above the village rose the chalk hills, on the summit of which she was usually flown; and to these, if she missed her prey, she would probably direct her flight. On these the danger from trees was lessened; for time and the hand of man have robbed the downs of timber. Here, from the Vale of the White Horse, commences the tract of Downs, the great chalk plateau lying between Wantage and Salisbury, the land of sheep. Travellers by the Great Western Railway see its outer wall between Didcot and Swindon and mark its main bastions, the White Horse Hill and Lyddington Castle. From the railroad it appears like a single range; but within this lies, ridge behind ridge, the mysterious Down country—a land of rounded outline and soft shadows, of shepherds' huts and sheepfolds. Even in summer few strangers penetrate this tract; yet, apart from the charm of space and solitude, it is not without beauty and interest. Much even of the highest land has been brought into cultivation; but great part has undergone no change. Here for miles lies the natural turf, elastic yet compact, studded at intervals with ancient thorns. Nor does the landscape want colour or the more subtle charm of scent. The turf is gay with unusual flowers, recalling the hill-tops of more distant lands. A tiny gentian dyes broad patches a brilliant cobalt. Harebells and blue campanulas fleck the green in contrast to the yellow crowsfoot and ranunculus. Blue butterflies match the harebells, yellow snail-shells lie among the crowsfoot. The scent of wild thyme rises heavy in the tremulous heat; and over all comes the sound of many sheep-bells. Nestling in the rounded hollows are rare farms, many of which are now occupied as training-stables. Not the least celebrated is that of the Seven Barrows, surrounded by the graves of heroes "whose souls went down to Hades" in the great fight of Ashdown, when Saxon and Dane contended for the mastery. Here the horse is still the *genius loci*, even as he was to his ancient worshippers, who cut his image on the great chalk hill hard by.

But snow and winter banish whatever of beautiful the land once owned. Nature's harmony is broken; nothing but a dull monotony of white remains. Colour is gone, and scent and even sound, except that of the icy wind that blows over the back of the great White Horse. All the sheep are folded down below, and even the birds have disappeared; only the sense of space and distance remains from summer's charms, as we see Inkpen Beacon and Highclere looming up in the leaden sky. Where a low plantation skirts the road the snow has drifted deep, calling to memory an incident of the last great snow-storm. Here a wagon was at last brought to in the drift, and the man and boy who accompanied it lay out all night in the bitter frost. In the morning the man with his remaining strength unharnessed the horses. Leaving one with the boy, he mounted the other and pushed through the drifts to a shepherd's hut. Here as the warmth relaxed his stiffened limbs he sank into a stupor. Meanwhile the boy remained forgotten; but the man's torpid brain was awakened by the arrival of the second horse, who had followed his companion. Full of self-reproach, he hurried back with the shepherd to the spot where the wagon was embedded in the drift. They found the boy standing with his hand still raised as though holding the rein; but the frost had done its work.

Seeing nothing of the falcon, we descended. On the lower terrace of the hills stood the homestead, surrounded by corn-ricks and cattle-yards; and as we approached it the absence of life and sound upon the hill was explained. The sheep, of course, were all here, bedded down in the warm pea-straw; the farm-horses also in their cosy stable, munching the oats of idleness. But here too were all the birds of the hill; for here only was *food*. Even the turnip-fields were covered by snow, though in one hard by several coveys of partridges were huddled. Here were all the rooks. In the morning they had made a combined attack upon a rick, and stripped the thatch. Now they were hastening to avail themselves of what light remained; as each black robber left the rick he carried off an ear of corn to eat in the field adjoining. But a barley-rick presented the strangest sight. The sides were black with small birds dragging out the straws with desperate energy; while beneath it the ground was covered by a fluttering, restless, feathery mass of birds, close-packed, eager, palpitating. The flock consisted of greenfinches, yellowhammers, buntings, and chaffinches; the sparrows had disappeared. By this time the light was failing, but hunger was not yet satisfied. On a sudden the mass of small birds rose as a kestrel swept round the stack and carried off one of their number, but instantly settled and were once more busy. A few minutes later a covey of partridges pitched down at a short distance; and after a few anxious calls, and stretching their necks as they reconnoitred the ground, they scampered over the snow to the stack. It was pretty to watch them fearlessly attacking the grain, jumping up now and then to reach a tempting ear, or chasing one another round the rick. Soon another covey joined them, and afterwards a third—all in frantic haste to make the most of their opportunity before nightfall. But by this time the light was disappearing—warning us to return and make arrangements for recovering our falcon next day.

Next day we again waded through the snow-drifts to the crest of the Downs. Close to the ancient "Ridge Way" stood a group of corn-ricks, and round these were gathered all the birds of the neighbourhood. Hundreds of rooks were on the snow round the stacks, or flying to and from the ricks. They were attacking the stores of grain, resolute to make the most of the only food available. A great number were clinging to the sides of the rick like martins under the eaves, and while some dragged out the straws (apparently quite aware that the ear would be at the other end), others shelled out the grain where they were. They had already made hollows a yard deep into the stack, and every minute made the work easier. The snow for a hundred yards around was littered with the stolen straws. But other and wiser rooks were "working the claim" in a more thorough fashion. They had quarried through the thatch deep into the stack, and were crowding into the hole in a black and busy throng, the place of those departing being at once filled, with much cawing and noise, by others who were waiting *en queue* all along the ridge of the thatch. "Then there came another locust, which carried off another grain of corn," was the burden of the Eastern story that was to last for ever. But judging by the hole already made in the stack, if for "locust" we had read "rook," the story would not have been long in coming to an end. Presently we approached so near, that the rooks rose reluctantly and flew off a few score yards on to the snow. Alarmed at the bustle, a covey of partridges which had been feeding on the opposite side of the rick to that from which we were coming, ran round to see what was the matter. After reconnoitring us for a minute, they also rose and flew a short way off, where they remained calling and running about anxiously till we should be gone. Some hurdles wattled with straw lay under a shed near, and by making a screen of these it was possible to remain close by, yet undiscovered.

Soon the birds began to call, and then flew boldly back to within twenty yards of the barley-rick. They stood upright, with heads raised for a minute, and then a fine old cock rushed up to the rick, clucking in an encouraging manner to the rest. These were not slow to join him, and soon the whole covey to the number of eight were pulling straw out with great energy, tugging and beating their wings when the work was more than usually difficult, and often *jumping up* to catch hold of any straw which hung out further than the rest. Another covey flew up to the other side of the rick, and the calling and clucking which notified their arrival made the first-comers cease feeding for a moment. The old cock bustled out from under the rick and was instantly confronted by the leader of the fresh covey. A fight seemed probable, but as their respective families fraternized and began to gobble barley together, the cock-birds seemed to think that enough had been done for honour, and were soon leading the joint attack on the grain. From our position we could see well the beautiful plumage of the birds, which looked even richer than usual on the white snow; and the strength and agility of the partridges, shown in the difficult task they had of dragging out deeply embedded straws, was very remarkable.

Besides the rooks and partridges, hundreds of smaller birds crowd round the stacks. On the sunny side, the ground is black with a fluttering, feathery mass of chaffinches, with a few linnets and greenfinches among them. After the recent snow had lain upon the ground for a week, these poor little creatures became so tame that we could not even drive them a few yards off, for the purpose of noting the wing-marks which they leave when rising,—perfect casts of the wing-stroke being sometimes left on the soft snow. They flew round us at a distance of a yard or so, and nothing would induce them to leave even for a moment the only spot where food could be obtained. Except the hawks and carrion-crows, none but grain-eating birds remain upon the hill. The rooks, which are not solely grain-eaters, do not thrive on a corn diet, and are obliged to cast up the outer husks of the wheat and barley, just as hawks and owls do the bones and feathers of birds. Even for those which, like the chaffinches and greenfinches, prefer corn, it is a hard matter to find enough. In good weather, the stock of food is so abundant that most land birds, except hawks, feed but twice a day, early in the morning and in the afternoon. In the snow they *feed all day long*. From dawn till dark the crowd round the stacks never lessens, and they feed until even the light reflected from the snow serves them no longer. Wood-pigeons, even in the deepest snow, manage to find seeds of some kind; and though their crops are generally full of turnip-leaves, there is always a mixture of some dark, shiny seeds, probably charlock. Red-legged partridges are much distressed by snow, not for want of food, for they burrow down to the turnips and eat both leaves and roots, but because they prefer running to flying, and the snow sticks in heavy lumps to their feathers. In Suffolk, where they are common, the unfortunate redlegs can be caught by a dog, or even by hand in such weather, and a heavy snow always thins their numbers sadly. Once the writer caught a brace of English partridges which had been flushed on the other side of a valley and pitched in soft snow near him. Instead of flying they crept deep into the drift, and made no effort to escape.

In the gardens and meadows the soft-billed birds suffer equally with the hardier sorts in lasting snow, even though in receipt of "relief" from kind friends in-doors. When the missel-thrushes come to eat crumbs under the window, as they have been doing lately, it is a sign that the last yewberry has been eaten, and the last thornbush stripped. The tits suffer less than other insect-eating birds, because the lower sides of the branches, in the bark of which they find most of their food, are always bare of snow. The cheerful "rap, rap," of the nuthatches is still to be heard, as they crack the nuts they have hidden away in better weather, or stolen from the squirrels. But such times are very bad for the birds. Half the blackbirds, thrushes, robins, and hedge-sparrows will die if not regularly fed, even though they spend all day turning over the dead leaves in the shrubbery in search of worms or snails. A three weeks' frost is more than they can endure, and already the thrushes are dying fast. But in great frosts, as a rule, those birds which stay with us run less risk than those which fly before the storm. Birds have no agencies to tell them the limits of the frost and snow ; and too often they arrive exhausted on distant coasts only to find that the frost has gone before them.

THE PEEWIT'S HOME

"There the winds sweep and the plovers cry."

THE return of the plovers to their nesting-grounds in the south is always watched with interest by those who are able to compare for any length of time the yearly increase or decrease of bird-life over the same tract of country. During the first weeks of May, when ploughing and sowing are over, and the land lies quiet awaiting the increase of the spring, the graceful peewits, and their "great relations" the stone-curlews, are occupied in the incessant care and protection of their young; and such is their anxiety and courage in endeavouring to mislead or frighten away intruders, that the number of pairs nesting on a given farm may easily be ascertained if the birds are disturbed. The writer has for many years been in the habit of devoting a few days at this time, partly to a careful observation of these and other birds, nesting on the open ground, near the White Horse Hill, with a view to ascertaining the conditions most favourable to their increase; and partly to searching the adjacent fir and beech copses, in order to take the eggs of the carrion-crows and magpies with which the plovers at this time wage fierce and incessant war; for if the crows have no family to provide for, they are, as a rule, contented to get their living honestly. The result of some nine years of observations so made, goes to show that the numbers both of the great plovers, or stone-curlews, and the peewits are decreasing, and the demand for "plovers' eggs," even though largely satisfied from abroad, must probably be held responsible for the diminished numbers of the last. The disappearance of the great plover is even more to be regretted, for its size and upright gait make it approach more nearly in appearance than any other bird to the great bustard, which used once to frequent the same ground; and its strange cry when on the wing is a wild and startling note among the sounds of the summer night upon the hill. It is difficult to account for the steady decrease of these birds. They generally choose the highest and barest ridges upon which to nest, and lay their eggs on some stony fallow, where it seems almost impossible to detect them, even though the particular field in which they lie is known. A friend of the writer's once endeavoured to aid him in discovering the nest by concealing himself at daybreak, and watching the ground with a telescope as the sun rose. But the birds quitted the field at his approach, and would not return. A week later the eggs were hatched, and we were so near to the young that the old bird settled on the ground within forty yards of us; but so closely did they conceal themselves, that the most patient search yielded no result. The eggs and young of the peewits are more easily found, for, unlike the great plovers, they make a nest which an experienced eye can quickly detect, and when we appear on the hill with staff and scrip for a long day among the birds, our first visit is generally paid to the peewits' nursery. This is a broad tract of rough ground dotted with stones and dead thistle-tops, among which the eggs can be laid without the danger which they incur on cultivated land from the modern practice of rolling the wheat in spring. The nearest pair of old birds instantly mark the danger, and in a few seconds the whole colony are wheeling, calling, and tumbling in the air in the wildest excitement and anxiety. No bird, not even a tumbler-pigeon, is a master of such feats of aërial gymnastics as the peewit, and their swift, fantastic circles and stoops inevitably arrest the eye, and divert the focus of vision from that careful and minute scrutiny which is necessary to detect the lurking young.

The best way to find the tiny creatures is to sit down and wait quietly, and without movement, when the anxiety of the old birds seems most marked. Then, after some minutes, a tiny head will be raised from the ground, and the watcher will be rewarded by seeing one of the prettiest sights in bird-life, a very young peewit. The little fellow is hardly larger than a walnut-shell, a tiny ball of speckled down, with large, bright black eyes, which he instantly hides from view, if the spectator moves, by gently pushing his head once more behind a weed or stone. But if perfect stillness is preserved, the whole brood of four will one by one rise, and move daintily forward on unsteady feet in the direction in which they hear their anxious parents screaming and calling, stopping now and again, and laying down their heads, as if to rest and regain courage for a further venture in the open. In no birds is this curious instinct for concealment, and the strange animal power of remaining motionless without discomfort, so early developed as in the young of the plovers and their kin, a power which nevertheless seems common even to the most restless animals. The writer has watched a squirrel on a branch remain as motionless as a hare in its form for half-an-hour, until his own powers of observation were exhausted. If it were not for this method of concealment, the young plovers would stand no chance of escaping the crows and magpies which swarm in the spruce-copses on the adjacent downs. Every copse holds yearly at least one crow's nest; and the population is seldom complete without a brood of hungry young magpies, and another of long-eared owls.

The great nests last for years in the tall spruces, and are occupied, like the castles on the Rhine, by successive generations of robbers, who, unlike the plovers, maintain their numbers undiminished. But the crows and magpies are a part of the natural inhabitants of the hill; and though we take their eggs, we leave the old birds in peace. But the hawks and crows are not the only robbers on the hill. The rich and juicy rye-grasses which grow on what was once corn-land, and is now laid down to pasture, naturally invite visits from the hungry sheep on the adjacent downs. Sometimes, when the coast is clear, their human guardian, unlike the "humble and innocent Abel" of Hooker's biographer, so far falls in with the wishes of his flock as to aid them in an organized raid into the heart of the neighbouring pastures; and the owner of the soil, when making a spring ramble on the hill, has occasionally the satisfaction of capturing a pirate-shepherd thus engaged. Farms intersected by one or more of the broad green tracks which do duty for roads on the downs are best suited for his operations, especially if he can secure the pasturage of some patch of land which gives him the right to drive his sheep along the track. When the shepherd concludes that the right moment for a foray has arrived, the conspirators—for the sheep-dog and the sheep seem perfectly intelligent parties to the scheme—approach the scene of action with due precautions. The dog quietly assembles the sheep on the edge of the down next to the highroad, and the sheep follow intelligently, the dog trotting quietly behind, with none of the officious barking and fuss which usually mark its behaviour when in charge of a moving flock. Arrived at the point where the green track leaves the main road, the shepherd makes a careful survey of the ground, and gives the signal for advance. Buried in the loose straw of a rick, we watch the foray through the binoculars with mixed feelings of indignation and amusement. Three hundred yards further along the track is a hollow, full of rich

Peewit's Nest. By J. W. Oakes, A.R.A.

grass, in which the flock might stay and feed all day unseen. To this point the invaders hurry, and in ten minutes have plunged into the hollow and disappeared. The shepherd and his dog lie down above them, and contemplate at their ease the success of their stratagem, ready to drive the flock unseen from the hollow on to the track on the appearance of danger. Though evidently an old offender, the shepherd is a stranger, so far as we can tell through the glasses; so we decide to trust to being mistaken for tourists, and thus endeavour to capture the robbers at their meal.

As we wander carelessly down the track the shepherd rises, and leaning on his staff, reconnoitres us with the keen eyes of a born son of the hills. The dog trots forward, and with one paw raised watches us also, ready at a sign from his master to rush back to the hollow and drive the sheep on to the track. "Towerists, for zartain," remarks the shepherd to himself, and prepares for a wayside chat. The collie, only partly convinced by his master's attitude, gives a short, defiant yelp, and trots back to heel. As we reach the edge of the hollow, we see the flock making the best of their time, eagerly pulling out and chewing the grass, and expanding in a rapidly widening circle up the sloping sides. The glimpse of the predatory side of an Arcadian existence becomes amusing. We feel that the approaching dialogue should take a classic form—

VIATOR.—"Tell me, shepherd, whose flock is this? Is it Melibœus'?"

SHEPHERD (politely, but conscious of being better

informed).—" No, zur ; 'em beant ; 'em be Mister Parkinses, zur ; the miller's sheep, zur, be at Up-Lambourne, zur."

VIATOR (tartly).—" Then if you and your sheep are here five minutes longer, we will run them all down to Cressington Pound."

SHEPHERD (realizing the situation). — " Great Apollo!" (or words to that effect.)

[The dog rushes off at a wave of his master's hand ; in a minute the flock are back upon the track, and in three more the enemy appear a white diminishing patch upon the distant down.]

MARCH DAYS ON THE DOWNS

GAME, and wild birds and beasts of all kinds show themselves more on a warm March day than at any other season. This is not because they are more numerous, for after the hardships of winter, and before the young are born, or the spring migrants have arrived, their numbers are at the lowest point in the year. Yet the bare fields and the edges of the copses seem to tempt every hare, crow, magpie, and hawk, to show themselves for a few days almost without fear of man. Even the tame cats leave the houses and gardens, and sit out in the meadows and on the sunny banks, neither hunting nor sleeping, but sitting up sedately enjoying the prospect, and licking their fur into summer glossiness. The dog-foxes do the same, though the vixens are already occupied in the care of their litters. On a rough hillside forming the outskirts of a park, dotted with patches of dried grass and brambles, I have often watched them at this time sitting up like a dog with ears erect and a boldness of demeanour which must be born of some vulpine recollection that the hunting-season comes to an end with the appearance of what the old huntsman called "them stinking violets," and that the days of peace and plenty are within measurable distance. Licking and cleaning their fur also occupies much of their sunny hours. No one who has watched them so engaged can believe that the fox is naturally an uncleanly animal, in spite of the disagreeable scent which it bears. But during the hunting season they become so wary and suspicious that every kind of food is dragged into the earths to be devoured. The skins and refuse parts are not eaten, the earths become foul and tainted, and with the approach of spring they are deserted, except as a place of refuge. The vixen digs a hole for her litter in some fresh haunt, or scratches out a deserted rabbit-burrow, and the male fox revels in fresh air, wind, and sunlight. In the long dry grass in the hollows on the downs, where what was once arable land has turned into coarse pasture, their seats may be found in numbers, round neat nests which the fastidious fox changes every day. "Grass burning" is an exciting minor branch of husbandry at this time, harmless to the ground-birds, which have not yet begun to nest, and pretty to watch, as the low flames creep crackling over the dry haulm above, and leave the good green undergrowth sprinkled with invigorating ashes. The March hares are wide-awake, and hop away to the adjacent slopes, whence they watch the progress of the flames with ears erect, and a very human look of curiosity. The partridges whirr off in pairs, and no one is the worse, except the singed and smoke-grimed bipeds whose business it is with branches and sacks to keep the sides of the fire from spreading too near to stacks or fences. Yet while directing this operation the writer once singed a basking fox. The grass had been lighted and relighted for more than an hour, and the successful laying of a long train of straw had at last produced a line of fire a hundred yards across, which was travelling slowly across the wind. The fox had chosen for its lair a hollow full of long grass from which rubble had been dug at some distant date, and was either sound asleep or unwilling to move, until the fire had passed on either side of its lair. When it sprang up in the middle of the smoke it was for a moment bewildered, and dashed through the flames with its fur on end, and every hair on its brush stiff with fright. A long-legged setter which was watching the proceedings at once gave chase, and it was not until after a long and close course in the open that the fox recovered presence of mind to make for a fence, and with one or two of the apparently simple ruses by which the fox always bewilders the slower dog-wits, that the setter was baffled. In a long day spent on the hills at this time it is possible to find every head of game, and all the winged vermin in a thousand acres, by sitting quietly opposite the sheltered slopes, or near the copses.

It is the only season at which animals are more restless than man; their power of sitting still deserts them under the genial influence of the unaccustomed sun. By the time that the peewits have ceased circling and calling, the little brown dots, which may be either hares or clods, begin to move. The distant ones look redder and larger. Presently one rises, not at once, but gradually, till its round back shows against the down. It creeps forward and nibbles at the grass, and at last hops gently down the slope. The rest take courage, and rise one by one; others appear in unexpected quarters, until the hillside is dotted with their cautiously moving forms. One, bolder than the rest, dashes up to its mate, and before long the whole party are busy courting, the lady hares nibbling at the young grass, taking little excursions to try another tuft, sitting up to watch the landscape, and pretending to be quite absorbed in the weather, or in anything but the affairs of the moment, while their suitors skip, run circles, or hop meekly after them, protesting that they have come miles to see them across the downs, and cannot take "No" for an answer. Some are already mated; but few of the young March leverets survive the dangers to which the short herbage and long light days expose them. The hungry sparrow-hawks, whose keen vision sees the tiny leveret far more quickly than the most practised human eye detects a bold March hare, must kill the greater number of these "rathe-born" litters. They seem to know the exact spots where the leverets are lying, and not to take them until such time as they consider to be necessary or convenient. While watching the hares at play and at the same time the progress of the horse-drills in a field in which spring corn was being sown, the writer observed a sparrow-hawk perched upon a tree, and also watching the progress of

Grass Burning on the Downs. By Lancelot Speed.

the work. The ground was in perfect order, dry, soft, and fine, and the horses were stepping briskly across the smooth, fresh-harrowed soil. At either end stood the open sacks of grain, ready to fill the seed-boxes, and the steady wind drove a cloud of good March dust —the dust of the field, not of the road—from the drills like spin-drift from a cutter's prow. More than half the area was finished when the hawk dashed from its tree, swept up a leveret from the edge of the field, and killed it before the sowers could run to the rescue. It had bided its time until, seeing that its prey must be disturbed, it at once made a bold dash to secure it. The magpies, carrion-crows, brown owls, and white owls, as well as the wood-pigeons and rooks, are all building; and by a curious coincidence, the largest of common English birds, the heron—the smallest, the gold-crest—and the most brilliant, the king-fisher—all lay their eggs in March. The frogs and pike are also spawning, and in the general scarcity of food the banks of the ponds and slow streams are a happy hunting-ground to nearly all the larger birds. The "breaking of the waters" under the first hot suns fills the stagnant pools for a few days with a thick infusion of green or red algæ. The mud smells, the frogs croak, the pike bask in pairs in the shallows, and as the water shrinks from the margin the carrion-crows are busy early and late in hunting for their favourite dainty, the fresh-water mussels. The meadows near the canal which flows through the White Horse Vale, and is there dignified by the name of the "river," are studded with the beautiful oval bivalve shells, their mother-of-pearl lining pierced by the crows' beaks; and near any favourite post or old stump, which the crows use as a dining-table, there is a pile of the dark-blue and opal fragments. It is not creditable to the rustic feeling for sport that the March shrinkage of the waters, which suggests to the crows their raids upon the mussels, usually prompts the whole village to a short-lived enthusiasm for "fishing." It never seems to occur to rustic anglers that autumn and winter are the proper seasons in which to take coarse fish. The sight of the young fry near the banks, and the big breeding pike in the shallows, sends every idle pair of hands with rods or poles to the stream. If the weather is unusually dry, the fish may even be hauled out with a hay-rake; and in any case, snares, or some "engine" not considered fair to the fish by anglers, is preferred. "Did you catch he with a snare?" was the first inquiry we heard addressed to an urchin who was discovered cuddling a 6-lb. pike in his arms like a baby. "No," replied the boy. "You groppled he?" suggested another. "Got 'un with a hook?" surmised a third. "Not exactly," was the answer; "I catched 'un wi' a *bung*." The big fish had fallen victim to a night-line, fastened to the cork of a mineral-oil cask.

"KITING" ON THE DOWNS

AFTER seven years' experience of the district, I may say without qualification that I have nowhere found partridges so impracticably wild late in the season as those bred on the high downs by the great White Horse. Apart from the known fact that hill partridges are generally stronger and fly further than those on lower and more sheltered ground, there are scarcely any fences on the downs; consequently there are no local limits suggested to the birds' flight other than those given by the natural lie of the ground. In an inclosed country a few brace may always be had by an active walker, even when single-handed, as they can generally be got to " fence." Such at least was my experience in Suffolk, when we as boys often made a Christmas bag when sturdy but short-winded farmers had returned almost empty-handed.

"Well, what sport have you had?" inquired my old friend Mr. Tom Barrett, as we met him walking rather sulkily home with the claws of one partridge sticking out of his covert coat-pocket.

"Oh, pretty good for us, thank you, Mr. Barrett,"

we replied, with the pride that apes humility; "we have shot six red-legs and a hare."

"Shot 'em!" replied our friend, with bitter irony. "Shot 'em! you don't shoot 'em, you walk 'em to dead!" and he stamped off home.

Whether this insinuation were true or not—and we certainly did rather tire our birds—neither shooting nor walking will command a bag in Berks in late December, and I have found that the only way to make sure of a few brace is to try the kite. This Christmas the frost fog settled on the hill, and the absence of wind to blow away mist and influenza made the kite impossible. But this was unusual.

A day marked by all the good and evil of "kite-flying" was that on which Eton restored some thousand young gentlemen to "make the home brighter" during the Christmas holidays. One of these was expected by an early train—a sporting youth of seventeen, who naturally did not wish to waste a minute of the precious time; and to meet this view it was arranged to begin so soon as ever the dogcart could deposit him at the cross roads, ready to take instant part in the business of the hour. It was a nice bright day, with enough wind to fly the kite, and sun to make the birds rather less anxious to shift their quarters than usual. Two coveys even rose within a long shot under a fence as we were getting the machine into working order, and a lively runner was claimed by all three of the party as the result of a general discharge. The kite was duly hoisted in the ancient road known as the "Icledon Way," and soared up clear of all danger from the few scattered trees near; and while it tugged and pulled at the string, it certainly looked very like some goblin falcon, as it swayed about and gazed with horrible scrutiny from its one eye on the ground beneath. The little tags in the tail danced and hovered like small birds mobbing a hawk; and a flock of rooks in a neighbouring field flew off into the vale in consternation at the invasion of so awful a fowl. Most people, when the kite is once up, fancy that the difficulties connected with its working are over. Though we did not quite share this view, the country before us was so easy, being a long and gradual ascent of four hundred feet with no timber, and a flat hill-top bare of trees beyond it, that we allowed the string to pass into the hands of a volunteer, who was an excellent farm bailiff, and rather jumped at the notion of working the kite for a few hours. It was not long before we discovered that the kite-flying part of his education had been neglected in his youth.

Before going up the hill we wished to try a large stubble field, on which several coveys were feeding. In the middle of this stood two large isolated elm trees; and we had not worked half the field before we were horrified to see the kite string caught in the largest and least "climbable" of the two. The kite struggled, fluttered, and then descended gracefully, casting the whole length of its tail across the topmost branchlets of the elm.

Now the trunk of the elm was large, and the lower branches had been carefully trimmed, so that there was nothing for it but "swarming"—a tiring exertion in any costume, and made worse in this case by one's heavy shooting boots. The tallest of the party, who was rather an expert at tree climbing, made the sacrifice, and, after a desperate effort, perched himself among the branches, some fifteen feet from the ground. But when he had reached the tree top, so far as that was possible for a man of his weight, the kite was still out of reach, so nicely was it balanced on the outer branches. We then sent for a ladder and a saw, and an active young labourer, who brought both, clambered up into the tree, and sawed the main branch, on which the kite was hung. But, as I waited, with our Etonian, at the foot, I suddenly saw an expression of alarm in the face of the latter, and, looking up, beheld the lad, who found sawing rather a slow job, "laying out," as the sailors say, along the half-cut limb to try and reach the kite. This was too exciting for our nerves, so we ordered him back, and, after a few minutes' vigorous sawing, the branch and kite came down together, without damage to the former.

Most people will agree that so far we had had our share of ill-luck. The hitch in the tree cost us an hour's delay. We had not started till eleven, and thus it was twelve o'clock before we could get under way again; worse than this, the tiring climb put one of the party off his shooting, and the fuss occasioned by the whole incident upset us all.

But straight shooting is never more wanted than with the kite. Birds fly fast, low, and twisting, and in this case there was a nice wind to help them, so that we soon had to laugh at ourselves and congratulate the birds.

Making straight for the hill-top, we passed over some long sloping stubbles, and before long one of the party held up his hand. "Come up quick," he said; "there is a whole covey squatting in this pit," and he pointed to a slight hollow in front of him, from which chalk had been taken. "Spring them," we said; and then watched him carefully pick up a clod, and shy it at the birds. Up they all jumped, with no end of a screeching and cackle, and then did our friend carefully miss them right and left.

After some remarks by an old shepherd who had joined us, to the effect that "when 'em's scared 'em twistës, and when 'em twistës 'em's bad to hit," we got the kite over a field of swedes. Now, a swede field in December, after the frost, means so many acres of hard round balls, with no leaf on top. But, bad as it was, it was the only cover we had, and the birds were there. Like prudent creatures, though afraid to fly, they ran as far as they could; and it was not till we got to the extreme edge that we had a rise. Then at least forty were flushed at once. Most flew low and fast, twisting; others rose high and went back, and one old cock waited till all our barrels were empty, and then got up with all the dignity possible and flew down the line. And what was the result of our volley?

Alas, two birds only; the pace had apparently been too much for us.

We then moved on to another swede field, and found that, as in the first, the birds had all run to the edge. Here we made the mistake of working the down-wind side first. The kite-flyer walked down the windward edge of the swedes, and soon flushed two big coveys, which flew away somewhere into the next parish but one. We then drew out, and taking up that side, had two good rises and bagged a leash! If the powder had only been decently straight, it should have been four brace. By this time it was past two o'clock, and the sun was already sinking towards the back of the White Horse Hill, and the misty vapours filling the hollow by Seven Barrows.

After tying up our kite, and eating some luncheon by a barn, we concluded to try some high rough grass for hares, and then have another turn at the birds. There is something very exhilarating in walking this high uncultivated land, far from houses, except scattered shepherds' cottages, and surrounded with memorials of a dead past in the shape of barrows and ancient camps. The hares were pretty numerous, and uncommonly wild; nevertheless, we shot three, and eventually a fourth. This last hare went on hard hit, but going fast; then, after travelling one hundred and fifty yards up hill, it gave three bounds and tumbled over stone dead.

We next unfastened our kite and tried some more swede fields. It occurred to me that, as we had sprung nothing but large coveys in the morning, we might have walked over some smaller lots. So we let the setter range, which had hitherto walked at heel; he very soon stood, and five birds rose. Of these our Etonian had a right and left, and I one, a fourth going on and towering over a copse, where we lost him. In the next field we rose two more coveys; but these were wilder, and we only had one bird.

By this time we had descended below the ancient "ridge-way," which marks the crest of the downs for forty miles, and the wind greatly lessened in force, so that the kite descended gently into a swede field on the steepest part of the hill-side. Then occurred a curious incident: one of the party went on to raise the kite, and, laying down his gun, stooped to pick up the mock falcon, while I took the string some forty yards away and higher up the slope. But as he stooped up bounced a covey all round him; so close were they, that he picked up his gun and shot the last bird.

It was evident that the kite had fallen right into the middle of these birds. They, true to their instinct, kept still. But when the wingless enemy, man, came among them, they flew. Of course the birds are quite right in their tactics. A peregrine is quite harmless as long as they are on the ground; and they seem to know it. But the sparrow-hawk will attack birds when running, if not when squatting. I witnessed this when shooting in Suffolk with my brother, Mr. J. G. Cornish, in severe winter weather. We were shooting red-legs in the snow, which had frozen on the top and enabled those wary birds to run, though they were of course very easily seen. We were watching a brace making across a roughly ploughed field, where the snow lay in the furrows and the ridges were bare, when a sparrow-hawk dashed from a tree, pitched beside the leading bird, and grabbed him by the back with one foot. The two scuffled along together for a couple of yards, and then the partridge shook himself clear, and got into the fence. Nor were his nerves at all upset by the encounter, for he got out of it before we could come within shot of him, and made off.

We killed another bird coming down the hill, and then wound in our kite, in case we might have another difficulty with the tree, having only bagged twelve birds and four hares. But if the powder had been straight, we ought to have doubled that number.

On the whole, shooting with a kite is unsatisfactory work. It is a nuisance to have a machine out shooting; and if it goes wrong or gets hung up, it disconcerts most people for the day. But if it is used, the success of the day will depend mainly on the judgment with which the man in charge of the kite works it. This means experience, and my own is not sufficient to allow me to dogmatize.

Kiting on the Downs. By Lancelot Speed.

WILD RABBIT FARMING

THE growth of " Wild England " has been going on by leaps and bounds during the years in which the price of wheat and oats have maintained their steady decline. It would be a most interesting experiment for the County Councils of the home districts to issue a map, on which the land withdrawn, not only from the plough, but from any form of cultivation, and running wild, was coloured in a bold tint and plain to the eye. Most of this will turn into rough pasture of a sort; but the question of how to gather some revenue from it meantime is a pressing one. Much of this land, especially that on the Berkshire downs, is thin light soil, well suited for the rearing of game; and as sporting rights let well, and the ground which rears partridges and rabbits is also suitable for running rough stock and sheep upon in winter, the new wilderness is likely to be fairly well peopled with its natural inhabitants. In some places wild rabbit farming has been taken up seriously. A partner in one of the large London provision stores told the writer that he had turned part of a farm in Essex—which he had taken to graze cattle on when the state of the market made it desirable to keep them for a few weeks before being turned into beef—into a rabbit farm, and that with the sale which he could secure, it answered well. This is a new departure in English rural economy.

The proverb that "what is one man's poison may be another man's meat" could not be better illustrated than by a comparison of an interesting little book on *The Wild Rabbit in a New Aspect*,[1] by Mr. Simpson, Wood Agent to Lord Wharncliffe's estate, near Sheffield, with the mass of rabbit literature which has appeared in Colonial Blue-books and Reports during the past few years. No one who is at all familiar with the feelings of resentment, irritation, and despair which find their way into Colonial prints on this subject can doubt that the character of the rabbit needs whitewashing badly. It is said that any person convicted of bringing the wild rabbit to any port of Cape Colony would be lynched as certainly as a Negro murderer of a White in the Southern States of America. In New Zealand, the sheep-farmer drives from one log-cabin to another on his "run" with a cartful of cats in cages, which are deposited at each, and taught to earn a living by keeping down the rabbit-plague. The demand for cats, fostered by the increase of the rabbits, even disturbs the domestic circle, when hearth-rug favourites of known home-keeping habits mysteriously

---

[1] *The Wild Rabbit in a New Aspect; or, Rabbit Warrens that Pay.* By J. Simpson, Wood Agent, Wortley Hall, Sheffield. London: Blackwood and Sons.

disappear, and bereaved housewives, on comparing notes, find a suspicious correspondence between the rise in the prices offered by the advertising farmers and the sudden loss of their household pets. In Australia, the rabbit has learnt a new accomplishment. In California it has forgotten an old one. The Australian rabbit has developed long claws, and climbs the scrub with ease, in order to eat the leaves when grass is scarce. In California it has forgotten how to burrow; and recently a rising *en masse* of the inhabitants of a rabbit-infested district succeeded by driving the creatures by thousands into an inclosure, where they were destroyed without a chance of escape. But in all the Colonies—and even in most parts of Germany, where the people will not eat rabbits, declaring that the meat was "too sweet"—the rabbit is looked upon as a pest, to be exterminated if possible, and so unremunerative as food as not to pay the wages of the men employed in its destruction. The "Ground Game Act," recently passed in England, reflected some such general feeling among our own middle and lower classes; and in many parts of the country where wild rabbits formerly swarmed they have completely disappeared. The contrary opinion, maintained within limits by Mr. Simpson, comes with a certain recommendation from the position and employment of its author. In the first place, "he comes from Yorkshire," writing from the park of Lord Wharncliffe, at Wortley Hall, near Sheffield, where his experiments were made; and in the next he is a "wood-agent," or manager of growing timber, young and old, upon a large estate, and, of course, looks upon rabbits *at large* as his natural enemies. His record of the means by which these creatures on a very large estate were maintained within bounds, and yet available as a source both of profit and sport, is all the more interesting. The Wortley warren consists of very old park-pasture, which had always been overrun with rabbits, on which the herbage was in many parts very poor and rough. Seventy-seven acres of this were surrounded by a cheap rabbit-proof fence, enclosing a strip of old wood, mostly of oak, with an undergrowth of elder, rhododendrons, and bracken. It is curious to notice that though the warren, which was divided by a wagon-road, was provided with artificial burrows on the side opposite to this wood, it took the rabbits a whole year to find them out; and for the first twelve months they fed almost wholly on the half of the pasture which adjoined their burrows. In the first year, 3000 good live rabbits were caught. Meantime, every other rabbit on the estate had been destroyed; and the annoyance of damage to woodlands and complaints from tenants ceased. For the succeeding three years the same average yield of 3000 rabbits has been maintained, in addition to which cattle have been fed on the warren to the value of £100 per annum. But omitting this source of profit, the ground has for four years produced over 40 rabbits per acre. The author makes the total 50; but this does not correspond with the figures in his acreage. But this is far beyond the return on less carefully managed or neglected warrens, where an average of from 15 to 20 rabbits per acre is by no means common. The expense of the Wortley warren is not stated as clearly as could be wished. But the returns from an "experimental acre," specially fenced-in and stocked with a view to ascertaining the number of rabbits which the standard acre would support, are given as follow—

Manure, lime, hay, labour, and interest on fencing at 5 per cent.	£1 10	0
Rent, rates, and taxes	1 14	0
Total cost	£3 4	0

Off this acre 110 rabbits were netted, whose market-value was 2s. 4d. per couple, giving a gross profit of £6 4s. 4d., and a net profit of £3 4s. 4d. per acre. It will be noticed that the number taken from this experimental acre was nearly three times that produced by the same quantity of ground in the large warren. On the other hand, the expenses of fencing and labour for the larger area would be far less in proportion than on the smaller; and the writer gives it as his opinion that, were he allowed to keep a larger breeding-stock at the end of the season his return over the whole 77 acres of the warren would not fall far below that of his experimental enclosure. Two facts in connection with wild-rabbit culture in England appear from the data which we have referred to. The creature is far less prolific in England than in the " new countries," where it now swarms in such uncontrollable numbers ; and it enjoys a reputation as delicate food among the working class of the North and of the large towns, which makes it always saleable at a high price. The wild rabbit, *in a warren*, does not multiply as it is reported to do in the Australian runs. A pair in an isolated burrow might, the author considers, produce 20 young in the season, which lasts from February till September; but in a warren, not overstocked, 10 young is the highest number which can be expected from a single pair. In reference to the great demand for rabbits, the author writes:—" In all towns and populous districts the demand is practically unlimited, and has increased since the Ground Game Act came into force. It might be supposed that the market would be glutted when the shooting season is in full swing, and thousands of rabbits are sold daily from many estates; but that is not the case, and game-dealers compete keenly with each other for the chance of securing the rabbits at shootings, and will attend and move them if shot, and pay cash down for them if required. The dealers find ready buyers at from 2*s.* 6*d.* to 3*s.* 6*d.* per couple, and a little less for the smallest and worst shot. But a considerably better price can be had for *hand-killed* rabbits than for shot ones." There can be no doubt that rabbits are the favourite luxury of the poor; and though we should be inclined to rate the constant market-value at from 2*s.* to 2*s.* 6*d.* per couple, rather than at the higher value given above, there is never any difficulty in disposing of them in any quantity, and at a constant price.

The reasons for the economic failure of rabbit-warrens hitherto are not far to seek. Opinion on the subject of the wild rabbit has long pronounced that any land—the worse the better—suits rabbits; and when this has been well stocked the pasture is left, without manure, or lime, or any of those restorative agents which are necessary to replace the waste caused by the sale of the rabbits which have built up their active little bodies from the produce of the soil. The result is that the catch grows yearly less, and the land is pronounced to be "rabbit-sick." Rabbit farming can only be conducted successfully just on the same conditions as any other form of stock-raising, with this exception, that the habits of the rabbit make it peculiarly suitable for such a purpose. It is, perhaps, the least wasteful feeder among all the rodent tribe. Unlike the hare, which is dainty and particular, and causes more damage to crops by wandering from place to place to satisfy its whims and fancies than by the actual needs of its appetite, the rabbits move slowly forward from the edge of the covert or burrow, going over the same ground every day. If the burrows are properly distributed over the warren, the rabbits will eat the grass down as it grows, keeping it short throughout the summer. If they do not, the warren is either ill-arranged or under-stocked. A few months cover the whole feeding period; and by the beginning of November most of the rabbits should be caught, and only the breeding-stock left through the winter, which can be provided with artificial food at little expense in long frosts or snow. Thus, beyond keeping up the fences and catching the rabbits, for whose wholesale and painless capture the author gives an ingenious and simple device in use at Wortley Park, there is little expenditure either on labour or food ; and the cost of protecting the warren against poachers need only extend through the spring and summer, before the young stock has been caught, for no one would think it worth while to attempt to catch the few rabbits left to breed in the winter. The only point of which we have to complain in Mr. Simpson's statement is, that his figures are less full and detailed than could be wished in what is otherwise a very suggestive and practical work. Rabbits are clearly in demand ; and the time is ripe for such an experiment as he suggests, which would probably yield a fair profit until the "rabbit pest" in the New World is converted into a source of wealth by some gigantic "canning" industry for the supply of the English market.

BIRDS IN THE FROST FOG

"And now there came both mist and snow,
And it grew wondrous cold."—*Ancient Mariner.*

THE sufferings which fell on the Ancient Mariner and his comrades for the wanton killing of the albatross were the penalty of a bird murder of the most aggravated kind, for in killing the albatross they broke the bond of an alliance formed between comrades in misfortune. The sea-bird suffered from the fog and mist in the same degree and in the same way as did the lost ship's crew. They saw in the bird a comrade, and the bird found in the ship and its crew both society and a home—

"At length did cross an Albatross,
  Through the fog it came;
As it had been a Christian soul,
  We hailed it in God's name.

In mist or cloud, on mast or shroud,
  It perched for vespers nine;
Whilst all the night, through fog-smoke white,
  Glimmered the bright moonshine.

It ate the food it ne'er had eat,
  And round and round it flew.
The ice did split with a thunder fit,
  And the helmsman steered us through!"

Poets have an instinctive feeling for the truth of natural life, and Coleridge caught and developed the probability that the bird was baffled and bewildered by the mist as well as the crew, and so heightened the feeling of good-will between the sailors and the white bird of the sea. For birds even more than mankind suffer in continued fogs and mist, even without the cold that generally accompanies or causes them. Men, and all things that *walk*, can usually find their way from point to point by working from one well-known landmark to the next. But a bird flying in the mist is like a ship in the sea-fog. The dull, grey cloud lies between it and the earth, and shuts out all guiding-marks from view; and when once it has lost its bearings, it becomes hopeless and distracted. This is more especially the case at sea, or on open plains or downs, and even in the homestead they seem torpid and afraid to move. The Berkshire peasants have a word for the condition of bees just before winter. They are said to be "droo,"—and this exactly describes the condition of the pigeons and fowls, especially the former, in a long frost fog. During such weather the white pigeons sit all day long under the dovecote eaves, huddled up as if asleep, not even coming to the ground to look for food; and on the high downs, where the frost-fog drifts all day like frozen smoke, neither the cry of a bird nor the stroke of a wing is to be heard. Great is the silence of the mist. No horses are at plough, the sheep are down in the straw-yards, and the wide hill-tops are all smoke and darkness. It is like the atmosphere before Ovid's cave of sleep—

> "Nebulæ caligine mixtæ
> Exhalantur humo, dubiæque crepuscula lucis."

Cobbett calls these fogs "dry clouds." But they are not always dry; oftener they condense on vegetation, and make everything dripping wet. Their area is very capricious. For many days in January, 1888, the vales were filled with dusky rolling vapour, rising to a level of 700 ft., while the hill-tops were in bright sunlight. Yet the larks and starlings and wood-pigeons dare not venture through the fog in search of the bright weather above it. The vapour condensed on *green* wood, but not on dead, and the woodlands were dripping and uncomfortable. The wood-pigeons were afraid to venture from the plantations, and remained in them all day, drowsy and stupid; and pheasants, which *run* in search of their food, and so feel no danger of being lost, did, in fact, wander away for miles, and scattered from their head-quarters in the preserves all over the country. On the downs, when a sudden drop of temperature covered the hill also with fog, and turned the water-drops on the trees into crystal tears, the birds all retired to the copses of beech and spruce-fir, and if disturbed, would flap on in scores for a short distance, or wheel back into the copse behind the intruder, not daring to leave the trees for the murky darkness of the fog. At such times, even the frequent discharge of a gun has fewer terrors for them than the unknown dangers of the mist, and numbers of these birds are shot in small plantations. But though this unusual tameness is partly due to their reluctance to leave the landmark of the wood, they have also another reason. Birds, looking *down* into the fog, as it lies below them with the solid earth for a backing, have far more difficulty in seeing objects *beneath* them, and so avoiding danger from below, than we have in distinguishing their forms against the sky, which must always be the lightest object even in thick fogs. The writer and a friend had once some curious evidence of the additional difficulty and danger to which fog exposes birds. We had gone up on to the top of the downs, where a long copse skirted the road, partly to see the curious effect of these mists freezing on the beech-trees, partly in hopes of shooting a couple of the wood-pigeons which had been eating the turnip-tops in safety during the open weather. For some time, however, the mist was so black that we could see little, and the pigeons, which were mostly in another and more distant plantation, were afraid to move. Soon, however, though the fog hung as thickly as ever on the ground, it was evident that there was a clearing in the vapours higher up, for the tops of some poplar-trees which grew by the side of the beech-copse, and rose some thirty feet above the level of the rest, could be seen bright with sunlight. These branches must have stood out from the dark sea of mist as trees do in a flood, and probably presented some such appearance to the pigeons. For the flocks, which soon began to fly about in the welcome light, settled on these trees, although we were standing below them. But we must have been quite invisible to the birds, for though we shot as many as we wanted, fresh numbers constantly arrived on the trees at the foot of which we stood in the open road. In this road, which was very cold and skirted by the copse, the fog hung closer than elsewhere, which perhaps accounted for our invisibility. On another occasion, the writer came across a bird really "lost in the fog." It was at Moor Allerton, near Leeds, a village which stands on a high hill, crowned by a large wood. By the road near the wood stood one or two of what were then the last gas-lamps of the town. Though it was not late in the afternoon, the fog was so thick that these were lighted, and round one of them was flying a large bird, either a wood-pigeon or a stock-dove, which had probably lost its way as it was making for the wood, and was helplessly flying round the twinkling light. It continued to do so as long as the writer cared to wait, but must have gone on later, as it had disappeared when he returned.

Wild geese, which like the wood-pigeons are most wary birds, often become very tame, and even bewildered, in a fog. St. John used to shoot them easily in the bay of Findhorn in such weather, waiting till they flew inland, when they would come cackling just over his head. But the oddest story of geese in the fog comes from Norfolk, and was told to Mr. Stevenson, the author of *The Birds of Norfolk*, by the Rev. H. T. Frere. A large flock of geese were attracted to the town of Diss on a foggy night by the lights, and from the sound of their voices seemed to fly scarcely higher than the tops of the houses. They came about seven P.M., and as it was Sunday evening, they appeared to be especially attracted by the lights in the church, and their incessant clamour not a little disturbed the congregation assembled for evening service. From that time until two A.M., when the fog cleared off and they departed, they continued to fly round and round utterly bewildered. One bird happened to fly so low as to strike a gas-lamp outside the town—probably, like the pigeon at Leeds, it was flying round the light—just as a policeman was passing by, who very properly, as the bird was making a great noise outside a public-house, took it into custody; and the next day it was with equal propriety sent off to a private lunatic asylum at Melton, where it lived for some years an honoured guest.

Rooks and partridges do not seem to alter their habits in the fog so much as other birds that seek their living in the open country. Partridges are, if anything, wilder than ever; and if the rooks keep nearer home than usual, they by no means refuse to fly; their wings make a great noise in the silence of the fog, and often the first notice of their presence is the flapping of the damp wings as they make off suddenly before the unwelcome presence of man. But all other wild birds keep still and moping till the darkness goes. The deprivation of light, which affects all animals so much, is particularly depressing to birds; and this may be another reason for their unwillingness to move in the frost fog. Naturally they are the first to welcome its departure. As the mist lifts from a Scotch hill-side, the cock-grouse begin to crow; and in the English fields, the rooks caw, the small birds twitter, and the cocks crow in the barn-yards. These sounds are as certain to proclaim the lifting of the fog as the "London cries" to begin when the rain stops.

ENGLISH ANIMALS IN SNOW

(The "White Horse" Downs)

As the first snow fell this year gently, steadily, and by day, instead of rushing upon us in a midnight storm, the sheep, not waiting until it pleased the snow-demon either to bury them or to pass on to mischief elsewhere, drew together facing the wind, and stamped the snow down incessantly as it fell, just as they stamp their feet when facing a strange dog,—but far more rapidly and continuously. Some of them were lambs of the year, that had never seen a snow-fall. Yet these creatures, so long domesticated, untaught by experience, were by instinct using the same means to combat the snow, their greatest enemy, as does the wild moose in the Canadian backwoods. The moose would perish like the sheep in the drifts, if the herds did not combine to trample out the "moose-yards"; and these sturdy Southdowns were showing exactly the same instinct in an English park.

But snow generally catches our animals unprepared—all but the hedgehog, who is comfortably asleep, rolled up in a coat of leaves,—and they are put to all kinds of shifts to find food and escape their enemies. The more open and exposed the districts, the greater their difficulties. Where there are thick woods and hedgerows, and, above all, running water, birds and beasts alike can find dry earth in which to peck and scratch, or green things to nibble, and water to drink. But on the great chalk-downs, a heavy snow-storm seems to drive from the open country every living creature that dares to move at all. For the first day after a heavy fall, the hares, which allow the snow to cover them, all but a tiny hole made by their warm breath, do not stir. Only towards noon, if the sun shines out, they make a small opening to face its beams, and perhaps another in the afternoon, at a different angle to the surface, to catch the last slanting rays. Walking across the fields after a violent snow-storm in January, the writer stepped on a hare, though the field showed one level stretch of driven snow; and later in the day, from the brow of a steep, narrow valley, the sun-holes made by the hares were easily marked on the opposite ridge. Four or five were discovered in this way; and on disturbing them, it was found that each had its two windows, one facing the south, the second and longer tunnel pointing further to the west, and at a sharper angle to the surface. But hunger soon forces the hares to leave their snug snow-house; in the bitter nights, as the icy wind sweeps through the thin beech-copses on the downs, and piles up huge ice-puddings of drifted snow and beech-leaves, they canter off down into the vale, to eat the cabbages in the cottage-gardens, and nibble the turnips in the heaps opened to feed the sheep in the straw-yards. Squirrels, which are often supposed to hibernate, only retire to their nests in very severe and prolonged frosts. A slight fall of snow only amuses them, and they will come down from their trees and scamper over the powdery heaps with immense enjoyment. What they do not like is the snow on the leaves and branches, which falls in showers as they jump from tree to tree, and betrays them to their enemies, the country boys. During a mild winter they even neglect to make a central store of nuts, and instead of storing them in big hoards near the nest, just drop them into any convenient hole they know of near. A pair took possession of an old, well-timbered garden in Berkshire, and when they found out, as they very soon did, that they were not to be disturbed, continued during the mild, open weather to exhibit a reckless improvidence quite at variance with squirrel tradition. In October they stripped the old nut-trees, but flung the greater number of the nuts on to the ground. Later in the autumn they spent the greater part of each morning collecting and *burying* horse-chestnuts, not in any proper store, but in all sorts of places,—among the roots of rose-bushes, under the palings of the lawn, or in the turf under a big tulip-tree. Almost every knot-hole in the trees of the orchard and walks had a chestnut or walnut poked into it; but there was no attempt to bring them together for a cold-weather magazine: and they even had the impudence to dig up crocus-bulbs under the windows, and leave them scattered over the lawn. Then came the snow, and the improvident squirrels had to set to work at once and call in all these scattered investments at an alarming sacrifice, for the nuthatches very soon found out their carelessly hidden property and made off with it. Fortunately the snow soon melted, or they might have been reduced to short rations.

Like the squirrels, rabbits seem rather to enjoy the snow at first. Like many men, they require a dry, bracing atmosphere, and sea-breezes and frost suit them; and the morning after a snowfall their tracks show where they have been scratching and playing in it all night. But after a deep fall they are soon in danger of starving. Though not particular as to quality, they like their meals "reg'lar," and with all the grass covered with a foot of snow their main supply of food is cut off. If there is a turnip-field near, they will scratch away the snow to the roots, and soon destroy the crop. If not, or if the surface of the snow is frozen hard, the hungry bunnies strip the bark from the trees and bushes. In the long frost of February, 1888, we saw nothing but bare white wood in the fences near the warrens. Ivy bark seemed their favourite food, and even the oldest stems were stripped, making a white network against the trunks of the big trees. Even these did not quite escape, for though the lower bark was too hard and dry even for the rabbits, broken limbs of a foot in diameter, smashed by the weight of snow, were peeled to the bare wood. In some places the rabbits had first stripped the bark from the lower part of a clipped thorn fence; then mounted to the top and nibbled the shoots; and lastly, using the thick top as a seat, had nibbled the ivy bark from the trees in the hedgerow, eight feet from the ground. It is easy to guess what damage the starving rabbits do in young plantations, if the drifted snow enables them to scramble over the wire fencing.

When snow melts on the grass, any one may notice a number of dead, frozen earth-worms lying on the flattened sward. This may account for a habit which moles have of working just between the earth and snow. When the thaw comes, the lower half of the burrow may be seen for yards along the surface of the ground, unless the upper crust was frozen before the snow fell. While all the harmless animals are obliged to spend the greater part of the day and night seeking food, their enemies profit exceedingly. The stoats and weasels find that they have only to prowl down the stream-side to catch any number of thrushes and soft-billed birds which crowd the banks where the water melts the snow, and little piles of feathers and a drop or two of red on the snow show where the fierce little beasts have murdered here a redwing and there a wagtail, or even a water-hen. The tracks show well their method of hunting. Once we followed the tracks of a fox for a long distance from a large earth on the downs. He had begun by visiting a farm near, going round all the ricks, and then close to the house. Apparently he had been frightened, for he had gone off at a gallop. Then after keeping along a high, steep bank where there was a chance of finding a lark roosting in the rough grass at the edge, he had diverged to examine a patch of dead nettles which had sprung up round a weed-heap. Next he had gone off for half-a-mile in a straight line to a barn, and there, after examining every bush and straw-rick, had caught a rat or a mouse, and then gone off into the vale. Not far off was his return track. He had gone a short distance on the track of a hare, but apparently had found a good supper before then, for in a few yards he had abandoned the trail and gone straight back to the earth. The same day we found the traces of a tragedy in rabbit-life: the footmarks of several bunnies just outside a thick brake, the traces of a fox creeping cautiously up the hedgerow between them and their earths, and the fox's rush from the bushes, ending in a broad mark in the snow, where a rabbit had been seized, leaving only a few bits of grey hair scattered about as memorials for his family. Walking along the road through the flat meadows one snowy night, we were startled by the noise of a covey of partridges rising and cackling the other side of the hedge. A fox had sprung right among the covey, but apparently missed his mark, as the next moment he crossed the road in front of us. Water-shrews, water-rats, and otters all dislike frost and snow, more, perhaps, because the streams are frozen, and food more difficult to obtain along the banks than from any inconvenience the snow causes them. The otters, even if the rivers do not freeze, have a difficulty in finding the fish, which in cold weather sink into the deepest pools, and, in the case of eels, tench, and carp, which form the main food of the otter in the slow rivers of the eastern and south-eastern counties, burrow in the mud. So the otters go down to the sea-coast for the cold weather, and making their homes in the coast-caves or old wooden jetties and wharves, live on the dabs and flounders of the estuaries. Rats also often migrate to the coast in snow-time and pick up a disreputable livelihood among the rubbish of the shore. Of all effects of weather, snow makes the greatest change in animal economy in the country-side, and weeks often pass before the old order is restored.

RUSTIC NATURALISTS

THE erection of the memorial to Richard Jefferies in Salisbury Cathedral, and the raising of a fund for the benefit of his family, are additional evidence of the favour with which the public looks upon the work of the prose-poet of the Downs country. His birthplace at Cote Farm has even become a place of pilgrimage; and his admirers doubtless imagine that they trace in the old farmhouse, and the daily life of its inmates, the natural and appropriate environment of a consummate writer on the wild life of the fields.

The inference is a very natural one. But if such a life and such surroundings thus predispose the mind to see what Jefferies saw, and to interpret nature as he interpreted it, why is it, we may ask, that so few of the writers who have treated of these subjects have sprung from the class to which Jefferies belonged? And why in the instances in which they have been born the sons of small farmers, or labouring men, have they been so reluctant to abide among the scenes which they and Jefferies so charmingly described? Thomas Bewick is one of the few instances of a farm-bred naturalist returning by an uncontrollable impulse to live near the scenes of his boyhood. "I would rather be herding sheep on Mickley Bank top," he wrote home, "than be one of the richest citizens of London." But Cobbett, the son of a labourer, abandoned the village when a lad; the Howicks, like the late Edward Bates, were citizens of "fair Nottingham," and Gilbert White, Charles Kingsley, and Waterton, were parsons or squires. Jefferies himself, like Cobbett, longed to shake off his early associations, and his mad enterprise of a walk to Russia when a boy, and failing that, of crossing the Atlantic, was only prevented by want of means. To the last he would rather have been a novelist than a naturalist, and declared that he knew London quite as well as he did the country. No doubt the sense of contrast so presented, painted the beauties of the country in more vivid colours in the mind of Jefferies, as in that of Cobbett. But it will be found that the rustic naturalist does not, except in rare instances, spring from the classes who spend their *serious* life in the fields. For the common labourer, his daily toil is too severe; for the farmer, the practical problems are too exacting. How exacting that strain is, mentally and physically, both for master and man, the reader may gather from Jefferies' description of the harvesting of the hundred-acre cornfield, in his essay on the "Loaf of Bread."

It is only the shepherds of the hills, while keeping their flocks as of old, who are free to see visions and dream dreams, or watch the stars and nature. For the rest, such contemplation fails to give the change of thoughts they need. Like Piers the Ploughman, they would turn their backs upon the fields and go

> "Wide into the world,
> Wonders for to hear."

It must not, however, be supposed that because the farmer and farm labourer usually confine their interests in outdoor life to the practical problems of the land, the rustic naturalist is a rare or eccentric character in village life. There are numbers of men employed in sedentary occupations in villages and small country towns, who find in the pursuit of natural history the same change and excitement which the London artisan does in his favourite hobby of angling in the well-fished waters of the Thames and Lea. Village tailors, cobblers, and harness-makers are among the greatest enthusiasts of this class. The most intelligent of the class whom the writer has known was, like Thomas Edward, the Banff naturalist, a shoemaker. His trade was hereditary, and accidental. Mechanical invention was the natural tendency of his mind; he learned the whole of Euclid, taught himself algebra, and became a rapid and exact calculator. Had he lived in Lancashire, and not in a country village, he would have improved the machinery in the mill or invented a new process. As it was, the sole mechanical appliances open to his observation were those used in making tiles and bricks. For this he invented new machinery, and went to London to exhibit his drawings. There his ideas were stolen; and he returned, in broken health and spirits, to become a naturalist, and so to "drive machinery out of his head." The change of ideas so obtained saved his health, and possibly his reason. By day he worked resolutely at his trade. Experience had taught him the value of silence; and he discouraged gossip by filling his mouth with wooden shoe-pegs, and hammering these one by one into the boot-soles, on the approach of a visitor. At night, "when the wheels began to work in his head," as he afterwards explained, he took his butterfly net, collecting-boxes, and dark lantern, and went out into the lanes to collect moths. His favourite hunting-ground was a dark and little-frequented road, bordered by trees, palings, and thick fences, which was avoided by most of the village people, except by lovers on June evenings. But there are moths to be caught in winter nights as well as in summer, and the shoemaker was as indifferent to solitude and darkness as the owls and nightjars which were his only companions. His garden was soon turned into a butterfly-farm. In it he planted the trees and shrubs whose leaves form the food of the rarer caterpillars, and as soon as the eggs laid by the females were hatched, they were turned out to pasture on the poplars, privets, and alanthus, and protected from the birds by ingeniously made coverings of muslin. One day he discovered that a certain old willow-tree was full of goat-moth caterpillars. This tree he bought "for fuel," and put aside until such time as the perforated trunk yielded a rich harvest of the rare goat-moth chrysalises. The boxes for his specimens he made himself. In the course of a few years he formed a complete collection of the butterflies and moths of the district, and became familiar with the other wild life of the county ; he also added music to his accomplishments, and learned the delicate craft of violin-making. Under the composing influence of his naturalist pursuits, his nerves recovered their balance, until his mechanical bent could be indulged without danger ; and he is at present said to be planning the illumination of his native village with electric lights.

The writer has more than once tried to enlist the services of the rural policemen to observe the habits of night-flying and night-feeding birds and beasts. In many counties these men are drawn from an intelligent class, and they often practise flower-gardening and bee-keeping with great success. But the village constable, though he often makes a useful assistant-astronomer, is less successful as a naturalist ; and though he can be educated to report the movements of comets and erratic meteors with professional accuracy, he generally prefers the starry company of the Pleiades to listening to the night birds in the dark shadow of the pollards, or by the still pools in the valley. In the periodical scares caused by the threatened introduction of some new pest, the lofty indifference of the rural constable to the insects and other "vermin" which he permits to crawl unnoticed on his beat, sometimes leads to trouble and perplexity. During the Colorado-beetle panic, a thoughtful Government caused portraits of the suspected insect to be circulated in rural districts, accompanied by other and highly magnified enlargements of its appearance in the grub and pupa stage. Naturally, the last were the more striking to the imagination, the "life-size" portrait carrying little conviction beside the large and variegated monster in the magnified plate. So guided and so informed, the rural policemen were all on the watch to arrest the delinquent beetle, as they would any other "party" who was "wanted," and whose portrait was circulated from head-quarters for identification. An opportunity for distinction soon occurred. Two enormous caterpillars (of the death's-head moth) were found by a labourer on his potato-patch, and by him carried to the house of a lady who took an interest in entomology. The caterpillars were received, and the labourer, praised and rewarded, took care to let his friends in the village know what a clever fellow he was. The discovery of strange caterpillars in the potato-bed was discussed ; and next day the local constable, in the absence of the lady, called, and demanded to see the creatures. These he compared with the illustrations in his possession, and pointed out that they were as big, or even bigger, than the awful monster there depicted. He then "took up" the caterpillars, and carried them off by the next train to the county town, where they were discharged after due inquiry, and returned, with apologies, to their owner. The policeman's ally, the gamekeeper, seldom lets his interests extend beyond the habits and requirements of the very limited number of creatures which it is his business to protect or destroy; but the close and accurate observation which these duties require make him in many cases an intelligent and useful auxiliary when properly directed. But the class which supplies the greatest number of *observing*, as distinguished from *collecting*, naturalists in the villages, is the brotherhood of shepherds upon the Downs. Partly from the solitude of their life, a solitude so great, that, in spite of the rural etiquette which forbids any one to pass a shepherd without speaking to him, these men often forget how to pitch their voices in the tones of ordinary speech, and partly from being concerned solely with animals and not with agriculture, the shepherds have the keenest eyes and most minute knowledge of animal habits of any class in the country-side. It may safely be assumed that no animal larger than a rat, and no bird bigger than a quail, appears upon the hill, even for a few days, unnoticed by the shepherds. They know the movements of the hares and foxes so exactly, that the writer has seen them point out the particular spot in a ten-acre field of barley or beans, in which the leverets or cubs would be lying. They know in which copse the long-eared owls, the sparrow-hawks, or kestrels are nesting, and the most likely stony patch for the curlew's eggs or plover's nest. They can foretell the approach of rain or wind, or judge the relative value of the herbage on one side of the down and on the other. They know the times when the springs will break out, the signs of plenty, and the tokens of dearth. Like the shepherds of Greece, they still play the pipe and strike the tuneful strings, though the instrument is the violin and not the lyre, and the scene the cottage on the Downs, and not the groves of Arcady. With them the love of Nature is neither a hobby nor an anodyne, but the hereditary and spontaneous accompaniment of the oldest and most primitive occupation of civilized man.

IN THE ISIS VALLEY

THE ISIS IN JUNE

ON the margin of a black-letter Herbal and Natural History, published early in the sixteenth century, and now in the library of Hertford College, I find this entry opposite to a quaint woodcut of a swallow: "This day, I did see a sea-swallow on Port Meadow."

Sea-swallows still find their way from time to time to the streams which border Port Meadow; and if any one desires a change from the tiring festivities of Commemoration, he may well follow the example set by the sea-swallow 300 years ago, and seek it by the Oxford river. The last time that I was there the backwater at Medley lock was covered by the boats of the rival establishments of Beasly and Bossom, families which have long been at the head of the riverine population of Oxford. A Beasly has for many years stroked the city four and city eight to victory. It was a Beasly—" Fighting Beasly "—who upheld the honour of Oxford against the bargee from the Potteries who had fought and beaten successively the local champions at each stopping-place by the canal on his way from the Midlands. Roused from his bed—for he was "in training" and had retired early—he met the insolent foe and defeated him in less than thirty rounds.

On the other hand, perhaps the boats of Bossom outnumber those of Beasly. The largest house-boat at Medley is inhabited by a Bossom. Behind it, in diminishing series, are other house-boats—his "cast shells," so to say, which he has outgrown, like a water-snail. I hired a gig, and placing in it my rod, rowed gently up to Rosamond's Bower at Godstow. On the left were the Wytham Woods; on the right the great flat of Port Meadow, covered with the cattle and geese of the freemen of Oxford. Half-way to Godstow is a marsh, noted for rare water-plants, where among beds of arrowhead and forget-me-not I found that beautiful plant the water-villarsia. It is not unlike a water-lily, but even more graceful, with the edges of its leaves scalloped and slightly upturned; the petals of its yellow flower are alternately opaque and semi-transparent, the latter delicately frilled. Here, too, was the flowering rush, tall as the iris, bearing a coronet of pale rose-pink flowers. By this time the geese had made up their minds that I was not to be trusted; and, forming a phalanx of some 200, with their yellow goslings in the centre, marched to the river and swam to the mud-bank which they occupy at night. I also took to the water, and rowed up to Godstow—once the fairest spot upon the upper river, but now disfigured by the works of the new Thames drainage scheme. The tiny lock stream is now a hideous straight cut, to make which the stone coffins of the prioresses were disturbed and displaced. The venerable walls of Rosamond's Bower, covered with thick ivy, are still standing; but many of the trees are cut down, and the position of the old bridge and inn has lost its meaning by the alteration of the river's course. In time the remains of Godstow will disappear, as those of Osney and the greater part of the castle have also gone. Collegiate Oxford flourishes; feudal and monastic Oxford seems doomed to neglect. It is strange that, while the buildings of Godstow perish, frailer relics of the nun's occupation remain. The medicinal herbs which they planted in the garden still survive in the fields and upon the broken walls.

In a copse near the ruins I found many nests of the reed-warbler, all placed in the wild hopbine which grows among the willows, and lined with the cottonlike down of some waterside plant. Over the shallow stream below the "Trout" a kingfisher was hovering in mid-air, his wings vibrating and invisible, till he plunged and seized his game.

In the garden of the inn I began my fishing. I say "in the garden," because it is a maxim among chub-fishers that to take the largest chub you must procure the biggest bumble-bees as bait. I look upon this as the most difficult part of the sport. Chub are not hard to catch, but bumble-bees are. A quick eye and steady hand are not required to catch chub, neither is nerve demanded in any measure: all these qualities are brought into play in taking bumble-bees. The snapdragons in the garden yielded some bumbles, and I presently attacked the less noble game, the chub, who were lying above in the Pixies' Pool, greedy but suspicious. In order to keep out of sight, I thrust my rod between the sides of a cleft willow, and made my bee play upon the water. After a few shy rises, a monster chub came slowly from the bottom, swallowed the bee, and whisked down again. We had a violent struggle for a minute, complicated by the awkward position of my rod. Soon, however, he came exhausted to the surface, and, passing the butt of my rod round the willow, I landed him. "Stuff him with pickled oysters," says Izaak Walton, "and baste him well with claret wine, and you shall find him choicely good meat." I doubt it, and doubt equally whether it is worth while to experiment with Izaak's recipe.

In the summer of 1893 the Upper Isis was almost vanquished by the sun. All its outlying streams were sucked dry. The long drought and heats burnt every meadow brown, and the foliage of the hedgerows were gnawed and bruised by the hungry cattle. Even the main streams and river were invaded, and not only the rushes and sedge upon the banks, but the water-lilies and arrowheads in the running water were browsed and cropped level by horses and oxen. Next year came the turn of the river and the land. The latter had drunk seven months of sun, and the summer rains of the next season brought the vegetation into life with almost tropical swiftness. The result was a crop not only of leaf, but of flowers, of the richest and most luxuriant growth. In the river-side gardens, the stems of the white lilies were six and seven feet high, the clustered roses almost broke their branches, the honeysuckle tore itself from the walls by its weight of blossom, and the second crop of grass was smothered with field-flowers. For the moment the gardens eclipsed the fields both in scent and colour, though the sense was almost oppressed by the heavy odour of the drying hay-ricks. But in the gardens there was a blending of delicate scents such as has not been known for years. There has grown up a fashion of preferring mere odours to perfumes, perhaps because the æsthetic perception, which has learnt to appreciate many things which it did not, is forgetting the value of what needed no teaching. The taste for wild-flowers is almost losing its sense of proportion, when ox-eyed field-daisies are bought in the streets by preference to roses, and at an equal price. But whatever the canons of beauty, that of scent can hardly change. The rose has still the purest perfume in Nature. Let those who are forgetting it, go down to the country, and walk among the rose-gardens in the morning, as the sun is drying the dew on their petals in mid-July. The flower fancies of the *Midsummer Night's Dream* were woven in the fresh hours of midsummer mornings, as well as of summer twilight, and it was then that the poet remembered to make his night-flying fairy-queen send her elves—

"Some to kill cankers in the musk-rose buds;"

while more true to fairy hours—

"Some war with rere-mice for their leathern wings."

It was the same hour which made Milton for once strike a note of gladness, unborrowed from the conventions of his classic store, and bid the Nymph of Gladness—

"At his window bid good-morrow,
Through the sweet-briar, or the vine,
Or the twisted eglantine."

And it was the rose-gardens of Damascus, in which, then as now, the Syrian lords sat among the damask flowers by the rushing stream from Lebanon, that Naaman had in mind when he asked if Abana and Pharpar were not better than all the waters of Jordan?

It is by the banks of English rivers that the natural beauties of the midsummer months are seen in their greatest perfection. The contrast of cool waters and sun-lit levels of meadow appeals equally to the sense of sight and the enjoyment of coolness, tranquillity, and repose. The Upper Thames, and its tributaries, the two Colnes, the Loddon, the Cherwell, the Windrush, and the Evenlode, are the natural summer haunt of those who can choose their locality to suit the months. To appreciate the beauties of the water-garden you must be on the water itself, and row among the lilies, and in front of the flower-set banks. The growths in the two have this contrast. All the plants of the bank are tall and upright; all those of the stream, except the arrowhead, are level and flat. Thus the purple and yellow loose-strife, the yellow iris, burr-reeds, the

Kingfisher. *From a Japanese Woodcut.*

St. John's wort, the bulrushes, and, above all, the pink flowering-rush, are set like sentinels to watch the stream, in which the lilies, water-plantain, and villarsia float and blossom, supported by the density of the water itself, which takes the place of the upright stalk, and leaves them free to spread themselves in ever-increasing areas of natural growth. Most of the upright water plants may be made to live and blossom indoors. If the yellow Iris or the flowering rush be pulled up by the roots from the river bank or the mud, and planted in a bucket, with plenty of river soil round them, they will flower even more gaily than when in the stream. Even the lily buds will open and last in perfection for days, *if they be set in the sun*, and the water be not allowed to drown the petals.

WILD-FOWL IN SANCTUARY

(BLENHEIM LAKE)

Just before the opening of spring, when the biting winds drive the shepherds down from the hill, and send even the gipsies to the shelter of the towns, wild birds and beasts seem almost to vanish from the open country, except the March hares—and they, we know, are mad.

Yet there is no time at which the rare and beautiful water-birds, now so scarce in England, are more tame or more easily observed than when they seek sanctuary for rest and pairing, before their long journey to their breeding-places in the high latitudes of the North. The scene on the few inland lakes and waters of any size in the south of England, where the fowl are unmolested, is at such times full of interest even to the least observant eyes, though a few weeks later the surface will be deserted by all but the nesting swans, and the few coots, dobchicks, and water-hens which remain throughout the summer. The lake at Blenheim, always beautiful from its setting and surroundings, gives a pleasing picture of the Lenten rest and quiet which the wild-fowl then enjoy. This lake, formed by the waters of the Gleam—all the tributaries of the upper Thames, the Colne, the Windrush, and the Evenlode, have harmonious names—winds for some two miles between low but steep hills, and naturally attracts to its quiet surface most of the wild-fowl of the Oxford vale. At my first visit to the lake at the end of March, it was evident that their numbers were as yet hardly diminished by departures for the North. Much of the surface was still covered by ice and snow, and just off the edge of the ice some twenty swans were feeding ; while from all parts of the open water were heard the constant musical whistle of widgeon and teal, the quacking of the mallards, the hoarse snort of the swans, and the croak of coots and moorhens,—sounds more suggestive of Poole Harbour on an August night, than of a Midland lake in March. On the further bank, sunning themselves on the sloping turf, and sheltered from the wind, were a score of mallards and their mates, which rose with much angry quacking and protest as a herd of deer came trotting down to drink at the very spot which they had chosen for their chilly siesta. It was, however, no wanton intrusion by the deer, for at that spot only was the shore free from ice, where some land-spring broke the frozen boundary. Meantime, the sun came out with a warmth which could be felt, and a second flock of wild ducks broke into sudden ecstasy at such an earnest of the coming spring. Beating its wings upon the water, each mallard rushed across the lake ; then diving, they reappeared beside their mates, and went through a kind of water-tournament, with much splashing and noise. In the course of this amusement, one of the performers came up from the depths almost under an old cock-swan, which was sleeping with its head "under the blankets"—that is to say, its wing-coverts—and resented the disturbance by a vicious bite which called the whole company to order. Most inland lakes, except those Surrey pools where the water seems to be held naturally upon an ironstone bottom, are river-fed, and shallow and sedgy at the head where the stream enters. Blenheim Lake is no exception to this rule, and some acres at its upper end are covered by yellow reeds, through which the Gleam cuts a winding channel of deep-green water. This is natural cover for the fowl, and, though frost and snow had beaten down the sedge, it was alive with coots and snipe and moor-hens. There, from behind a tree, we watched for some time a snipe courting, at least so we judged, for the object of its attentions was concealed in a little tuft of sedge. The snipe ran round this bower setting up its wings, and flirting its tail in very gallant fashion, turning round and bowing with all the airs and graces of a pigeon making love. At the extreme head of the lake, in the swift, narrow current of the Gleam, a fleet of swans were feeding, one behind the other, an old cock-swan taking the post of danger—and of profit—next to the conduit from which the water enters. By hiding behind the bridge-parapet for some time, and then carefully peering over, it was possible to observe exactly the way in which a swan feeds in water just deep enough to make it necessary for it to invert its body in order to reach the bottom. The neck was partly bent, and the crown of the head touched the bottom, its head and neck being used exactly like a bent-handled *hoe* to search among the gravel and stones. Its head was deeply tinged with red, from the iron in solution in the water and mud. The result of stillness and partial concealment in watching wild animals was well illustrated during the ten minutes spent in observing the swan. Water-hens seemed to spring from the flattened sedge by magic, as if rising from the ground, and launched themselves on the stream, or tripped about feeding among the sedges, where the ground was rapidly thawing.

The head and western bank of the lake are fringed with a narrow belt of young plantation, made partly with a view to sheltering the wild-fowl, partly to screen the guns when the birds are shot in the winter. The lake-keeper, whose cottage stands at the head of the water, quoted as an example of the number of fowl that collect in severe weather at Blenheim, that on one occasion three guns shot a hundred and twelve snipe, and between forty and fifty wild duck and teal. But the birds are seldom shot, and at the time of our visit seemed quite aware that no harm was intended; and as we passed close to the water on the opposite side to that from which we had approached, partly screened by the belt of young trees, they showed little inclination to leave the water, with the exception of a solitary heron, which, after watching us uneasily for some time, rose with a croak, and after flapping some way, with its dangling toes touching the ice, rose high into the air, and flew steadily in the direction of Wytham Woods, where the hen-birds were already sitting on their eggs.

Viewed from the western shore, the scene was in bright contrast to the prevailing steely monotony of an English landscape in March. The tops of the overgrown osiers which fringed the lake wore the polished scarlet bark of early spring, and shot up in a stiff line of red rods. Beyond them lay the surface of the lake, under the sun, in three zones of colour, following the sweeping bays and curves of the ice. Next to the shore, the ice was dazzling white with snow, which had melted on the earth, but still lay deep on the thickest ice; and against this white background stood up the thousands of scarlet osier rods. Next to the snow was a zone of clear ice, blue-grey and snowless; and beyond the margin of the ice-fringe lay the deeper waters of the lake, of the deep translucent green of jade, on which some fifty shining swans were floating in every attitude of motion or repose. Beyond, on the hill, the long colonnades and shining cupolas of Blenheim stood solemn and severe, like some "Palace of Silence," against the sky.

A great number of duck and teal, and a flock of widgeon, were floating near an evergreen-covered island, in separate groups; and a score of coots, conspicuous by their white heads and velvety black bodies, were feeding near the shore. At the sound of a stick struck upon a paling, all but the coots rose from the water, the mallards showing to the greatest advantage as they spread the fanlike white feathers below the dark-green tail, and mounted high above the lake. The widgeon kept in a compact flock, turning and wheeling like starlings, and passing and repassing in a symmetrical and monotonous course through exactly the same evolutions in the air to an accompaniment of melodious notes. The teal soon settled down in pairs, some dashing boldly into the water, others alighting with rapid backward beats of the wing upon the ice. A careful stalk brought us near enough to see that the teal, like most of the ducks, had evidently paired for the summer, as the cock-birds were swimming round their mates in a restless, fussy fashion, and did not allow any other bird to come within the circle of water so appropriated. The view of the lower lake which we caught through the wide and beautiful arch of the stone bridge, showed that the fowl were there even more numerous than on the upper waters. From the parapet of the bridge we counted seventy-four duck sleeping on the edge of the ice. Under and upon the steep and sloping bank near Rosamond's Well, quite three times that number were crowded together, and as a sudden snow-squall came over the hill, they all rose with a loud roar of wings, and, joined by the flock from the ice, settled on the open water, preferring, apparently, to endure the squall on their native element than on the ice or firm land. No doubt the numbers of wild-fowl on the tidal harbours of the coast in winter are many times greater than those collected at Blenheim and on similar lakes in March. But such opportunities for watching them in their happiest moods cannot be obtained by the sea, or anywhere except in places where man combines with Nature to protect them in the season of sanctuary.

IN HIGH SUFFOLK

SUNDOWN IN SHOTLEY WOOD

Shotley Wood is marked on the county map. Sometimes, though rarely, when there was enough spare money in the county to keep a three-days-a-week pack, it figured among the less popular meets of the season. Now it is forgotten by the world, even the world of county sport. Yet it has stood—or rather it has been felled and risen again—since the days of King John. From the time of Magna Charta till the present day, no plough or harrow has cut the virgin soil within its fences; and every decent piece of building in the parish, from the church roof—set on in the year of grace 1507—to the newest barn floor, has been fitted with the timber grown on its seventy acres of deep yellow clay. "Us be all despret poor now," as the exciseman (the only rich man in the parish) truly says; and those who had sense to read the signs of the times have made treaty with necessity, and stepped back, with a rough and rugged insistance on the change, to the plain living of Saxon times.

Are our tables worse furnished, or is our roof-tree colder? I think not. We kill our own swine, brew our own ale, and press our cider; bake our dark but palatable bread, and pay our men and our dwindling "tradesmen's bills" from the narrow yield of our own fields. The owner of the "big wood" finds it a little silver-mine. Frugality begins at home—a coy but lasting friend—and when once won is never lost by the countryman who lives on his own acres. The coal-grates have been pulled out in hall and dining-room, and the old bars rescued from rust in the out-house are piled with the surplus branches of the oaks; and on Christmas-day the green ashen faggot will blaze and sputter with a lively warmth that mocks the dull caloric of the coal, as young laughter leaps above the book-bound wit of ages. The wood supplies our table with its daintiest fare. Never was there such a year for wild-bred pheasants; and the stub-rabbits are no longer despised. In December the wood-pigeons come in to roost in large flocks, and pay a daily tribute to the gun. The poor still look for rabbits at Christmas, and on our way to the wood before dusk, to lie in wait for the pigeons, we overhear the rabbiter and the bailiff in consultation: the former deep in the yawning ditch, under the stubbs, the other with his ear to the bolt-hole in the field above. The rabbiter is calm and professional, as becomes one finishing a long day's work. The bailiff—a school-boy friend of the poorer man, long since risen in the social scale, a stern and unbending Noncomformist, but with a suppressed but uncontrollable love of sport—is as excited as a boy. They have dropped the ceremonious "Mister" of East Anglian address, and for the moment have forgotten that the world contains anything but themselves, the hapless rabbit in the bury, and the ferret at the end of the line. "Eddard," says the bailiff; "Eddard, I can hear it a-scrabbin'!" "Can you?" replies the rabbiter. "Do you cop me your 'dabber.'" The "dabber," an implement with a spade at one end and a spike at the other, is "copped" and dexterously caught. "Do you fudge him a bit," urges the rabbiter; and the bailiff "fudges" vigorously. Then the ferret is withdrawn. "Lor' bless me, if I hain't been a-fudging the ferret!" he exclaims; and the ill-used and gasping ferret is exhibited. "Oh, ah!" says the rabbiter, "we'd best go back, I reckon." And the pair wind up nets and bags, and splash home through the mud. They are almost the last to leave the open fields, and as we enter the high wood the sounds of daily human labour die with the waning light—when the plough-teams, with looped-up splinter-bars banging against the trace-chains, plod homewards to the stables. The grey light wanes and the wind rises, angry and sighing in the tree-tops. A wide avenue of Scotch firs runs down the length of the wood. The ride is still strewn thick with acorns, for this has been the most prolific year ever known for the seeds of trees; the husks are already splitting here and there, and the red shoots are sprouting from the pointed end; but many are mere crackling shells nibbled by squirrels and mice. The wood-pigeons have been feasting for weeks, pheasants have helped them, sacksfull have been carried home by the woodman to grind and mix with bran for the sheep, and pigs have forced their way through the fences to munch their fill, yet the quantity on the ground seems now as great as ever. In the ride we met a hedgehog, almost the last creature to be expected on such a chilly day. Generally piggy spends the winter coiled up in a bed of leaves in a rabbit-burrow, under a root, or in the centre of a thick bush, and sleeps till spring comes. Perhaps this hedgehog had been idle in the summer, and not laid up a store of fat to last him through the winter; so he was awake, and obliged to forage. He was hunting eagerly, taking half the width of the ride, and quartering it to and fro—not very accurately, for he did not keep straight lines, like a setter, but still rarely going twice over the same ground. We approached slowly, for if a hedgehog is not disturbed by a heavy footfall or sudden movement, it simply disregards men. To and fro he went, poking his long snout into every hoof-mark, and routing among the oak-leaves. He seemed to find little, and to be very hungry. Once or twice he put up his head and sniffed, and stared at the figure above him; but as it did not move, he went on searching for a supper. As he passed, we touched him *a tergo* with the gun-barrel. He whisked round with prickles up, looking angry and quite at a loss to understand what had happened. He then examined the boots and tried to climb the leg above, but could not get a foothold for his hind-feet.

Down again to the boots. The blacking smelt nice, so he gnawed at them steadily, with far more force than might be expected from so small a hedgehog—for he was not larger than a cocoa-nut. Having tasted one boot, he then tried the other, and did not take alarm till he was suddenly picked up. Then for a minute he closed his eyes and rolled into a ball. A curious change of expression takes place when the hedgehog draws his heavy eyebrows down. At other times his face is impudent and rather savage. Then he looks meek and gentle, a nice little fellow, who eats bread and milk, and is regarded as a pet for children. Unrolled he is his true self—a creature that kills adders, drives the partridge from her nest, and eats the eggs; a sturdy omnivorous little animal, afraid of few things except a badger. He had not been held a minute before he began to uncurl, wriggled over on to his back, gave the nearest finger a bite which reached through the buckskin glove, dropped on to the ride, and scuffled away among the brambles. By this time it was almost dusk, and the pigeons were arriving in small flocks, and settling into the fir-tops in different parts of the wood. Each flock circled high overhead twice or thrice before alighting. The fieldfares followed, squeaking and chattering from tree to tree, and the cock pheasants went up to roost one by one, telling the whole wood about it. Small woodland birds feed till dark in these short winter days, and a whole flock of tits and bullfinches were climbing and flitting among the ash-poles, eager to use the last minutes of twilight.

A pair of sparrow-hawks were anxious to make their supper on the tits, and their silent gliding forms crossed and recrossed among the stems from minute to minute, winding among the closely growing ash-poles with astonishing powers of steering in full flight. So quick were their movements, and so close to the stems, that though the bold birds took no alarm at the motionless human figure, it was almost impossible to fire a shot at these worst poachers of the woods, with any certainty of killing. They had carried off more than one of the tits when a third hawk swept over the wood, seized a small bird in its claws, and sailed off up the ride. A shot and a red shower of sparks was followed by the fall of the hawk, and the clatter of a hundred pairs of wings as the pigeons left the trees. The hawk was dead, with the finch still in its claws, apparently unhurt. In a few minutes the wood is quiet again, and the pigeons return, and during the last few minutes before dark pay heavy toll to the gun, as they fly low and sleepy and bewildered over the pine-tops. There is hardly a better bird for the table outside the true game birds, than these plump Christmas wood-pigeons after months of plenty and open weather. Even when the lingering twilight has almost gone, and the bright planets shine with eager eyes through the lacing oak-boughs, while " echo bids good-night from every glade," the wood is not yet silent. The grey crows have come from the north to tell us that it is Christmas. They have crossed the North Sea, and skirted the shore southward from estuary to estuary, past the mouths of the fen rivers and the marshes of the broads, and arrived, as they always do, in the last week of the old year, to croak their warning tale into the winter night.

> "I sent forth memory in heedful guise,
>   To search the record of preceding years;
> Back like the raven to the ark she flies,
>   And croaks disaster to my trembling ears,"

the poet writes. The cry of the grey crows, like the voice of the raven, has an evil sound. But they have croaked in the wood at each year's ending, and if the next be no worse than those which have gone, we shall not cease to enjoy the sounds of the winter wood at sundown.

ANCIENT MEADOWS

PROBABLY there are no meadows in the world so good as those in England, or so old. They are the sole portions of the earth's surface, with the exception of the barren wastes and cliffs, which modern agriculture respects and leaves in peace. Hence the excellence of the English pastures, and the envy of the Continent. When I look at one of these fat and smiling meads, the pride and stay of the farm in which it lies, I like to think that it and its like are probably survivals of old England's surface remaining unchanged since the days of Canute and Edward the Confessor, with a fixity of type as enduring as that of the wildest parts of the New Forest or of the great park at Windsor.

From the early Saxon times, old meadow has been distinguished from mere grazing-ground, and has always been scarce. Two-thirds of what is now established meadow-land still shows the marks of ridge and furrow; and from the length of time needed to make a meadow—ten years on the best land, a hundred on the worst—men have always been reluctant to break up old pasture. Ancient customs survive even in the tenure of these sacred spots of earth. "Joint holdings" exist in meadow-land long after they have disappeared in connection with the cultivated portions. The Thames valley is still full of such joint tenancies. In the Stour valley, with Essex on one side and Suffolk on the other, are numbers of "common meadows" in which several men own portions, which they agree to feed or mow, as they may decide, every year. At Bampton, in Oxfordshire, the sections of the "common meadow" are annually redistributed by lots among sixteen owners.

The flat meadows by the sides of rivers, level as a table, are so exactly alike in one particular, their absolute conformity to the level line, that an explanation of their history seems demanded by their shape. The story is simple enough as geologists read it. All the flat meadows have been made by floods, which, as they retired, left a uniform deposit of mud. This went on till the level rose even with the highest flood-mark, and as rivers tend to wear their own channels deeper the flat meadows were left. These, however, are in many cases only in course of being made—they are not always the sweetest or most ancient pasture, like that on the good warm marl and loam round the inland farms.

"St. Barnabas mow the grass" is an old country saying. But although St. Barnabas' day falls when the meadows are generally ripe for mowing, there is no crop so "tickle," as the Yorkshire farmers say, as to the time at which it must be cut. Hay must fall when the grasses are in flower. Walk into a hay-field, in the second week in June, and you will see the pollen dropping from the fescue and timothy, and the yellow from the buttercups lodges on your boots. Then the beauty of a good meadow can be seen and understood. The trefoil and yellow suckling are ankle deep, and a little above rises the perennial red clover—the white being not yet in full bloom. The true grasses reach to the knee, the growth becoming less dense as it rises higher, and the crowning glory of beauty is the wide, ox-eyed daisies—more dear, however, to the artist than the farmer. Dotted among the grasses are carmine meadow vetchling, and a dozen other small *leguminosæ*, golden weasel-snout, buttercups, and wild blue geranium. In a picture of Albrecht Dürer's, which we once saw, the artist had evidently painted the *section* of a hayfield. One seemed to be lying on the cut grass, and looking at the wall left after the last sweep of the scythe. Every flower, every stalk of grass was painted, the white daisies filling the top of the canvas. Not only sight but scent is needed to judge the maturity of the crop. In a walk through the "mowing grass," to determine the condition of the blossom, the fragrance of the odours from the almost invisible flowers of the grasses, and of the tiny clovers, crowfoot, and trefoil, that "blush unseen" in the thick growth at the bottom, is almost stupefying, and is certain, in some cases, to bring on a violent attack of hay-fever at night. If the flower is out, then the hay must be cut, no matter how threatening the weather, and no crop lies so completely at the mercy of the skies as does the hay. If the crop be short, it cannot therefore be left to grow. The grass must fall while the blossom is upon it, or the cattle will refuse it. "Better let it spoil on the ground than spoil as it grows," is a country maxim. For the latter is a certain loss, and a day's bright sun and wind may always dry a fallen crop.

How and when men first learned to make hay will probably never be known. For hay-making is a process, and the product is not merely sun-dried grass, but grass which has partly fermented, and is as much the work of men's hands as flour or cider. Probably its discovery was due to accident, unless men learnt it from the *pikas* or calling hares of the Eastern steppes, which cut and stack hay for the winter. That idea would fit in nicely with the theory that Central Asia was the home of the "Aryan" race, if we were allowed to believe it, and hay-making is certainly an art mainly practised in cold countries for winter forage.

But the old meadows only supply a part, though probably the most valuable part, of the yearly crop of hay. The change from arable to pasture, which has marked the last twenty years of English farming, has covered what were once cornfields with sown grasses or "leys." No one travelling by rail over any of the high plateaux of the south of England, such as the Berkshire downs or Salisbury Plain, can fail to notice the hundreds of acres of waving "rye-grass," which has taken the place of fallows and turnip-fields. On the

R

chalk land the lovely sainfoin spreads its crimson flowers over an ever-growing area ; for sainfoin hay is the best of all food for producing milk, and is saved for the ewes in lambing time, and for the dairy cows. Seven years is the life allotted to a sainfoin "ley," after which it is ploughed up and used for other crops. Hardly any sown pasture is so beautiful or so profitable as this on soil which suits its growth. It gives two crops in the year, and the hay can often be sold for £6 or £7 an acre. The broad-leaved clover grows on most soils, and though it stands for two years, is generally ploughed in after the first year's cutting. For agricultural chemists have discovered that the delicate clover leaves gather in nitrates from the air, and so, when ploughed into the ground, give food to the young wheat-plant. "Field-hay," as the produce of the rye-grass, sainfoin, clover, and trefoil is called, is a new feature in the country. Its beauty is less refined, bright though the masses look in early June ; and the pleasure it gives is less. It is part of modern husbandry, and lacks the poetry of the old.

Half the beauty of the "haysel" has been lost since the mowing-machine was invented, and the other time-saving appliances of modern farming. For the most picturesque sight in the cycle of rural toil was to watch the mowers. But the steady rushing of the steel through the falling grass, the rhythmic movement of the mowers, as they advanced *en échelon*, right foot foremost, down the meadow, and the ring of the whetstones on the scythes, have almost given place to the rattling machine. Yet there is more pleasure in "haysel" than "joy in harvest." The weather is not so hot, and the grass does not attract the sun as does the stubble. Every one is ready to lend a hand. There is the sweet scent of the flowers when fresh, and of the grass as it dries. The big horses munch happily while the workmen rest for their "elevenses" and "fourses," and eat their white currant-loaves and drink their cider. The wives help to rake the swathes together for the men, and the children roll about and bury themselves in the haycocks. If the weather is very catchy, the farmer is sometimes thoughtful; but the stake is not so great as at harvest-time, and the anxiety proportionately less.

The cutting of the grass leads to a sad disturbance of the wild creatures which the meadow shelters under its tall crop. As the machine or the mowers make the circuit of the outer edges, the nests of landrails, larks, partridges, and pipits, are uncovered; and even missing bantam-hens and guinea-fowls from the farm may often be found sitting on a stolen nest in the hayfield. The shining blades of the machine cause cruel destruction among all these confiding creatures, and the close-sitting partridges are more often killed than saved. Doe-rabbits and field-mice—or rather the "voles" which are destroying the Scotch pastures—have their nests in the grass, and in the very centre of the field an old hedgehog and her young and prickly family are found rolled up like dumplings, and presenting their spines to the inquisitive sheep-dog that has discovered them. The ground, of course, swarms with insects that have fallen from the grass; and the whole surface of the newly-cut field is one great table of food for birds and beasts. They do not wait to be invited. Starlings and sparrows rush down upon the grubs and spiders, and eat till they can eat no more. The rooks march over the field in black battalions, and gobble up every lark's, landrail's, and partridge's egg uncovered, pull to pieces the voles' nests, and swallow with infinite relish the young and helpless voles. The dogs do their best to eat the young hedgehogs, and thereby prick their mouths sadly; and then scratch out the young rabbits and catch the moles, which, being stupid and subterranean, are not aware that the covering grass has gone, and work too near the surface. In the evening the cats come shyly to the field, and catch the disconsolate mice which venture back to look for their children. But perhaps the most curious evidence of the universal attractiveness of a hayfield which the writer has yet seen, was the invasion of a meadow by fish! A summer flood had come down the upper waters of the Cherwell, and spread over the meadows near Kidlington Church, drowning millions of insects and small animals. The water still lay among the haycocks, covering the ground to the depth of a few inches, and of course filling all the ditches and deeper channels. Up these the fish had come, leaving the muddy river, and had spread themselves in shoals over the field; great chub and carp and roach were pushing and flapping among the haycocks, their backs partly out of the water, and swallowing greedily the drowned creatures which floated in thousands on the surface or lay dead at the bottom. When frightened, they struggled back to the ditches, from which, however, they soon returned to their novel feeding-ground.

SHOOTING RED-LEGS IN THE SNOW

FRENCH partridges, or "Red-legs," as they are called in Suffolk, grow so cunning after the end of October, that on ground where game is scarce, or driving not practicable, they escape the gun entirely after the heavy covert has disappeared, and in this case sportsmen are only too pleased when a heavy fall of snow brings them once more within reach. A sudden snowstorm disconcerts these birds infinitely more than the grey partridges. Accustomed as they have been for months to run rather than rise on the approach of danger, the new obstacle to their progress seems to baffle them entirely. Their usual cunning forsakes them, and the coveys remain huddled under the fences, or more often in the ditch itself, sometimes all together, but more often in twos and threes, and rise within easy shot of the guns. Usually they do not repair to the fences until they have made some futile attempts to run about the fields, and this may perhaps account for the fact that those shot have often large lumps of frozen snow hanging to their thighs and bellies. In a few days they get thin and poor should there be fresh falls, but generally the surface of the snow is frozen hard enough on the second morning for them to run as usual, and any one who will watch them may then form some notion of what one of these birds is capable of doing on its feet.

There is no need to start very early in the morning after the fall; it is best to begin about ten o'clock or half-an-hour later, when the birds have given up their attempts to travel over the snow, and will be lying up snugly under the hedges. An old setter, who will not mind going into a fence to flush a bird if necessary, is the best dog for the work, or a good hunting retriever. But not every one keeps one of these "dogs of all work," and an obedient spaniel is equally good, provided he will keep close. If not, he is apt to spoil sport by running on ahead and flushing the birds, which, according to the habit I have mentioned, often lie scattered for some distance along the brow of the ditch.

It is a pleasant and exhilarating experience to step out, well wrapped up and thickly shod, into the fleecy powder-like snow, and tramp across the fields, or rather round them, while the icicles tinkle on the bramble sprays and glitter in the pale winter sunlight. Before starting, however, it is well to remember that shooting in the snow is accompanied by certain chances of accident which are not so likely to occur in ordinary weather. Two of the most dangerous are the blocking of the muzzle by chance contact with snow, which will burst it as effectually as if plugged with a wedge of iron;

and, secondly, the danger of slipping on ice which is rendered invisible by the loose snow fallen upon it, and so risking an explosion by the gun flying out of the hand. Both these mischances have occurred to the writer, although in the fall the gun did not go off. The concussion was, however, so severe that a deep dent was made in one of the barrels. In the former instance the barrel burst about two inches from the muzzle, the metal opening evenly down the centre. It must be remembered that hares as well as "red-legs" lie very close the first day after a heavy fall. Often they will allow the snow to cover them entirely, and not move until almost trodden on.

One of the most amusing day's red-leg shooting in the snow which the writer recollects was in Suffolk, after a very heavy and sudden fall, accompanied by a fierce wind from the east. The snow fell all one afternoon and night, and next morning the drifts were as high as the fence tops in some places; while all ditches, gullies, and drains were filled up level and smooth like the top of an iced cake. The wind had dropped, and the sun shone brightly, but the cold was intense, and the sun had not the least effect in consolidating the dry and powdery snow. No better weather could have been desired for forcing the birds to "fence," but the walls and ramparts of snow cast up against the hedges made it an exceedingly difficult matter to get from field to field. A couple of well-trained retrieving Clumber spaniels were our aid on this occasion, and we fortified ourselves against the cold by taking with us a plentiful luncheon of cold mutton chops, cold plum pudding, and two large flasks of cherry brandy, enough for my brother and myself and for the man we took with us. The dogs too were not forgotten.

The first half-mile along the road was easy enough, and we stepped out briskly, the dogs racing about and rolling over each other, every now and then eating mouthfuls of snow; but the moment we stepped into the fields we realized that not a little judgment would be required to make a bag. The fences running from east to west, and therefore facing the sun, were the likely places, but all the cross hedges which ran at right angles to the direction of the last night's gale were piled high with many feet of snow. Thus in many places to "double" the fences properly was impossible. On the other hand, we knew on which side the birds were likely to lie, and the piles of snow in the hedge foot made it difficult for them to slip through on the wrong side.

Our first effort was made along a tall hedge covered with snow on the windward side; on the leeward was a tiny stream, and the water had washed a little margin clear of snow. The spaniels soon began to feather, and a track here and there showed that birds had been there that morning; then one of the dogs paused a moment on the bank, cocked his ears, and plunged into a mass of brambles, tall grass, and teazles, and out of the cascade of snow and tiny icicles a couple of big "Frenchmen" bounced, looking as large as pheasants. Both birds flew across us, and fell. Three more rose at the shot, and, though they were rather wild, a partridge against the snow is a clear mark, and a careful long shot brought the last bird down. He would have been a runner had the snow allowed, but, finding it impossible to make any way, he poked his head under the snow, and submitted to be caught by Rebel, the retrieving Clumber.

Following the little stream up to the higher land, we secured another brace of red-legs—old birds, with legs knotted like a blackthorn stick. One of these was a towered bird, and made a beautiful picture on the snow, the coral legs and beak and beautiful shades of buff, French grey, and chestnut showing up against the white background. We also flushed several coveys of grey birds; but these were quite wild, and seemed only extra wary on account of the difficulty of concealing themselves. On the higher ground we had some difficulty in finding our birds; but at last we discovered a sunny fence, under which four or five coveys had collected. This we were able to double; and though they were wilder than we expected, as birds generally are when collected in any number, we had very good fun. These birds were all lying in the ditch, or rather just below the level of the field, as we could see by the holes in the snow where they had been sitting. My brother secured a right and left, and I two single shots, and two birds were marked down in hedges at no great distance. One of these the spaniels caught, he having thrust himself under brambles covered with snow, and so became entrapped. The other bird rose, and was shot by my brother through the hedge. The dogs could not get across to retrieve on account of the piles of snow, so he walked down some way until he came to what seemed a level crossing, though the absence of gateposts in the opening in the fence ought to have warned him. Stepping boldly across, he at once sank into the ditch up to his shoulders, only his head and arms appearing above the snow. The dogs were dreadfully upset at the incident, one of them howling with excitement and sympathy. Nor was it an easy matter to get him out, for the brambles beneath the snow laced him in. However, after taking his gun, I managed to get a hurdle and throw it on to the snow, by means of which he extricated himself, and then got the bird. By this time we were pretty hungry, and were making our way to some stacks to eat our luncheon, when the sun, which had been shining brightly, was obscured by a fall of the finest and driest snow. Then followed a beautiful snow scene. A small whirlwind, like those which often travel across the cornfields in harvest time, and twist up straws and barley swathes to great heights in the air, swept round the high plain on which we were, and wreathed the light snow into fantastic clouds. Presently we found ourselves in the centre of the vortex, and stood surrounded by the eddying rime, through which the sun dimly penetrated. As we approached the stacks we could see that we were not the only creatures repairing to them for warmth and shelter. Hundreds of yellow-hammers, chaffinches, and greenfinches were hopping and fluttering beneath the stacks. The rooks were pulling away the thatch, and a covey of grey partridges rose close by, and one fell a long shot to my brother's gun.

The bag, eleven red-legs and one grey bird, were laid upon the snow, and admired, and we fell to upon the luncheon. As for the cherry brandy, we could drink it like claret, and feel no ill effects in such a frost. The birds which we had laid upon the snow were frozen hard and fast to the surface when we once more started to shoot.

Our idea was to take down a long boundary fence, some three-quarters of a mile in length, which marked the limit of a three-hundred acre farm. Most of this had, in accordance with modern notions, been stripped of its hedges, and laid into one monotonous stretch of corn land. Many strong coveys of French birds had been on it all the season, and had hitherto laughed at all our efforts to touch them.

To-day, as we expected, they were all along the boundary fence, and not choosing to desert it for the white and covertless expanse of snow, they simply flew on, and pitched in again. The first covey rose wild, but we saw them all drop in pairs and singly along the fence, so calling the dogs in, we hurried onwards. A hare then bounced out from the ditch, looking as big and brown as a fox, and fell to my gun, and before we reached the spot where the other birds had dropped, another covey rose, straggling from the fence, and left three of their number kicking on the snow; these also went forward, and we began to have great hopes of a bag. Soon the spaniels came to the place where the covey had begun to drop in. It was easy to find them, for the place where each bird had alighted was plainly marked in the snow, with his track leading to the deep ditch, and thick straggling hedgerow. The spaniels grasped the situation at once, and, instead of floundering about in the snowy hedge bottom, went up to the place which we indicated, and soon pushed the birds up. Five of this covey were secured; but, even in the difficulties of the snow, their usual cunning did not altogether forsake them, and many a chance was spoiled on my brother's side of the fence by their rising just when he was engaged in scrambling over the cross fences which were pretty numerous on that side of the boundary. Further on we put up two fresh coveys, and picked up several single birds, which were by this time well scattered. The last twenty yards of the fence yielded three, and, counting our bag since luncheon, we found that we had ten red-legs and a hare. Some of these we decided to take to a large farmhouse which stood in some park-like meadows surrounded by a moat, like so many of the large farmhouses of Suffolk. A good many moor-hens or "water-cocks," as they are called in the eastern counties, frequented this moat, and "water-cock pie" is a dish which any one who has tasted it will wish to try again. The moat was frozen tight as an iron safe, and we rightly conjectured that the water-hens would have left it, and be hiding in the deep ditches in the meadows. Both the spaniels were immensely keen in hunting these birds, which give them all the pleasure of running the foot scent, as they slip up and down the ditches, with the final excitement of a flush. To-day the snow wreaths so weighed the brambles down that the birds could slip along underneath them, though the dogs could not. Several, however, must have run forward to a small pond further on, for from the banks of this the dogs flushed five, first "setting" them, and then making a rush. The water-hen, unable to dive or flutter across the water, rose high, and flew back over our heads towards the house and moat, giving very pretty shots, and we secured all five.

After leaving some of the game at the farm, and getting our cherry brandy flasks refilled, we decided to send the man home with the rest of the game, and go ourselves to a small spinney near at hand to wait for wood-pigeons. Twilight was coming on fast, but the light was reflected from the snow, and an early moon was already up, looking silvery and white.

Waiting quietly under the fir-trees, I could hear the sounds in the farmyard as the horses were watered and taken to the stable, and the calls of the partridges before going to their roosting-places in the snow. Then an inquisitive jay came down the plantation to have a peep at the intruder, and was shot. A flock of fieldfares then next arrived, with squeaks and chattering, and I was tempted to try and add a few of these excellent birds to the projected "water-cock pie." Just then I heard the "swish" of wings, and a flock of pigeons circled round, and settled in the larches near.

One I "potted," and as the flock dashed off, I heard my brother's gun, and surmised that they had paid toll in passing. Before long I had two more, and found that he had also secured a couple. By this time, though not too dark to shoot, the cold was so intense that we decided to go home. It was time, for when we got there our stockings were tight frozen to our boots.

Apropos of shooting in the snow, I may mention a strange experience that occurred to me when shooting in the snow near Pangbourne. It had been intended to drive partridges on a neighbouring property that day, but a deep fall of snow the night before caused this to be postponed. In the afternoon I went out with another gun, more for exercise than with any expectation of killing game. We found one or two hares buried in the snow in the way I have mentioned, but the birds, which were numerous, were much too wild to approach, and the immense quantity of snow on bush and branch rendered any attempt to beat even the smallest spinney impossible. Eventually my companion and I separated, he walking along one side of a valley, while I, with the keeper, took the opposite brow, with the hope that one or other might put birds across, and so give a chance of a shot. After some time I was far ahead, when I heard a distant cry of "mark," and a covey of seven birds was seen flying across the valley in our direction. The wind was dead against them, and it was some time before they reached the field we were in, and pitched some sixty yards from us, the first pair close to the fence, the rest at irregular intervals of from one to twenty yards from each other. The snow was quite soft and powdery, but my surprise was great to see the birds, instead of rising as I approached, gradually sink out of sight in the soft mass. By the time I reached them only the backs of the first pair were visible, and both let me come within ten yards before rising. I shot both, and looked for the others. They had disappeared. Presently I saw two small depressions in the snow, about an inch lower than the rest. When I was quite close, up jumped a partridge, which I shot; and then another from beneath the snow. Ten yards further on was another little mark in the snow, which also yielded a bird; and a sixth the keeper caught under the fence. The seventh rose close by, but I did not shoot. They were in splendid condition, plump, and strong.

SOMERSETSHIRE COOMBS

A WHIT-MONDAY FISHING

Mountain, sea, and stream are the natural features which most invite tired men from town; and for our part we could never understand where lay the difficulty of choice. The human fancy which saw in every stream the intelligible form of a god, a nymph, or a saint, will not be lightly blamed. There are rivers in England to suit every mood of man, and suggest every impulse whether of melancholy, merriment, or repose. But no one would consciously choose a sad stream as the scene of a sojourn, however short, upon its banks. The sight of the

> "full-fed river winding slow
> By herds upon an endless plain;
> The ragged rims of thunder, brooding low,
> With shadow-streaks of rain,"

is apt to breed melancholy and depression, as it did in the Soul which owned the "Palace of Art." Nor do we love best, even as the companions of a day, those quiet, slumbrous streams which poets' fancies have ever painted as singing the lullaby of sleeping gods. The

> "Rivus aquae Lethes, per quem cum murmure labens
> Invitat somnos crepitantibus unda lapillis;"

the

> "Rock-born flow of Lethe's streams,
> With muffled murmur of a thousand tongues,
> Of tinkling pebbles soothing Somnus' dreams."

Merriment, not repose, is the best and brightest gift of the young summer; and we must seek it, not by the solemn rivers of the plain, or by the dropping springs of the rocks, but by the brooks that come dancing down from the hills, and overrun in a thousand tiny channels the sloping meadows of Somerset or Devon.

There are thousands of such rivulets in the west country, not brown and peaty, like the becks of Yorkshire or the burns of Scotland, nor white and glassy, like the Hampshire chalk-streams, but honest little home-spun brooks without a history, though rarely lacking a name, some running through the homesteads of the upland farms, some filling the fish-ponds of the old manor-houses, others mere channels in the broken faces of the hills. But whatever the nature of their upper course, all are alike controlled at last by the ingenious western farmer, and carried along the ridges of the coombs in a network of terraced rivulets, by a system of engineering which tradition has made almost perfect for its purpose, until they reunite at last and rush through the wooded bottoms to the waiting sea. In early summer, these water-meadows are the chosen resort of every form of wild life in the neighbourhood. The leverets come down to nibble the rich grass at night, and play along the sides of the tiny dykes; and in the early morning the cock-pheasants slip out from the covers to drink and feed. The peewits are tamer there than on the hills above, and the wood-pigeons, rooks, and jackdaws bathe in the shallows, and leave their broken feathers and footmarks on the soft mud. Big trout leave the main stream and slip into the cuts, where they grow fat on the grubs and insects and little trout, and even young salmon force their way up to the upper waters, until they reach the utmost sources of the stream.

Owners of the ancient fishponds once attached to every house of consideration in the country-side, remembering the old saying that an acre of water is worth four acres of land, often take advantage of the chance offered by the subdivision of these streams to re-stock their home waters with young and lively trout; and if the streams are not too high, a "Whit-Monday fishing" with this object will convince the most sceptical visitor that the fun and merriment of the good old days in the country have by no means passed away, and that master and man may still unite in the common pursuit of sport and amusement. For sport it is, though catching, not killing, be the object, and the quarry only lively little brook-trout, and eels, and lamperns, destined, however, to grow strong and lusty fish in the fat waters of the manor pond. Nor need the Hampshire fly-fisher share the feelings of resentment which the writer once saw excited by the simple narrative of a method of taking trout in the water-meadows, given by an Andover rustic : " When us sees a big 'un, us shuts down the sluice ; and then us runs he up and down until he be that blowed he can't a-move ; and then us gropples he." For the " fishing " entails hard and enduring toil before the trout can be transferred from the brook to the tub on the cart which waits to carry them to their new home. Such, at least, was the experience of the last occasion of the kind in which the writer assisted.

The scene was in a narrow coomb, down which ran one of the minor tributaries of the river Yarty, on whose banks Sir Francis Drake was born, and beyond which lies the Tudor manor-house, which was part of the grant awarded to him by Queen Elizabeth, with an estate, held, like the house, by his descendants, within sight of the birthplace of the first circumnavigator of the globe. The stream ran almost beneath the windows of an even more ancient manor-house,[1] dating from the days of Henry VII., on the Somerset side of the Yarty, and the trout-pools below the mansion were yearly filled from the young fish taken from the lower waters. Close by were the remains of a Roman gentleman's comfortable villa ; and it is not improbable that our Whit-Monday fishing may have been a repetition of yearly scenes of country economics, supervised by the polite Roman, whose interest in domestic comfort doubtless extended from

[1] Whitestaunton Manor.

the arrangement of his hypocaust and neatly constructed Turkish bath, still remaining, to the "stagna," or fish-ponds, which gave him grilled trout for breakfast.

The spot selected lay in a wood, at a point where the brook divided for some distance into two streams,—the one, straight, deep, and rapid; the other, a succession of small pools, joined by miniature cataracts, in which the water danced down from pool to pool over lumps of flint and brown chalcedony. Early in the morning, the men—for this is no boy's work—had dammed the last stream at the fork, and turned most of the water down the straight channel; and when we tramped through the squashy meadows, and the thick growth of wood-elder, wake-robin, wild garlic, and blue and pink comfrey in the wood, to join the workers, the chain of pools was only connected by an inch of trickling water. But the instinct by which fish detect and follow the first warning of scarcity, had already caused them to withdraw to the deepest holes and hollows, and even the groping of a practised hand under the banks detected no sign of a trout. No one who has not tried to empty it, would believe the quantity of water which a small pool holds. When a dam of turf cut from the banks has been thrown across, to prevent the waters below running back as the surface sinks, two men step into the pool, and rapidly and steadily, like machines, fling the water forward and over it, until the sweat rolls from their foreheads, and we volunteer to take their places. Stepping into the cool water, we do our best to imitate the mechanical swing and cast of the practised hands, until the pails strike the bottom, and only a few gallons remain. Then, as we grope in among the rocks and stones, the water seems alive with fish, and the excitement grows. Half-a-dozen pairs of hands are busy feeling among the slippery roots and hovers, and shouts of laughter rise, as the nimble trout spring from the grasping fingers, or are held and carried full speed across the brambles and under-growth to the tub. Nothing could exceed the beauty of these small brook-trout, streaked with yellow, olive, and silver, and studded with vermilion spots, and showing their contempt for the temporary discomfort of their capture by a violent jump and fling of their tail as they drop from the hands of their muddy captor into the clean water of the tub. But the trout, though the main object of the foray, are not the only denizens of the pool. Eels and lampreys and the odd little " miller's thumbs " abound, and the pursuit of the eels is an endless source of laughter and mishap. A big yellow eel slips through half-a-dozen pairs of hands, writhing round and under rocks, in and out of the tree-roots from which the water has worn the soil, and back into the deepest hole left in the pool. "Drat he!" exclaims an old labourer, looking at his bruised knuckles, "he be so nimble as a little pig," citing appropriately the most difficult creature to catch—next to an eel—in his experience. But at last the trout and eels are all caught, and nothing left in the pool but the " miller's thumbs," or " bull-heads," and certain tiny and game-like little fish, which we suspect to be, not troutlets, but young salmon. In the larger pools which hold the finest trout, it is often impossible to throw away enough water to make the capture.

The closing scene of the "fishing" was a swan-hunt, in order to capture and shut up the royal birds, which would have given little law to the young trout when turned, tired and bewildered, into the strange waters of the manor ponds; and it was not until after much manœuvring and strategy that the swans were driven from the water, and shut up, hissing and indignant, in the pen which is reserved for such occasions. But the fish soon become accustomed to the spacious waters of their new home, and there thrive and grow fat, until they fall victims to the rod, and form not the least welcome of the "kindly fruits of the earth" which a well-managed estate provides for its owner's table.

In a similar enterprise in a different part of Somersetshire, at which the writer assisted, a number of fine trout took refuge in a deep hole under the bank, where the tips of their tails only would be reached by the hands stretched to the utmost limit which the water allowed. One of the party, fired by the enthusiasm of the moment, divested himself of all raiment, and lying down in the water, drew out, one by one, the reluctant fish. Meantime, the "water" became a thin red paste, deeply coloured by the red marl of the district, and when the successful bather emerged, he stood like an interesting example of terra-cotta statuary, until a dip in the mill-pool enabled him to resume his costume.

The pools which it was intended to stock were a chain formed in one of the lovely coombs that run down from the Quantock Hills towards the Bristol Channel. At the head of it is a pass which the red-deer stag usually take when hunted in this neighbourhood, and making for the sea. Lower down, where masses of deep purple heather and bracken almost hid the little stream, the owner had made one or two small pools, by throwing a few stems of Scotch fir across, and banking them with turf. The experiment grew more interesting the lower down the valley he descended. The pools grew larger, the trout more numerous, and the satisfaction which attends minor engineering feats, prompted further efforts. At length he plunged boldly into building, and made a fine stone wall across the coomb, and gained an additional pool larger than a tennis lawn. All went well during the summer, though the farmer who lived lower down sometimes expressed a doubt as to what might happen in winter rains. There was a small farmyard and piggery below, and a kitchen garden, and further down a long narrow lake in the grounds of the owner's house. One night the farmer was awakened by dismal sounds, and a sound of waters. The stone dyke had given way, the water was rushing down, and had washed the pigs into the gooseberry bushes. Soon it tore these up, and pigs, garden, and gooseberry bushes went rolling on to the lake. The lake burst its lower end, and went on an excursion down the road, and far into the valley, taking with it thousands of tench and eels, which were picked up, wriggling and perplexed, in the newly-formed river-bed in the road. This was an unfortunate result of amateur engineering; but the business of making fish-pools is now better understood, and the results are beyond measure satisfactory to the owners of these artificial lakes.

THE EAGLE IN ENGLAND

IN November 1891 a spotted eagle was caught at Elmstead near Colchester. It appears to have alighted exhausted in a field, and to have been there chased and caught, after weak efforts to fly, by a labourer, who sold it to a gipsy, from whom it was bought by a benevolent bird-stuffer; and as it is reported to have eaten in three days a rabbit, a large fowl, and many pounds of mutton, it may be taken that its health was perfectly restored, after its involuntary flight across the German Ocean. For the spotted eagle is amongst the rarest stragglers to England, and the bird should by this time be far on its journey to the south, or making its way with others of its kind up the Nile Valley, towards the mountains of Abyssinia. But though the spotted eagle is so rare a visitor to this country, eagles are less uncommon in England than might be supposed, and hardly a season passes in which they are not seen, even in the south. Two are said to have been seen flying over Westminster during the frost of February 1895; and though this report is not corroborated, it is certain that during the past few years, sea-eagles have been seen frequently in the Isle of Thanet and in the great flats and marshes near the estuary of the Thames; and though there were constant notices of their appearance in the local papers, owing to the open nature of the country, and the absence of game-preserving and vermin-traps, they have generally escaped destruction. In other parts of Kent, they have been less fortunate. In 1887, one was shot at Minster, and one at Eastwell Park. But a third which was seen was not destroyed, though the dangerous attraction of the game-preserves must naturally tempt the hungry young eagles from the safer but almost foodless marshes[1] by the coast. Most of those killed in the south are young sea-eagles, which seem to follow a general line along the east coast, and sometimes so far adhere to the ancient instincts of their race as to make some stay in the Norfolk warrens and marshes, where they were once so common as to be known as the "fen-eagles." But eagles appear in other parts of England, and it is probable that if they could be protected from those who, unlike shepherds and gamekeepers, have neither lambs nor game to suffer from their ravenous appetite, some might come once more to nest in their ancient breeding-places in the cliffs of the south and west.

An eagle which was clearly not a passing autumn traveller, but which remained till late in the winter, appeared a few years ago on the Quantock Hills, a

[1] Those marshes near Rochester, where the Cliffe coursing club hold their meetings, and on the Essex coast near Southminster are an exception. They swarm with hares.

district quite apart from the line of migration of the coasting eagles, and one in which the cliffs and coast of the Bristol Channel, and the open country on the Quantock and Brendon Hills and Exmoor, offer a home as suited to the sea-eagle as the coasts of Jura. "We first saw the eagle," writes a correspondent, "on Christmas Day, circling above the carcass of a sheep on the side of the hill. For several days we observed the bird wheeling over the moor, mainly on the high hills; but once or twice it was seen flying over the low lands near the villages. It had evidently been feeding upon the sheep, which was freshly killed, but probably not by the eagle; it was too early for lambs upon the hills, so it probably fed upon carrion and rabbits. It remained for about a month after we saw it, but towards the end of January it was wounded by some gunner, and afterwards picked up dead by a labourer." If this eagle had escaped, it might perhaps have found a mate and occupied the old eyrie in Lundy Island, and the eagle and the red-deer might have once more become neighbours on the coasts of Devon and Somerset. Since the death of the bird mentioned, another is said by a good observer to have haunted the Quantocks, near St. Audreys; if so, it has so far escaped the fate of its predecessor. Culver Cliffs, in the Isle of Wight, are said to have been an old eyrie of the erne, or sea-eagle; and the Arnescliff, a mass of stone jutting from one of the hills in Wharfedale, in Yorkshire, still recalls its former presence south of the border. But as most of those which might settle again in the English cliffs are young birds driven by their parents from the eyries in the north, we must look to Scotland as the source of supply; and there it is to be feared that the sea-eagles are dwindling in numbers, mainly owing to the incessant war waged upon them by shepherds and "oologists." It may be doubted whether the bribes offered by the latter are not more stimulating than even the loss of their lambs in springtime to the egg-robbing ardour of the shepherds. Still, the sea-eagles are by general consent ill neighbours to the young lambs which are born on the hills, and lie out scattered on the moors. On the poor and barren Highland coast there is little farm stock to be injured, except the lambs; but where they are to be found, little pigs are said to offer great temptations to the sea-eagles, and one was caught in the Hebrides in a stye into which it had descended, but which was too narrow to allow it to spread its wings and escape. What a scene such a foray among the pigs would cause in a well-regulated English farmyard! The statement of a shepherd that in one season more than thirty lambs were killed by eagles on a single sheep-farm has been doubted, on the ground that it would be impossible to judge the actual loss, or the cause, on the wide area of a Highland "farm." But perhaps the critics know more of the eagle's habits than of those of the sheep, or of the minute and careful knowledge possessed by the shepherds as to the numbers of the flocks, and the particular spots in which the ewes drop their lambs on the hills.

Even when half-tamed and provided with food, the sea-eagle does not lose its predatory habits. A full-grown young bird, which had met with some injury, was kept for some weeks and fed by the gardener at an old castle in the West, which has been the home of the chiefs of a highland clan for perhaps as long as the cliff of which it forms almost a part has been the eyrie of the sea-eagles. When cured and released, it returned to be fed, and in time grew so familiar as to enter the house. The dining-room, as in many ancient Scotch houses, was at the top of the castle, with several windows looking out over the Atlantic. Breakfast was laid, and many of the guests were in the room, when an open window was suddenly darkened as the eagle flew in from the sea, and, folding its wings, alighted on the sill. It then flapped on to the table, and after looking at the guests standing in the room, it made its way down the table, and swallowed the butter, which was set for use at intervals down the board. For two years the eagle lived about the castle; but its visits to the farmyards were not less frequent, and though "indemnity" for these outrages was freely paid, it is to be feared that the eagle's disappearance was due to a reprisal from an injured flock-owner. There is, however, good reason to believe that the golden eagle, which at one time seemed destined to extermination, is rapidly increasing in numbers. By a fortunate chance, its powers of destruction, which incurred the revenge of the shepherds and grouse-preservers, are of certain service to the deer-stalker by keeping down the numbers of mountain-hares which live on the hills, and often spoil the success of a hard morning's stalking by jumping up and alarming the deer. For once, the sportsman and a bird of prey can exist together, and the eagles are carefully protected in order that they may aid in keeping the forests clear of all other animals but deer. In these vast preserves—quiet, secluded, and untrodden by sheep or shepherds—the golden eagles are now suffered to rear their young, and have so far increased in numbers that it is rare to meet with a deer-stalker who is not familiar with their appearance, and in some degree with their habits. They occasionally kill a deer-calf, and have been known to attack the full-grown deer. But their main food is the blue hares, and these are so numerous that the problem of maintaining in any numbers a carnivorous bird which will swallow five or six pounds of meat at a meal presents no difficulties. It is quite likely that, where several of these protected districts adjoin, the golden eagles will once more become numerous. In California, where they find an inexhaustible supply of food in the land-tortoises of the plains—a curious commentary on the story of the death of Æschylus, caused by a tortoise let fall by an eagle—they are not only common but exceedingly tame, building their nests near roads and houses. One nest was found in a small live-oak near a road, and only thirty feet from the ground, built of sticks of the poison-oak and sage-brush. An old nest was close by. Another eagle had decorated its nest with a large " soap-root " by way of ornament;

and the next year the same bird built close by, and also procured a "soap-root" to place on the side of its nest, which showed some individuality in taste. A third eagle had a fancy for sacks, and after its old nest, which contained a corn-sack, had been blown out by a storm, it built a fresh one close by, and in this was found another and a new sack. The eagles seem to be, at any rate in some parts of California, almost as common as the kite was in England, and to have the same propensity for carrying to their nests any object which strikes them as ornamental or interesting. It is not to be supposed that, under the most favourable circumstances, the golden eagle will increase to such numbers in the Highlands. But there is every probability that, as its area extends in the North, some of its earlier breeding places in the South, such as the Cheviots, the Peak of Derbyshire, or Westmoreland and Cumberland, where it nested as lately as 1838, may be revisited, and that we may before long see the golden eagle re-established in England.

The following extracts from a letter communicated to the writer by one who has unequalled facilities for acquaintance with golden eagles gives an idea of the great increase in their numbers, and of their boldness in the "protected areas" of the deer forests where they live. "Eagles are more plentiful now, I should imagine, in this forest than anywhere else in Scotland, as they have always been carefully preserved. Three years ago, indeed, while I was stalking hinds in the winter, I saw eight in one day. One rarely goes out stalking without seeing one or more in that beat of the forest. On the other side of the river also they are comparatively plentiful. Their food consists of all sorts of game, sheep, and lambs. They seem to prefer young deer and hares to anything else. These they kill, though they prefer the former sick, and unable to help themselves. They are also rather destructive among lambs. An eagle, unless hungry, seems to be a cowardly bird, and rarely attacks anything that seems likely to give it much trouble. Last year I was stalking, and shot a calf by accident, which was coming up beside a hart, in a sort of gulley formed by a rock, thus—

I was at the point x, and shot the beast at D. The remainder ran over the ridge, about twenty or thirty feet high above them, and I ran after them. I shot a hart at about Q, and ran back to see what I had done at D. There I found my calf, with his eyes already torn out by an eagle, which was sitting on him, and just about to begin a good meal. It must have been very hungry, as after I had shot the calf I was never twenty yards from it, and fired a shot, though I was on the other side of the hill. It was a misty day, which would make a little difference.

"We often shoot grouse under a kite at the end of

the season, when it would otherwise be impossible to get within shot of them. The kite is made in the shape of an eagle, and causes the birds to sit better, and rare sporting shots they give when they rise. This kite is a sure draw for any eagles in the neighbourhood. They come swinging round it, completely puzzled, and cannot make it out at all. The other day we were accompanied for two or three hours by an eagle, a falcon, and a merlin, all at the same time."

CLIMBING IN ENGLAND

It is more difficult to sympathize with other people's amusements than with their troubles in this world. The reflection is not new, but so many amusements are, that we are constantly invited to recognize its truth. The attraction of mountain-climbing, especially in the minor form in which it can be enjoyed in England, is a case in point. Yet the admiration for our mountain scenery is a semi-modern sentiment. Speaking of the beautiful Lune Valley, Defoe wrote, "This part of the country seemed very strange and dismal to us (nothing but mountains in view, and stone walls for hedges, some oatcakes for bread, or clapat bread as it is called). As these hills were so lofty, so they had an aspect of terror. Here were no rich pleasant valleys between them as in the Alps; no lead-mines and veins of rich ore as in the Peak; no coal-pits as in the hills about Halifax!" The pleasure of climbing for climbing's sake is almost as little understood by many minds at the present day, as the picturesque forms of the mountains were by Defoe. Yet it is increasingly popular, as may be seen from the work on this amusement as now practised in this country, which Mr. Haskett Smith recently published,[1] though it is not in the Cumberland Fells that the taste for mountain-craft usually originates. It is the High Alps that make the first and obvious appeal to the uninitiated. The gratification of the sense of sight is the main inducement held out by the mountain-tops. The rims and peaks of the ice-capped walls which rise so high and so steep that the eye does not readily see clear of their summits, unless the natural poise of the head be altered, promises a view so boundless and majestic if once the barrier be topped, that the imagination is kept in a constant crescendo of excitement and curiosity until the summit is reached. To stand level with the heads of twenty Alps, whose glittering peaks stud the horizon like a *rivière* of brilliants, or to see the plains of Lombardy spread, like a carpet, ten thousand feet below, and thirty miles beyond, or the rising sun " stand tiptoe on the misty mountain-top," or the " bright white lightning " leap from the thunderstorm in the valley below, or, best of all, to look from some untrodden peak from which no human eye ever yet gazed,—these are the promises which beckon the climbers to the mountain. Experience often shows them to be delusive; but it is not experience which issues the first summons. That is the work of imagination, though experience often transforms it into a longing which outlasts the ability to gratify it. The exhilaration of the air is such that

[1] *Climbing in the British Isles—England.* By W. P. Haskett Smith. London: Longmans.

at reasonable heights of from five to ten thousand feet, a buoyancy of spirits and strength of body seem to accrue such as is only felt elsewhere in rare and happy dreams. All sights and sounds are new and beautiful. The flora changes, and the climber finds himself among flowers and plants unknown, in a setting equally unfamiliar. Sounds gain a strange clearness and resonance, and the mere effort of producing the voice has an effect of sonority such as nothing but some mechanical instrument could render in the dull air which creeps on the level ground. Then at the last comes the need for physical exertion, coolness, and skill, under the very circumstances of atmosphere and mental exhilaration most likely to secure their successful development. The extent to which the English mountains are now used as a training-ground for the delights of Alpine climbing is evident from the familiarity with particular spots which Mr. Haskett Smith's book presupposes in his readers. The delightful difficulties which may be found and surmounted in the ascents of the Pillar Rock, of Pavey Ark, Napes Needle, and Moss Gill, are given with the minuteness of detail which is usually bestowed on the climb of some High Alp without a guide. Ice-climbing needs special practice in the glacial regions. But rock-climbing can be learnt almost as well on the mountains of the Lake district as on any others. There, according to recent experience, it "may be enjoyed by amateurs without incurring the reproach of recklessness, while they may at the same time enjoy the exquisite pleasure of forming their own plans of attack, of varying the execution of them according to their own judgment, and finally of meeting obstacles, as they arise, with their own skill and by their own strength, and overcoming them without the aid of a hired professional." The peculiar charm of these mountains, to the initiated, consists in the cracks, or "chimneys," which seam the precipices from top to bottom. Sometimes these are damp with trickling water, and Nature has thoughtfully lined them with moss. Too often they are only hard and angular crevices, like three sides of a chimney-top. Up these the climber wriggles, like an eel in a pipe. In reading the records of their ascent, one is tempted to muse on the relative nature of pleasure. It is not long since master-sweeps were sent to prison for sending their apprentice boys up real chimneys, not nearly so high, nor so dangerous, as those of Moss Gill. It was in the interest of these human victims that a philanthropist made the happy suggestion that a live goose pulled up the flue with a string would do just as well,—or, if not, that a couple of ducks would answer the purpose. Now, amateurs in climbing go to Cumberland to experience the sensations which must have been part of the every-day lot of the chimney boy, and record their enjoyment in print. The high spirits and serious fun which underlie these accounts speak volumes for the benefits of mountain air. Winter climbing adds the pleasures of surmounting snow and ice in considerable quantities, in addition to the difficulties of the natural rocks. The "Lakes" have now a winter season, entirely devoted to the best class of English climbing. "There is no time," writes Mr. Haskett Smith, "at which a trip to Lakeland is more thoroughly enjoyable. In the first place, there is no crowd. You can be sure that you will get a bed, and that the people of the house will not be too overworked to make you comfortable. You will have no companions but life-long lovers of the mountains, and robust young fellows whose highest ambition is to gain admission to the Alpine Club, or having gained it, to learn to wield with some appearance of dexterity the ponderous ice-axes which are indispensable to the dignity of their position. How different are the firm outlines of the distant peaks from the hazy indistinctness which usually falls to the lot of the summer tourist! What sensation is more delightful than that of tramping along while the smooth crisp snow crunches under the feet, and gazing upward at the lean black crags standing out boldly from the long smooth slopes of dazzling white! Christmas in Cumberland is usually dry and fine, as is pointed out triumphantly by those who resent Mr. James Payn's sarcastic allusion to "dry weather" in the Lakes, "which is said to have occurred about the year 1824."

The Yorkshire dales, Cornwall, and Dartmoor, though their beauties are not disparaged, have less attraction for the ardent learner in mountaineering. The axiom that "a very fine hill may be a very bad climb," applies both to the "tors" and the limestone carrs and crags of millstone grit. But the great sea-cliffs of England offer a peculiar and natural playground to the devotee of climbing. Old-fashioned cragsmen, who, unlike the modern school, risked their necks with a purpose, if only for the very inadequate one of gathering sea-fowls' eggs, or taking a falcon's or raven's eyrie, chose an exactly opposite method of attack to that now in favour. They accepted the fact that it is usually easier to reach the juts and ledges of a cliff from the top than from the bottom, and that scrambling about on slippery chalk or treacherous limestone was quite dangerous enough for glory, if the rope were made fast to a crowbar above, and not to the waists of a line of climbers tied together like bits of paper on the tail of a kite. Of course, these men sometimes grew over-confident, and paid the penalty with their lives; but the margin of safety is usually ample, and there is no reason why the particular cragsman who has taken the young ravens from the Culver Cliffs, in the Isle of Wight, for the last seven years, should not do so till he is too stiff to climb. But the modern athlete prefers to treat the cliffs as training-grounds for practising manœuvres likely to be useful in recognized mountaineering. The use of the rope is not discountenanced, but only in Alpine form, as a link between the climbers. Some of the directions for the " use of cliffs " seem horribly dangerous; and the art of climbing is considered so entirely an end in itself, that the precipices are merely mentioned in the terms of the material for the exercise of a fine art, chalk being described rather quaintly as a " treacherous and difficult *medium*, and one which is likely to lead those practising on it to be very careful climbers." The uses of the magnificent cliffs of Dover, and between that place and Folkstone, with the precipices of Beachy Head, and the vertical cliffs to the west of it, are thus indicated for the enjoyment of seaside visitors who may think of a visit to the English lakes next year, and of qualifying for the Alps the year after. "As a rule chalk is only sufficiently solid for real climbing for the first 20 ft. above high-water mark, though here and there 40 ft. of fairly trustworthy rock may be found. These sections of hard chalk are invariably those which at their base are washed by the sea at high tide." "Traverses," or scrambles sideways, are the proper exercises in these delightful spots; "a good *objectif* may be found in the endeavour to work out a route to the various small beaches that are cut off by the high tide and the cliffs." The discovery of these little hidden bays and rock-gardens is always interesting; but though Mr. Haskett Smith properly cautions his readers that in climbing the upper precipices of the chalk slopes, "a slip would almost certainly prove fatal," he omits to mention that if not killed the modest "passager" who breaks his leg by a slip from the sea-washed base is also pretty certain to drown at high tide. Nor should it be forgotten that climbing, even on Cumberland fells, is perhaps the severest form of exercise known, and that the results of overstrain are almost equally dangerous with those of a fall, when the exhilaration of mountain air has led to an overtax of a frame fresh from the sedentary life of professional work.

THE YORKSHIRE FEN

THE Yorkshire Fen is less well-known than those of Cambridgeshire and Lincolnshire. Yet its history is not less interesting, and its present appearance, especially in those parts which lie in the narrower valleys, and were formerly arms of the great marshy sea, is far more picturesque, owing to the number of woods and plantations which flourish on its black and rotten soil. It was the first of all the large fen areas to be reclaimed, and the history of its reclamation is one of singular interest. For the details the reader should consult the life of Sir Cornelius Vermuylen, in Dr. Smiles' *Lives of the Engineers*, and the story as told by Abraham de la Pryme, F.R.S., in the MS. *History of Hatfield* in the British Museum. This is not the "Hatfield" owned by Lord Salisbury, but the ancient fen of "Hatfield Chase," which with the Isle of Axholme, and the marshes lying between the Don, Thorne, Idle, and Trent rivers, constitutes the Yorkshire fen. Sixty thousand acres of this great tract were drained by Cornelius Vermuylen, the Dutch engineer, in 1626, who in two years completed a task which

Taking Cormorants' Eggs. *From a photograph by* M. AUTY

a commission appointed to report on its possibility had declared impossible. The nature of the ground at that time may be judged from the fact that when James I. visited the country five hundred deer were collected from the drier parts of the fen, and made to swim across the waters, where they were caught from boats. The scene must have been much like that of hunting the swamp deer of Borneo. The local name for the upper levels of the reclamation is the "Carrs," and each village usually has attached to it a part of this reclamation which bears its name, such as Loversall Carr, Wadworth Carr, Balby Carr, and others. The portion with which the writer is best acquainted is that which lies south-west of Doncaster, in the valley, or what is now the valley, but was once the marsh, of the rivers Thorne and Idle. This was an outlying branch of the great fen, which originally extended on the north to the river Humber, on the east to the lowlands of the Trent, and on the south into Nottinghamshire, and included the Isle of Axholme, Thorne Waste, Marshland, and the Fen of Hatfield Chase. Before the end of last century, according to a most interesting article on this fen by Mr. Eagle Clarke, which appeared in the *Field* of November 26, 1887, there were not only vast numbers of duck breeding in the fen, but in addition the bittern, ruff, and reeve, the black-tailed godwit, the marsh harrier, the great crested grebe, and the water-rail, all bred *commonly* on the "Potterick Carr" above Doncaster. In 1762 John Smeaton, the builder of the Eddystone Lighthouse, showed how the lingering surface waters might be made to disappear. The drainage and enclosure of the flats, now separated by deep and impassable streams, and planted with wide and enduring woods by private owners, extends a natural protection to the remaining species which still in countless numbers make the "carrs" their home. In no inland region that the writer has yet seen are the larger birds found in such astonishing numbers, or so easily observed, as in the wooded portions of the "carrs." Nor need this be matter for surprise, where food, water, shelter, and quiet are found over vast spaces of land. The farms and villages are far removed on the higher ground, seated, as it were, with their feet in the quiet marshes, where breadth and solitude are broken only by the thick and silent woods, and the slow-running rivers: a dark country, with dark skies, and trees, and waters. The very mole-hills are black, and the dykes bridged by heart of oak, black as coal, and dug from the peat of the fen. Even on the sound land on the border of the marsh, where the ancient trees survive, the giant poplars which fringe the pools have leaves as dark as those on which the vapours of invaded Tartarus left their mark for ever. Yet, unlike most marsh-lands, the "carrs" are neither gloomy nor deserted. But birds, not men, people the flats; and to meet them the visitor must keep early hours, and be abroad by sunrise, or in summer a little later; for it is possible to be too early for the birds, even after day has broken, and at four o'clock on a summer's morning even they are scarcely awake. Here there is no sudden leap of

Nature from sleep to active and eager life as in the tropics, where the beginning and ending of light and darkness are as rapid as the lighting and quenching of a torch, and the hour of disappearance of the creatures of night is fixed by the quick and tyrannous invasion of the sun. The early visitor to the streamside will surprise the wild ducks and herons before they leave their feeding-grounds for the day. In that part of the "carrs" with which the writer is best acquainted, the heronry lies in the centre of a thousand-acre wood, from which the birds sally in all directions to hunt the streams at night. In the early morning their grey and ghostly forms may be seen, as they stand quietly in the long meadow-grass, resting after their night's fishing, or wading about in the long, wet herbage. Seen among the white and curling vapours which lie upon the dripping aftermath, they seem like the spirits of the fen, as they slowly spread their wings and sail away towards the sunrise to their sanctuary beyond the stream. The departure of the herons is the signal for a general awakening of the main bird-population of the "carrs." Though the sunbeams have scarcely penetrated the lower levels of the mist, the tree-tops in the plantations are already glowing with the morning rays, and the noise of the birds is astonishing. The tree-tops are full of rooks and jackdaws, wood-pigeons and stock-doves; and like children, their first impulse on awakening is to chatter. The rush and clatter of wings as the flocks leave the wood for their feeding-grounds is like the sound of the sea, and their numbers beyond conjecture. The fallow fields, where the roughly ploughed clods are dry and warm, are first visited, not only by the rooks, jackdaws, and pigeons, but also by the flocks of peewits which have been feeding all night on the wet marshes. The last come, not for food, but, as it seems, for rest and company, remaining quite still and quiet, and apparently enjoying the warmth of the morning sun. But the great flocks of day-feeding birds are eager in search of food, the rooks and jackdaws prying beneath every clod, while the pigeons fly over each other's backs, struggling for a place in the crowd like their tame relations in a London square. Perhaps the latest birds to awaken to the business of the day are the partridges. Even in August the coveys do not seem to move till six o'clock, when they may be heard calling and making up their minds to leave their roosting-places for the first-cut stubbles. By eight o'clock in August or September, the birds have ceased feeding, and fly to the river to bathe and drink, by some common and well-understood impulse, which brings the flocks in noisy and cheerful companies to the water-side. When coming down to drink, their flight and manner of approach is altogether different from that which marks their descent upon the fallow fields which are their morning feeding-grounds. The serious business of the day is over, and they go down to the water in great companies and processions, flying low over the ground and constantly alighting for a short time, then rising and flying onwards with much cawing, chattering, and gossip. Several different kinds unite in these bathing-parties. On one occasion the writer saw a flock which must have numbered at least a thousand rooks and jackdaws approaching the water in this manner. With them were scores of wood-pigeons, a flock of turtle-doves, and a number of peewits, all of which flew or alighted at the same time in the same direction. The stream was flowing rapidly and smoothly between high embankments, and it was only here and there that the cattle, or some careless weed-cutter, had trampled down the edges sufficiently to make the access to the water easy for the birds. All these " bathing ghats," as we could see by looking up the straight cut from behind the decayed stump of the last great tree that stood upon the marsh before the forest disappeared, were occupied by crowds of rooks and pigeons drinking and bathing, until others came down and pushed them forward till they were obliged to fly across the stream. There they sat in long rows on the rails which run by the side of the dyke, drying themselves or preening their feathers, until the whole row of fencing was covered with black lines of cawing and chattering birds. In no long time the water brought down traces of the bath, in the shape of hundreds of floating feathers, lightly cushioned on the surface of the stream. Not even the floating thistledown lies more gracefully on the water, than do these little fleets of feathers from the morning toilet of the birds, the crisp and curling black plumes from the breast of rook and jackdaw sailing by like fairy gondolas, while here and there a feather from a pigeon's wing, with a drop of water for ballast in its curve, catches the wind at every gust, and sails among the lesser craft and dances on the ripples like some miniature yacht.

The pheasants and partridges also visit the stream to drink, though not to bathe. Hidden near one of their favourite drinking-places, the writer has more than once observed the care and anxiety which the wild pheasant exhibits when bringing her brood to the water. Men are so rarely seen upon the "carrs," that her fears must be due, not to the danger from human interference, but to the attacks of the hawks and magpies, foxes and stoats, which enjoy almost the same freedom from disturbance as the other wild creatures of the fen. The pheasants invariably approach the stream from a wood near by a long hedgerow, which runs down to the water, and gives complete protection from winged enemies. The old bird then ascends the bank, and after some moments spent in surveying the neighbourhood with head erect and motionless, she descends and drinks, raising her head like a fowl after each draught. A low call then summons the brood, who descend in turn, while the old bird once more mounts guard. If disturbed, the whole brood run into the fence, with a speed and silence more to be expected from some nimble four-footed animal than in a bold and strong-flying bird like the wild pheasant. The partridges, on the contrary, drink at the most open spots, flying in a body with much noise and calling to the waters, and returning as hastily when their thirst is satisfied. By nine o'clock the "carrs" are almost deserted by the birds. The pheasants are in the corn, or hidden in the plantations. Rooks, jackdaws, and pigeons have flown far up into the cultivated ground, the plovers have followed them, the herons are asleep in the thick woods, before the shepherd drives his flock to feed on the drying grasses of the fen.

In the great frosts the running streams which flow from the upper ground into the "carrs" are an almost certain haunt of wild-duck, and the writer was for many years accustomed to visit the fen before breakfast, when the only light was the topaz glow in the sky before the winter dawn, and the moon had a planet opposite its curve, as bright as that which shone when the Turks stormed the city of Constantine. The way to the fen lay along the side of a wood, below a park in which warm springs rose from the limestone almost at the edge of the flat. No frost, even those recently experienced, ever froze this "dyke," to which the contrast of green weeds, running water, and, in such weather, clouds of warm vapour rolling from the surface, gave an almost tropical appearance, while all the ground round was crusted with snow and frost needles. The rush and flutter of the water-hens in the thick rushes, the thin dry sound of the reeds as they rustled and bent in the cold morning gusts, and the darkness of the wood which fringed one side of the water, made this one of the most unusual scenes I have ever met with in English cultivated districts. A brook below was the favourite haunt of the duck, which fed in the warm dyke by night, and then lay in the brook which was still more removed from the ordinary paths of the labourers on the farms. In the half-light every splash of a water-rat or rail suggested the immediate rise of duck ; and when they did fly up from the deep brook, sometimes in a flock of from eight to a dozen, over-anxiety and the dusky light often made the shooting less straight than it should have been. By the time the true "carrs" were reached the sun was well risen, and the view across the flat "line landscape" with its level waste of snow, long black lines of dyke, and straight walls of trees fringing the distance was very striking. The drains and rivers were almost without bridges ; there are no more roads than when the marsh was impassable, and the farmhouses and villages to which the "carrs" are annexed lie far away. Consequently there are neither men nor houses on the marsh, and the early visitor is absolutely alone. When the duck had been disturbed in the higher levels of the "carrs," it was not unusual to see a "wedge" flying steadily down the fen, seeking open water in the main river. This was an exciting moment, for if they pitched, owing to the high banks, a shot was certain. On one occasion the writer and another watched seven duck come down the level, and suddenly descend into the river where it is joined by the brook. Here there is always open water even in hard frost, and the duck will even lie in the rough grass in the angle between the streams.

> " Ille terrarum mihi praeter omnes
> Angulus videt."

It is a favourite corner. We crept up to the place. Thirteen fine wild-duck rose, for a previous party had evidently acted unconsciously the part of "decoys," and three were shot. One, a beautiful drake, fell across the stream, which was deep, and icy cold. Local knowledge here came in usefully; a sheep-trough on wheels was fetched and run out into the water, and with the pier so made, and the aid of the shepherd's crook, the fine mallard was secured.

Mr. Eagle Clarke, in the interesting paper referred to above, has given a history of an ancient duck decoy about three-quarters of a mile from the junction of the St. Catherine's brook and the river Thorne, which was owned by the Corporation of Doncaster. He thinks it probable that Sir Cornelius Vermuylen's Dutchmen, who settled on the reclamation, first introduced the art of decoy-making into England. The decoy on these "carrs" "dates from at least as early as the year 1657, when it was either erected or acquired by the corporation of Doncaster as an investment for certain moneys intrusted to it for the benefit of the poor. It is curious that in the very earliest days of decoys in England we should thus find a public body selecting such an innovation as an investment." Mr. Clarke supposes that the success of the Dutch in other decoys in the Yorkshire fen encouraged the Doncaster corporation to construct one. In any case they devoted two sums of £100 and £60, money left for the poor, to making the decoy, and made a special embankment of over three-quarters of a mile in length, still called "Decoy Bank," to reach it. The decoy pond was circular, with six acres and a half of water and six "pipes." In 1662 it was let for twenty-one years at an annual rent of £15 —not a bad return on a capital of £160. But in 1707 the rent had fallen to £3. Yet there must have been plenty of wild-fowl still upon the "carr." Smeaton did not complete the drainage till after 1762; and the lessee of 1707 made a specialty of catching pochards— one of the best ducks for the table, though not often seen in English poultry-shops at this date—by means of nets which were raised by pulleys on poles after the pochards had settled on the water.

The last decoy-man died in 1794, and all the pipes were in existence in 1778. Now the Great Northern railway runs straight through what was the decoy; part of the wood which surrounded it remains, but few visitors from London to Doncaster imagine that just as they approach the busy town they are running through the site of the old corporation decoy. But south of the line the "carrs" are still secluded, solitary, and a very paradise for birds. Mr. Clarke's interesting and full account of the archæology of wild-fowling in the district should be read by all who know the Yorkshire fen as it is, and would like to picture what it has been.

DUCK-SHOOTING IN A GALE

THE wind was sweeping across the great level of the Humber valley, tearing slates from the barn roofs, twisting up the rick thatches, and whirling loose straw and rubbish from stackyard to field, while squalls of rain and sleet or driving hail sent everything that had legs or wings to covert and shelter. As I was walking out between the showers, I was hailed by the shepherd, riding up on the battered old horse which he has the use of when the flock is far afield, from a visit to his sheep in the marshes. A fresh-flayed fleece flung across the saddle in front of him, the wool inside against his thighs, with the red exterior presented to view, showed that at least one of his flock had succumbed to the rigours of the night. But it was not to give news of his sheep that he smote the old horse with the hedge-stake in his hand and jogged across the path to address me. "Eh," he said, "ye suld ha' been wi' me an hour back wi' your double-barril goon. Such a sight o' dook! I believe there wur forty came over me and pitched in the drain by the black wood, and t' dyke is fair *wick* (alive) wi' 'em. They'll be come some way, I'm thinking, for they made nought of me, but just settled and bided where they were."

Though this sounded rather like exaggeration, it seemed, on reflection, likely enough that the storm had brought duck into the "carrs." Flights of plover, pigeons, gulls, and fieldfares had been passing all day, and no doubt the duck on the large pieces of water in the neighbourhood would find them rough resting-places, while shore-loving widgeon and teal might well have shifted inland. The great flats, though drained and in places cultivated, were once a paradise for fowl, and in the particular corner in which I was, the quiet dykes and drains were in many places bordered by tall plantations, and fringed by deep beds of reeds and bulrushes. In some, where the water hardly ever freezes, duck may be found at all hours in a hard frost. At any rate it seemed worth trying, so unchaining an old half retriever, half water spaniel, and putting on a covert-coat, comforter, and cap with flaps to keep the rain out of my ears, I started for the "carrs." At the bottom of the park, where the flat land begins, a stream bubbles up, and flows by the side of a dark plantation for half-a-mile before joining one of the drains of the "carr." The water seems to be warm, for all through the winter cresses and other green weeds grow there, and in a hard frost the steam may be seen rising from it like smoke. Naturally, it is a favourite feeding ground at night, and to-day was more than likely to give a shot. The wind was howling so loud through the tree-tops that even the wary moor-hens failed to hear my steps, and hurried off alarmed to bury themselves in the thick reeds on the opposite bank, but for some time I saw no duck. Presently I approached a favourite spot, never more likely than in a storm. Here the stream is joined by a smaller rill, and the two form a deep circular pool, sheltered partly by the plantation and partly by a thick clump of black poplars on the neck between the streams, whose gnarled and twisted stems look like those in the foreground of some picture by Poussin, and form a remarkable feature in the flat landscape. Slipping up between the poplar stems, I peered over towards the pool. A dozen duck were swimming across to the far side, evidently uneasy, but loth to move. Just as I saw them they saw me, and rose. The noise in the branches was so great that I could hear nothing of their clatter, but I fired into the thick of them and got two, and sent a third away hard hit, for so quickly did the wind take them that the last bird put fifteen yards further between us than he would on an ordinary day. I watched the struck bird, and saw him fall about 300 yards further down the dyke; so, picking up the first brace, and tying their heads together, I hung them across a bough in the plantation, and proceeded down the dyke. More moor-hens and a solitary coot were all that I saw for some time. Meantime the gale increased, and the stinging hail beat down like shot, rebounding from the gun-barrels, and making the old dog whimper and poke her head between my legs for shelter as I stopped and turned my back to the blast.

Then it lulled, and as I walked on, my dog, who had

been longing to go in and beat the reeds, splashed in, and in a minute a teal rose and flew low across the meadow. He fell, and at the shot a second rose also; but wild, and I failed to get him. Then came a *contretemps*. We had arrived at about the place where the wounded duck had fallen, and after some hunting in the reeds, which the furious wind was bending and beating almost level with the water, the old dog emerged with a splendid mallard in her mouth. The bird was alive, and I had some difficulty in giving him his *quietus*, which the dog took advantage of to hunt down the stream on her own account. Turning round to pick up my gun, I saw, for I could hear nothing for the noise of the wind in the branches, first three and then five duck rise and drift away before the wind. Then the dog came sneaking back, looking ashamed of herself, as she deserved. This brought us to the end of the stream which we had been hunting, and we were now upon the "carrs" themselves. Here, away from the shelter of the belt of trees, the full force of the gale was apparent; and it seemed pretty certain that any duck there might be there would be in the dykes which ran at right angles to the direction of the wind, and not in those which were swept lengthwise by its full force. The main stream was that which bounded the property, and was in most parts exposed, though here and there was a bend which seemed worth trying. Accordingly, I made directly across the "carr" to one of these spots, tramping, with my hands in my pockets and head bent down, across the wet tussocky pastures, whence the big Lincolnshire sheep had been driven by the gale to huddle beneath the stacks of coarse, stemmy hay. On my way I kicked up a hare, and was stupid enough to shoot him; an awkward load at the best of times, this one was doubly so, for I had not a large game bag, and so tied his legs together and hung him to the strap of my cartridge bag. With this animal bumping against my thighs, I cautiously approached the first bend, but it held nothing. The next held a single duck, which fell an easy shot, but on the further bank. The dog, however, made up her mind that it was in the water, and it was at least five minutes before I could get her to mount the further bank and search. Then she dropped it in the stream and refused to take any further notice of it; consequently, I had to coast along by the bank watching it drift, until it should please chance to put it my side of the stream, if it did not stick on the other. Just as I was thinking of giving up the duck the dog changed her mind, and, jumping in, retrieved it.

About 500 yards lower, the drain made a sudden twist, beyond which was an old stump, the remains of one of the great trees which seem once to have covered this curious country; at any rate, the plough constantly strikes on trunks, often of oak or yew, more or less sound, in such parts of the " carrs " as farmers choose to plough.

Though there is nothing, to judge by appearances, to make this part of the straight uninteresting drain more attractive to duck than any other, the neighbourhood of this old stump, worn smooth and polished by the rubbing of generations of cattle, is a favourite place with them, and I crept up full of hope. But I was not to succeed. The duck were there, but some fifty yards to the left of their usual place, and thirteen rose just out of shot, and flew down stream, disturbing a pair and a single bird on their way.

This was dreadfully disappointing, but there was still another chance. At the very end of the estate is a plantation of about fifteen acres, by the side of which for some eighty yards runs a tolerably wide drain. It was not on the sheltered side, but there seemed a possibility of finding birds there, especially as some of those I had sent on had wheeled, and shown an inclination to alight. One or two herons flapped away from the trees as I came up, with their noisy croaking cry, but as the wind was from the dyke to them it did not matter.

Passing through the plantation was rather nervous work. The trees, tall and spindly, most of them spruce firs and ashes, were ill rooted in the loose, rotten, peaty soil, and more than one had fallen during the day, not broken, but uprooted. However, I made my way through the tangled growth of unhealthy, green-looking brambles and white shimmering reeds, and looking through a screen of the latter, which grew on the dyke side,—I was a little above the water,—I saw not wild-duck proper, but a small flock of widgeon swimming about forty yards to the right. Pulling in the dog, and giving her a small cuff by way of admonition, I stepped back into the wood, and crept carefully up to the bank again; I had hoped to get a sitting shot, for the noise of the wind drowned any that I made. But, as I was within a few yards of where I hoped to shoot from, they sprung up—there must have been thirteen or fourteen —and drifted back over the wood. My first barrel missed, but the second brought one down with a crash into the brambles behind, whence I extracted him, stone dead. The widgeon must have come inland from the sea, for the surf mark was on the breast of the bird shot. He was in excellent condition, and storm, not hunger, must have brought them inland.

It was a weary trudge back, soaking wet, with the wind cutting through damp clothes, and the hare was a gruesome object, more like a drowned cat than a smart jack hare, when I arrived at home. But the duck were an ample reward. One lesson to be drawn from the experience of the day is that, in a widely distributed storm, affecting large areas of land and sea, it is worth while to take a walk in the marshes.

IS COUNTRY LIFE STILL POSSIBLE?

To ask if country life is still possible may seem mere paradox. That every sound-minded Englishman is at heart a countryman, has been for so long a fixed idea that we have hardly realized that what was once the inborn bias of a nation has perhaps dwindled to a sentiment. There are good grounds for thinking that the old belief (to which we would still most gladly cling) was based on fact, and not on fancy. Lord Burleigh's axiom, that "he who sells an acre of land sells an ounce of credit," was respected long enough to become a guarantee for its transmission. Men who made fortunes, large or small, clung to the habit of investing them in land, and their sons, to whom they left their " money "—that is, their land—were brought up to live on it, and there learnt that strong love for country life which seems almost inseparable from early association with the soil. They were countrymen in the best sense, and knew how to reap the most conscious and complete enjoyment which their manner of life could afford. Of the general tendency of a nation, there is no quicker judge than an intelligent foreigner;

and even so late as M. Taine's first visit to England, his diagnosis of the end proposed to himself by the average successful Englishman—namely, the possession of a country estate, with the social and political prestige which it conferred—was probably not wide of the truth. The change had already begun, but not for the generation with which M. Taine was probably most in contact during his visit. For most of them, "modern life" had begun too late to destroy the tradition of the past. Those of his hosts who were engaged in commerce, probably took as it came the huge rush of "business" of the first half of the present reign, with its rapid increase of wealth, its bustle and excitement, and wisely made the most of it. But their ideas of leisure were those of their fathers. The form which their enjoyment of that leisure should take was determined by the ideals of their youth. When the money was made and the time came to enjoy it, they bought estates, or added new acres to the old ones, settled down naturally to country interests and country sports, the taste for which had been early formed; and shook off the dust of the City without regret. There was no cause for them to feel *ennui* or isolation, for they merely exchanged one set of occupations for another, with which early associations made them not unfitted. They did not leave affairs to dawdle through the morning with the *Times*, or potter with vineries and early asparagus, but found work in the management of their property and amusement in field-sports, or more rarely in the observation of the wild life which urrounded them. In the last, they renewed their youth;

in the first, they found employment for the energies of maturity.

But though this reaction towards the country was partly due to early sentiment, it must be remembered that London life was then infinitely dull for the busy man, and especially so for the "business man." Office-hours were much longer, and holidays very rare and short. Mr. and Mrs. John Gilpin's

> "Twice ten tedious years that we
> No holiday have seen,"

was the common experience not only of decent tradesfolk like the hero of the ride to Edmonton, but of merchants and professional men of standing. We were told by the head of an old City business, who is now, excellent man, enjoying his country house in old English fashion, that the first day on which he so far complied with modern habits as to take a "half-holiday" on Saturday, he made bold to go so far as Hampstead Heath; and when there, was so overcome by the enormity of the thing he had done, that he went back to his office, though he knew that he should find it shut up, and his younger employés taking their holiday without any scruples of conscience. Again, we still recall the memory of two old partners in a leading firm of solicitors, whose sole form of enjoyment for twenty years was a solemn drive round the Park together in a yellow chariot at half-past six, as a preliminary to dinner, whist, and bed. There was little or no mixing with other men and other interests; no journalists or artists to chat with; no mixture of the leisured class with the busy class; no "society" for the business man. If he wanted a change, and a chance of meeting fresh ideas in others, "e'en from the peasant to the lord," he could only find it in the country; and to the country he went.

That neither of the two causes which mainly kept up the old English taste for the country retain their old force, is certain, though the effect of their gradual weakening is curiously sudden. Early association certainly has less hold on the imagination of the present generation than it had on their predecessors, mainly because it is allowed so little time to act before it is supplanted by rival interests. When the author of *Tom Brown's Schooldays* complained that "young England" did not know their own lanes and fields and hedges, he found a reason in the "globe-trotting spirit" which sent young men abroad travelling, instead of returning to the old country haunts. By a curious irony, the later chapters of his book, in which the author has so vividly painted the delights of organized athletics, have appealed so powerfully to "young England," that, with our usual instinct for doing one thing with all our might, games of every kind have not only in a great measure supplanted the old interest in wild life, but even threaten to rival the taste for field-sports which once seemed innate in every Englishman. To be able to ride fairly, to throw a fly, and to shoot with some skill himself, and without danger to his neighbours, were the common accomplishments of an English gentleman. Excellence at cricket, tennis, and golf are now more important social qualifications; and if "young England" has a marked taste for riding anything, it is probably the safety-bicycle. Organized athletics do not flourish in the country nearly so well as in a London suburb or a fashionable watering-place. But these counter-attractions are mainly, though not wholly, for young men and—it must not be forgotten —for young ladies. Later, the disabilities of country life, and the necessity of the hourly fillip given to the mind by close and easy contact with the executive centre of the world at Westminster and the financial centre in Capel Court, become more and more imperious. To the man who has really been engaged in affairs, the mere perusal of the morning papers is a poor substitute for the day-long possibilities of telegrams and special editions. Even if he secures a constant supply of "news," he wants the right people with whom to talk it over. In London, he can generally find the man he wants. In the country he is often at a loss to find a kindred spirit with whom to discuss subjects unconnected with the petty interests of rural life. Hence the country house tends to become a mere annex to the town establishment, reserved for brief intervals devoted to recovery from town life.

But rest, repose, and beauty are not the only enjoyments which rural life has to offer. The country is not solely a playground and a sanatorium, a tame and temporary recruiting-ground after the excitements, great or little, of the town. Even its beauty may pall and fade, as Wordsworth found, and Mr. Ruskin has confessed, unless the conditions which make country life possible are better understood than they are by some of those who have tried it and failed. Now, the first of these conditions is that we should really *live* there, and not make the country house a mere basis and depôt for excursions elsewhere, but make it, in the true sense of the word, a home. If this be established, it is wonderful how quickly the accessories of rural happiness group themselves round it. To one who has known a country home, any other seems but a dim and distant shadow of that reality. Town life is only a huge co-operative society where we all subscribe to pay jointly for cabs, horses, gardens, and the rest.

But the country house must be self-supporting; and it is in the provision and maintenance of such accessories as it requires, that one of the chief interests of the country life is to be found. "Live not in the country without corn and cattle about you," says Lord Burleigh; and in the well-ordered country house, animals which in town are often useless pets or mere machines for locomotion, not only "justify their existence" by the share which they contribute to the comfort of the establishment, but generally manage to assert a separate and amusing individuality which seldom fails to exact due consideration from master and men. As for the dogs and riding-horses, whose share in country sports is as personal as that of their owner, there is no limit to the interest which their training and well-being may afford to a skilful and sympathetic master, or to the return of cleverness and affection which their simpler natures are willing to make.

Now, the welfare of horses, cattle, dogs, chickens, and pigeons, not to mention the pigs, which, if overlooked by the masters, are generally very dear to the servants, is a thing not lightly to be trusted to subordinates without supervision; and it is not too much to say that if all these are to thrive and be happy—and there is no more depressing sight round a country house than sick and ailing animals—the master may rise at half-past six, and still feel that by eight o'clock breakfast he has not done more than the supervision of his animal dependents requires. It is only too common in country houses to see hungry horses and cattle and famished poultry, which ought to have been fed at six, and are kept without food till eight by the neglect of careless servants. Besides the welfare of the animals, this early rising offers two other "compensations for disturbance,"—health, and the beauty of the garden, which is never so lovely as in the early morning, when the flowers seem half-asleep, and all the wild birds in it are tame and confiding. Never, since the great revival in Queen Elizabeth's days, has the garden had a greater store of pleasure to offer than now, when all good flowers, old and new, are cultivated and cherished for their single and separate beauty, instead of being banished to distant borders to make way for curly cactuses and paths of pounded brick. The garden is the one pleasure of country life which stands unquestioned and alone; it is a pleasure which never palls, which makes demands upon our time rather than our purse, and is dearer to women even than to men. From March till October the flowers last, from the first tulip that raises the signal of spring to the last Michaelmas daisies drenched with autumn dew. In the late autumn mornings the garden is perhaps dearer than ever, when the squirrels are collecting nuts, and the rooks, which have been stealing walnuts since dawn, are cawing as contentedly as if they had gained their breakfast honestly, and the late autumn flowers linger, not as part of the chain of production, but as gracious things in themselves, with nothing to offer us but their beauty.

The garden is ill-stocked which provides only flowers and fruits. With due management, there is hardly any limit to the birds and animals which will freely and gladly haunt the lawns and shrubberies of a country house. The modern Eden should be a home for animals as well as plants, and the lawn their playground. There is no reason why even the wilder creatures should be banished to woods and plantations, when, if not molested and encouraged, they will gladly take sanctuary under the protection of man. October sees the last of the flowers; but the pleasure of the garden may be continued, in a slightly different form, even while the flowers sleep. Trees are only flowers of a larger growth, and though the satisfaction gained by planting trees is part of the "joy that cometh of understanding," the art of forestry is now well understood, and is not difficult to learn. A wood, properly planted, will in thirty years be worth the freehold of the land on which it stands, and no monument to the ability of a past resident is more durable and more honoured in the memory of the country-side than that left by woods and plantations of good and beautiful trees. Jacob in Palestine dug a well, and left it to posterity.

In England, he would have planted an oak-wood. Trees, plants, and animals, none of them are to be neglected if the country life is to be developed to the full. Cobbett, who, though not a naturalist, was a keen and practical observer of all sides of rural life, and probably took a more comprehensive purview of the relation of all he saw on his rural rides to the human welfare of the country-side than any other writer since his time, surrounded his whole farm with a broad belt of trees of the newest and most valuable kinds, planting not only oaks and ashes, and such English trees as were suited to the soil, but acacia, plane, Italian poplar, hickory, and walnut. The growth of the acacia in this country is mainly due to Cobbett, and many cottage industries, such as straw and grass plaiting, which he introduced, have increased the comfort of thousands of villages.

Cobbett, though very sensitive to the beauties of landscape, was not an observer of the ways of animals like Richard Jefferies. But the habit of observation can be learnt, when it has not been gained by early association, much more readily than the love of the beauties of landscape. It is far more concrete and conscious than the subtle suggestions of natural scenery, though it is so mixed up in the minds of countrymen with sport in all its forms, that it is often difficult to say where the liking for observation of animal life ends, and its use as a means to their destruction begins. Perhaps the truest view is that the habit which begins in the case of animals which are the objects of the chase, is extended to the case of all others, though often this process is reversed. To many dwellers in the country, the possibility of close and intimate acquaintance with the wild life of the district is one of the most lasting pleasures which it affords. Much has been written and much has been read upon the subject; but what has not been *seen* is always new, and what has once been seen never loses by being seen again. But much has never yet been seen or understood.

Our eyes are barely open to the facts of the flight of birds. We know little of the changes in animal life wrought by the sudden influences of wind, rain, cold, and heat, and next to nothing of parts of the life of some of our commonest quadrupeds. No doubt sport fills a great place in the life of countrymen. "From February to September I fish," said one noted sportsman, "and when it is wet I make flies. From September to February I shoot, and when it is wet I make cartridges." But though sport does, and always will, hold a prominent place among country amusements, the care of domestic animals, gardening, planting, and the observation of wild life and scenery, with the due ordering of a household, give a guarantee that part of the time spent in the country shall be both pleasant and profitable. But country life has more to offer than this. To the health and vigour of the body, which make the mind elastic, it adds another condition without which study and mental effort are at a disadvantage. Real leisure and freedom from interruption are nowhere so easily obtained as in the country. "It is a good year for the grouse," remarked a visitor to Sir Walter Scott's old servant at Abbotsford. "Yes;

and a *gude year for our books*," was the reply. But in the country it is always a "good year" for books, whether for writing or reading them, and Sir Walter's pen might never have run with such astonishing ease and quickness had he not been supported by the bodily and mental vigour gained by his country life at Abbotsford. Charles Kingsley is another instance of a good and vigorous worker who did his task the better for his country surroundings. Yet even in his active nature the inroads upon his leisure made by his parish and pupils were, in the literary sense, a burden; and his pen never showed such charm and freedom as when, in a brief holiday, he wrote *The Water-Babies*. So long as it has such gifts to offer, the country can never remain long discredited; and the reaction from town and suburban life will be all the stronger because it has been for a time deferred. Even now there is in many minds a half-unconscious repulsion to the sustained strain of modern life, which will before long find expression in a new exodus to the fields; and in others the tastes of Wordsworth and his followers have never died. The unbought beauty of the country which so strongly influenced them is still its main and most potent charm, and at the same time we comfort ourselves with the thought that country life, with all its beauty and repose, may be one of vitality and vigour, and not of "calm decay."

THE END

[*R. Clay & Sons, Ld., London & Bungay.*]

LIST OF PUBLICATIONS

Issued in Demy 8vo. Third Edition. Price 12s. 6d.

LIFE AT THE ZOO

NOTES AND TRADITIONS OF THE REGENT'S PARK GARDENS.

BY

C. J. CORNISH.

Illustrated from Photographs by Gambier Bolton.

Opinions of the Press.

"Mr. Cornish not only knows his dumb friends in Regent's Park institution and beyond its limits well enough to have acquired a profound understanding of their varying habits and peculiarities, but he is able to do the humour of the animal world an amount of justice such as it very rarely obtains . . . . In its graver, as in its lighter portions, this absorbing work is without a single dull or superfluous line, and its value is not a little enhanced by the several beautiful reproductions of photographs by Mr. Gambier Bolton. Alike for young people and for children of 'a larger growth,' the pleasure of a visit to the 'Zoo' will be enhanced tenfold by a study of Mr. Cornish's equally diverting and instructive book."—*World.*

"Mr. Cornish is manifestly a keen lover of animals and a close observer of their habits and humours, and he records his observations in a very attractive fashion, genial in tone, curiously felicitous in description, and with frequent touches of quiet humour."—*Times.*

"He gives in short compass the results of long and patient observation, and in doing so displays to an envious degree the faculty of critical, but easy, exposition."—*Standard.*

"A charming series of sketches that form a pleasant medley for the lover of animals."—*Saturday Review.*

"A more companionable book than 'Life at the Zoo,' for a visitor to the great menagerie, we cannot imagine . . . . Interesting, thoughtful, and teeming with acute and often minute observation, and the sympathy of a true naturalist."—*Spectator.*

"The articles on 'Animal Colouring,' 'Patterns on Living Animals,' 'The Speech of Monkeys,' 'The Temper of Animals,' and many others we might also mention, show startling insight and much originality. Mr. Cornish writes well, and, if we mistake not, this should place him high in reputation amongst his brother naturalists."—*Black and White.*

"The book is beautifully illustrated, and one of the pleasantest introductions to popular natural history we have seen for some time."—*Daily Telegraph.*

"The book gives an account of the habits and nature of the inmates of the lordly prison-house in the Regent's Park, and of some of their past or future companions. It is of absorbing interest throughout."—*Daily News.*

LONDON : SEELEY & CO., LIMITED, ESSEX ST., STRAND.

EVENTS OF OUR OWN TIME.

A Series of Volumes on the most Important Events of the last Half-Century, each containing 300 pages or more, in large 8vo, with Plans, Portraits, or other Illustrations, to be issued at intervals, cloth, price 5s.
Large paper copies (250 only) with Proofs of the Plates, cloth, 10s. 6d.

THE LIBERATION OF ITALY. By the COUNTESS MARTINENGO CESARESCO. With Four Portraits on Copper. Crown 8vo. Price 5s., cloth.

THE WAR IN THE CRIMEA. By General SIR EDWARD HAMLEY, K.C.B. With Five Maps and Plans, and Four Portraits on Copper. Fifth Edition. Crown 8vo. Price 5s., cloth.

THE INDIAN MUTINY OF 1857. By COLONEL MALLESON, C.S.I. With Three Plans, and Four Portraits on Copper. Sixth Edition. Crown 8vo. Price 5s., cloth.

THE AFGHAN WARS OF 1839-1842 AND 1878-80. By ARCHIBALD FORBES. With Five Maps and Plans, and Four Portraits on Copper. Second Edition. Crown 8vo. Price 5s., cloth.

THE REFOUNDING OF THE GERMAN EMPIRE. By COLONEL MALLESON, C.S.I. With Five Maps and Plans, and Four Portraits on Copper. Crown 8vo. Price 5s., cloth.

*ACHIEVEMENTS IN ENGINEERING DURING THE LAST HALF-CENTURY. By Professor VERNON HARCOURT. With many Illustrations. Crown 8vo. Price 5s., cloth.

*THE DEVELOPMENT OF NAVIES DURING THE LAST HALF-CENTURY. By Captain EARDLEY WILMOT, R.N. With Illustrations and Plans. Crown 8vo. Price 5s., cloth.

Of Volumes so * marked there are no Large Paper Editions.

LONDON: SEELEY & CO., LIMITED, ESSEX ST., STRAND.

BY THE REV. A. J. CHURCH.

THE FALL OF ATHENS. A Tale of the Peloponnesian War. With Sixteen Illustrations. Large Crown 8vo. Price 5s., cloth.

STORIES FROM THE GREEK COMEDIANS. With Sixteen Coloured Illustrations. Price 5s., cloth.

'The broad humour of Aristophanes is most effectively given in this little book, and the flashes of brilliant irony not less vividly.'—*Spectator.*

THE STORY OF THE ILIAD. With Coloured Illustrations. Crown 8vo. Price 5s., cloth.

THE STORY OF THE ODYSSEY. With Coloured Illustrations. Crown 8vo. Price 5s., cloth.

'One of the most beautiful pieces of prose in the English language, as well as one which gives a better notion of Homer than any one, probably, of our many meritorious metrical and rhymed versions.'—*Spectator.*

STORIES FROM HOMER. With Coloured Illustrations. Twenty-second Thousand. Price 5s., cloth.

'A book which ought to become an English classic. It is full of the pure Homeric flavour.'—*Spectator.*

STORIES FROM VIRGIL. With Coloured Illustrations. Sixteenth Thousand. Price 5s., cloth.

'Superior to his "Stories from Homer," good as they were, and perhaps as perfect a specimen of that peculiar form of translation as could be.'—*Times.*

STORIES FROM THE GREEK TRAGEDIANS. With Coloured Illustrations. Tenth Thousand. Price 5s., cloth.

'Not only a pleasant and entertaining book for the fireside, but a storehouse of facts from history to be of real service to them when they come to read a Greek play for themselves.'—*Standard.*

STORIES OF THE EAST FROM HERODOTUS. With Coloured Illustrations. Ninth Thousand. Price 5s., cloth.

'For a school prize a more suitable book will hardly be found.'—*Literary Churchman.*

THE STORY OF THE PERSIAN WAR FROM HERODOTUS. With Coloured Illustrations. Fifth Thousand. Price 5s., cloth.

'We are inclined to think this is the best volume of Professor Church's series since the excellent "Stories from Homer."'—*Athenæum.*

STORIES FROM LIVY. With Coloured Illustrations. Sixth Thousand. Price 5s., cloth.

'The lad who gets this book for a present will have got a genuine classical treasure.'—*Scotsman.*

THE STORY OF THE LAST DAYS OF JERUSALEM FROM JOSEPHUS. With Coloured Illustrations. Seventh Thousand. Price 3s. 6d., cloth.

'The execution of this work has been performed with that judiciousness of selection and felicity of language which have combined to raise Professor Church far above the fear of rivalry.'—*Academy.*

LONDON: SEELEY & CO., LIMITED, ESSEX ST., STRAND.

BY THE REV. A. J. CHURCH.

HEROES AND KINGS: Stories from the Greek. Sixth Thousand. Price 1s. 6d., cloth.

'This volume is quite a little triumph of neatness and taste.'—*Saturday Review.*

THE STORIES OF THE ILIAD AND THE ÆNEID. With Illustrations. Seventh Thousand. Price 1s., sewed, or 1s. 6d., cloth.

'The attractive and scholar-like rendering of the story cannot fail, we feel sure, to make it a favourite at home as well as at school.'—*Educational Times.*

THE BURNING OF ROME: A Story of Nero's Days. With Sixteen Illustrations. Price 5s., cloth.

'Is probably the best of the many excellent tales that Mr. Church has produced.'—*Athenæum.*

WITH THE KING AT OXFORD: A Story of the Great Rebellion. With Coloured Illustrations. Fifth Thousand. Price 5s., cloth.

'Excellent sketches of the times.'—*Athenæum.*

A YOUNG MACEDONIAN, in the Army of Alexander the Great. With Coloured Illustrations. Price 5s., cloth.

'The book is full of true classical romance.'—*Spectator.*

THE COUNT OF THE SAXON SHORE: A Tale of the Departure of the Romans from Britain. With Sixteen Illustrations. Third Thousand. Price 5s., cloth.

'"The Count of the Saxon Shore" will be read by multitudes of young readers for the sake of the story, which abounds in moving adventures; older readers will value it for its accurate pictures of the last days of Roman Britain.'—*Spectator.*

THE HAMMER: A Story of the Maccabean Times. By Rev. A. J. CHURCH and RICHMOND SEELEY. With Illustrations. Second Edition. Price 5s., cloth.

'Mr. Alfred Church and Mr. Richmond Seeley have joined their forces in producing a vivid picture of Jewish life and character.'—*Guardian.*

THE GREEK GULLIVER. Stories from Lucian. With Illustrations. New Edition. Price 1s. 6d., cloth. 1s., sewed.

'Every lover of literature must be pleased to have Lucian's good-natured mockery and reckless fancy in such an admirable English dress.'—*Saturday Review.*

ROMAN LIFE IN THE DAYS OF CICERO. With Coloured Illustrations. Sixth Thousand. Price 5s., cloth.

'The best prize book of the season.'—*Journal of Education.*

THE CHANTRY PRIEST OF BARNET: A Tale of the Two Roses. With Coloured Illustrations. Fifth Thousand. Price 5s., cloth.

'This is likely to be a very useful book, as it is certainly very interesting and well got up.'—*Saturday Review.*

TO THE LIONS: A Tale of the Early Christians. With Coloured Illustrations. Fourth Thousand. Price 3s. 6d., cloth.

LONDON: SEELEY & CO., LIMITED, ESSEX ST., STRAND.

EIGHTEENTH CENTURY WRITERS.

SIR JOSHUA REYNOLDS AND THE ROYAL ACADEMY.
By CLAUDE PHILLIPS. With Nine Plates after the Artist's Pictures. Price 7s. 6d., cloth ; large paper copies (150 only), 21s.

'Mr. Phillips writes with knowledge, insight, and original inspiration—full of accurate information and sound criticism.'—*Times.*

DEAN SWIFT: LIFE AND WRITINGS. By GERALD MORIARTY, Balliol College, Oxford. With Nine Portraits, after LELY, KNELLER, etc. 7s. 6d. ; large paper copies (150 only), 21s.

'Mr. Moriarty is to be heartily congratulated upon having produced an extremely sound and satisfactory little book.'—*National Observer.*

HORACE WALPOLE AND HIS WORLD. Select Passages from his Letters. With Eight Copper-plates, after Sir JOSHUA REYNOLDS and THOMAS LAWRENCE. Second Edition. Crown 8vo. 7s. 6d., cloth.

' A compact representative selection, with just enough connecting text to make it read consecutively, with a pleasantly-written introduction.'—*Athenæum.*

FANNY BURNEY AND HER FRIENDS. Select Passages from her Diary. Edited by L. B. SEELEY, M.A., late Fellow of Trinity College, Cambridge. With Nine Portraits on Copper, after REYNOLDS, GAINSBOROUGH, COPLEY, and WEST. Third Edition. 7s. 6d., cloth.

'The charm of the volume is heightened by nine illustrations of some of the master-pieces of English art, and it would not be possible to find a more captivating present for any one beginning to appreciate the characters of the last century.'—*Academy.*

MRS. THRALE, AFTERWARDS MRS. PIOZZI. By L. B. SEELEY, M.A., late Fellow of Trinity College, Cambridge. With Nine Portraits on Copper, after HOGARTH, REYNOLDS, ZOFFANY, and others. 7s. 6d., cloth.

'This sketch is better worth having than the autobiography, for it is infinitely the more complete and satisfying.'—*Globe.*

LADY MARY WORTLEY MONTAGU. By ARTHUR R. ROPES, M.A., sometime Fellow of King's College, Cambridge. With Nine Portraits, after Sir GODFREY KNELLER, etc. 7s. 6d.; large paper copies (150 only), net 21s.

'Embellished as it is with a number of excellent plates, we cannot imagine a more welcome or delightful present.'—*National Observer.*

LONDON: SEELEY & CO., LIMITED, ESSEX ST., STRAND.

POPULAR SCIENCE

RADIANT SUNS. A Sequel to 'Sun, Moon, and Stars.' By A. GIBERNE. With Illustrations. Crown 8vo, cloth. Price 5s.

SUN, MOON, AND STARS. A Book on Astronomy for Beginners. By A. GIBERNE. With Illustrations. Twenty-first Thousand. Crown 8vo, cloth. Price 5s.

"One of the most fascinating books about astronomy ever written."—*Yorkshire Post.*

THE WORLD'S FOUNDATIONS: Geology for Beginners. By A. GIBERNE. With Illustrations. Sixth Thousand. Crown 8vo, cloth. Price 5s.

"The exposition is clear, the style simple and attractive."—*Spectator.*

THE OCEAN OF AIR. Meteorology for Beginners. By A. GIBERNE. With Illustrations. Fifth Thousand. Crown 8vo, cloth. Price 5s.

"Miss Giberne can be accurate without being formidable, and unites a keen sense of the difficulties of beginners to a full comprehension of the matter in hand."—*Saturday Review.*

AMONG THE STARS; or, Wonderful Things in the Sky. By A. GIBERNE. With Illustrations. Seventh Thousand. Price 5s.

"We may safely predict that if it does not find the reader with a taste for astronomy it will leave him with one."—*Knowledge.*

THE GREAT WORLD'S FARM. How Nature grows her Crops. By SELINA GAYE. With a Preface by Prof. Boulger, and Sixteen Illustrations. Crown 8vo, cloth. Price 5s.

"A fascinating book of popular science."—*Times.*

THE STORY OF THE HILLS: A Popular Account of the Mountains and How they were Made. By the Rev. H. N. HUTCHINSON. With Sixteen Illustrations. Price 5s.

"Charmingly written, and beautifully illustrated."—*Yorkshire Post.*

LONDON : SEELEY & CO., LIMITED, ESSEX ST., STRAND.

FAMOUS SCENERY

THE RIVERS OF DEVON. From Source to Sea. By JOHN LL. WARDEN PAGE. With Map, 4 Etchings, and 16 other Illustrations. Crown 8vo, cloth. Price 7s. 6d.

"The book is a capital one to read as a preparation for a tour in Devon, or to take as a companion on the way."—*Scotsman.*

AN EXPLORATION OF DARTMOOR. By J. LL. W. PAGE. With Map, Etchings, and other Illustrations. Third Edition. Crown 8vo, cloth. Price 7s. 6d.

"Mr. Page is an admirable guide. He takes his readers up hill and down dale, leaving no corner of Dartmoor unexplored. An enthusiastic lover of its rough beauties, he infuses his book and friends with something of his spirited energy."—*Morning Post.*

AN EXPLORATION OF EXMOOR. By J. LL. W. PAGE. With Map, Etchings, and other Illustrations. Third Edition. Crown 8vo, cloth. Price 7s. 6d.

"Mr. Page has evidently got up his subject with the care that comes of affection, and the result is that he has produced a book full of pleasant reading."—*Graphic.*

THE PEAK OF DERBYSHIRE. By JOHN LEYLAND. With Map, Etchings, and other Illustrations by HERBERT RAILTON and ALFRED DAWSON. Crown 8vo, cloth. Price 7s. 6d.; Roxburghe, 12s. 6d.

"Altogether, Mr. Leyland has produced a delightful book on a delightful subject, and it is impossible to lay it down without regret."—*Saturday Review.*

THE YORKSHIRE COAST AND THE CLEVELAND HILLS AND DALES. By JOHN LEYLAND. With Etchings, Map, and other Illustrations by ALFRED DAWSON and LANCELOT SPEED. Crown 8vo, cloth. Price 7s. 6d.; Roxburghe, 12s. 6d.

"Written with judgment, good taste, and extensive knowledge."—*Spectator.*

"Unique in itself, 'The Yorkshire Coast' should be in the hands of every person who professes interest in the history of Yorkshire."—*Yorkshire Gazette.*

LONDON: SEELEY & CO., LIMITED, ESSEX ST., STRAND.

PICTURESQUE PLACES
A SERIES OF ILLUSTRATED BOOKS

THE BRITISH SEAS. By W. CLARK RUSSELL, and other Writers. With Sixty Illustrations, after HENRY MOORE, R.A., J. C. HOOK, R.A., COLIN HUNTER, A.R.A., HAMILTON MACALLUM, and other Artists. 6s., cloth.

LANCASHIRE. Brief Historical and Descriptive Notes. By LEO GRINDON. With many Illustrations by A. BRUNET-DEBAINES, H. TOUSSAINT, R. KENT THOMAS, and others. 6s., cloth.

PARIS. In Past and Present Times. By P. G. HAMERTON. With many Illustrations by A. BRUNET-DEBAINES, H. TOUSSAINT, JACOMB HOOD, and others. 6s., cloth.

THE RUINED ABBEYS OF YORKSHIRE. By W. CHAMBERS LEFROY. With many Illustrations by A. BRUNET-DEBAINES and H. TOUSSAINT. 6s., cloth.

OXFORD. Chapters by A. LANG. With many Illustrations by A. BRUNET-DEBAINES, H. TOUSSAINT, and R. KENT THOMAS. 6s., cloth.

CAMBRIDGE. By J. W. CLARK, M.A. With many Illustrations by A. BRUNET-DEBAINES and H. TOUSSAINT. 6s., cloth.

WINDSOR. By W. J. LOFTIE. Dedicated by permission to Her Majesty the Queen. With many Illustrations by HERBERT RAILTON. 6s.

STRATFORD-ON-AVON. In the Middle Ages and the Time of the Shakespeares. By S. L. LEE. With many Illustrations by E. HULL. 6s., cloth.

EDINBURGH. Picturesque Notes. By ROBERT LOUIS STEVENSON. With many Illustrations by W. E. LOCKHART, R.S.A. 3s. 6d., cloth; 5s., Roxburghe.

CHARING CROSS TO ST. PAUL'S. By JUSTIN M'CARTHY. With Illustrations by JOSEPH PENNELL. 6s., cloth.

A few Copies of the Guinea Edition of some of these volumes, containing the original etchings, can still be had.

LONDON: SEELEY & CO., LIMITED, ESSEX ST., STRAND.

www.ingramcontent.com/pod-product-compliance
Lightning Source LLC
Chambersburg PA
CBHW020229240426
43672CB00006B/469